Christopher McMahon's *Understanding Jesus: Christology from Emmaus to Today* . . . is a refreshingly direct Christological overview in which McMahon allows the debates, concerns, and questions not only of scholars but also of the faithful to emerge from the texts and then to be addressed in a balanced and thoughtful manner. . . . McMahon offers crisp summaries, poignant questions for discussion and reflection, helpful charts, and sidebars, which serve as pedagogical tools. The book's open and inclusive approach invites readers from any background or perspective to make the journey and to encounter the richness and impact of Christ's life in the world.

—Shannon Schrein, OSF
Lourdes University
Sylvania, Ohio

With its explanation of the successive quests for "the historical Jesus," [*Understanding Jesus*] provides a learned and comprehensive antidote to conspiracy claims about Jesus of Nazareth. . . . The author helps students make sense of an often-bewildering array of scholarly voices. . . . Christopher McMahon's accessible prose is supplemented with helpful charts, questions for reflection, topical bibliographies, and a glossary.

—Christopher Denny
Associate Professor, Department of Theology and Religious Studies
St. John's University
Queens, New York

D1571120

AUTHOR ACKNOWLEDGMENTS

At the outset, I would like to express my gratitude to those people in my life who have boldly modeled their faith in Christ and challenged me to be a more faithful and consistent disciple. My families, students, and so many friends, especially Julie Pomerleau, to whom this small book is dedicated, have powerfully illuminated my world with their dynamic witness to the central conviction of the Christian community: "In Christ God was reconciling the world to himself, not counting their trespasses against them" (2 Corinthians 5:19). Without such witness, the Christological doctrines and the theological tradition that seeks to make sense of those doctrines will at best remain mere curiosities and will leave Jesus as a historical figure standing on the shores of an ancient and distant landscape.

I would like to thank the publishing team at Anselm Academic, especially Jerry Ruff, Paul Peterson, Brad Harmon, and Maura Thompson Hagarty, as well as the anonymous readers and instructors who have given feedback over the years. They have helped to revise this text (originally titled *Jesus Our Salvation*) and have made it a more effective teaching tool. Among those who gave helpful feedback in the formation of the first edition were Terrence Tilley, Ralph Del Colle, Mary Ann Baran, SND, and Shannon Schrein, OSF. My colleagues at Saint Vincent College have provided me with feedback along the way and guided me to many useful sources. Rene Kollar, OSB, the Dean of the School of Humanities and Fine Arts, Jason King, the chair of the Department of Theology, and my colleague, Patricia Sharbaugh, have provided constant encouragement, friendship, and support, as have Nathan Munsch, OSB, Campion Gavaler, OSB, Tom Hart, OSB, and Elliott Maloney, OSB.

Scottdale Mennonite Church, my wife's church community and mine by marriage and fellowship, afforded me the opportunity to teach an adult Sunday school class and to preach during the long months of revising this book, and they provided valuable feedback on my presentation of the material. As a non-creedal church, they helped me to articulate more precisely the value and limitations of the dogmatic tradition. The blessing of sharing in two church communities, one Catholic and the other Mennonite, has challenged me and left me doubly blessed over the years.

Finally, no one has imaged Christ in my life more consistently or nobly that my wife, Debra Faszer-McMahon. Her patient endurance and steadfast love as well as her skill as a teacher and writer have improved every aspect of this book in both its first and second editions. Words cannot express the debt I owe her. As always, the efforts of those mentioned here do not diminish my responsibility for this text, and any errors or oversights are my own.

Understanding Jesus

CHRISTOLOGY FROM EMMAUS TO TODAY

CHRISTOPHER MCMAHON

Created by the publishing team of Anselm Academic.

Cover image royalty-free from iStock.com.

The scriptural quotations contained herein are from the New Revised Standard Version of the Bible, Catholic Edition. © 1993 and 1989 by the Division of Christian Education of the National Council of the Churches of Christ in the United States of America. All rights reserved.

Vatican documents and translations are taken from *vatican.va* unless otherwise noted.

Quotations from the *Catechism of the Catholic Church* are taken from English translation of the Catechism of the Catholic Church for the United States of America copyright 1994 and 1997 United States Catholic Conference, Inc.—Libreria Editrice Vaticana, available at *usccb.org/catechism/text/*.

Printed in the United States of America

7047

ISBN 978-1-59982-426-0, Print

To Julie,
in gratitude for your friendship and humble witness to Christ's saving love
(Romans 5:5; Galatians 2:19b–20)

CONTENTS

LIST OF CHARTS AND SIDEBARS

Chapter 6

Chapter 7

Chapter 8

PREFACE TO
THE REVISED EDITION

The motivation to offer a revised edition of a textbook can often appear simply to be financial, a means of addressing economic issues on the side of the publishers or the author. Yet, at times, circumstances demand a book be revised, and I hope that readers of this text will appreciate the many reasons for this revision of *Jesus Our Salvation*.

First, the original edition was well received by instructors and students, earning the book praise and numerous course adoptions. Yet, the book was crafted in the early stages of Anselm Academic's foray into the college textbook market, and the precise editorial voice of the press had yet to be established. Moreover, it was my first book, and the combination of these two factors played a role in the shortcomings of the original edition. The opportunity to revise the text in light of my experience and the insights of the experienced editorial team at Anselm could not be ignored. It is my hope that the current edition will preserve the virtues of the first edition, correct any of its errors, and provide both instructors and students with an even more useful tool for engaging the questions surrounding the religious significance of Jesus within the Christian tradition.

Second, the original edition seemed to take an explicitly faith-centered stance on Christology, and many readers thought that it presupposed (or even imposed) a faith stance. Feedback from instructors indicated that this perception hampered the book's usefulness in settings where a significant number of students did not share the same faith traditions or convictions. The new edition seeks to remedy this problem by adopting a "faith friendly" perspective, one that articulates basic Christian and often Catholic convictions on Christology without presupposing these convictions are shared by the reader. The title and design of the book have been changed along with the artwork and the questions for reflection so as to accommodate a wider audience. While no text will please all readers, I believe that the current edition represents a strong and consistent attempt to address this important issue in a balanced way—in a way hospitable to readers representing a wide range of faith convictions.

Third, in this revision I have added some new material and revised much of the original. For example, although many readers appreciated the sidebar discussions, a few sidebars seemed either inordinately long or otherwise distracting. Several such sidebars have been deleted, and others have been revised and abbreviated. Additionally, the presentation on the various quests for the historical Jesus in chapter 1 has been tightened and incorporated into a discussion of the paradigmatic shift in Christology that has taken place over the course of the past century. The reconstruction of Jesus' life and ministry in chapter 3 has been tightened, and the material on the resurrection of Jesus in chapter 3 has been expanded slightly. The discussion of NT Christology in chapter 4 includes additional material on the provenance and complexities associated with the term *messiah* within late Second Temple Judaism. Additionally, the discussion of soteriology in chapters 6 and 7 has been improved with an expansion of the approach offered by Aquinas and a fuller presentation of Rene Girard's contribution to contemporary soteriology.

This revised edition will, I hope, continue to serve college students with a useable, approachable, and engaging text that will help focus and direct further inquiry into the central claim of the Christian tradition, namely that in Christ, God is reconciling the world to himself. The book takes a theological rather than purely historical or social-scientific approach to Christology. I hope that this theological presentation resonates with both believers and nonbelievers in a way that makes Christian claims about Christ a compelling and fruitful topic for inquiry and discussion.

CHAPTER 1

Contemporary Christology and the Historical Jesus

The Western world, which for more than fifteen hundred years had defined itself in relation to the Christian tradition, is rapidly being redefined, largely by a globalized and distinctly post-Christian culture. Today all religions, and Christianity in particular, struggle to promote the integration of a life of faith with daily economic and political concerns. The broader culture tends to define the values people hold, leaving religious values marginalized or blended and indistinct.

Standing twenty centuries removed from the life of Jesus of Nazareth, Christians struggle to articulate the relevance of his life and the doctrinal statements about him that emerged in the intervening centuries. What remains is often pious religious sentiment or technical theological study, as the claims about Jesus made in the history of Christian theology fade into obscurity. Indeed, the history of theology is in some ways a history of forgetting. This is especially true of the discipline known as "Christology," i.e., critical reflection on the religious significance of Jesus. Many Christians regard the Christological tradition as irrelevant for contemporary faith, and many choose to ignore it or simply forget it. A number of theologians in the nineteenth and twentieth centuries have even attempted to drive out what they regarded as the "demons" of medieval and ancient Christology and its creeds.

Dissatisfaction with what might be called "creedal Christianity"[1] and a cultural move away from organized religion in the West has turned many contemporary Christians away from classic Christology to focus exclusively on the Bible, hoping thus to arrive at a simpler, clearer understanding of Jesus. Such a maneuver has its own problems, however, for how do we know that the Gospels give us a true picture of Jesus? The desire to get behind the canonical Gospels to

---

1. This phrase will become clearer in the course of this text; for now, it is sufficient to identify "creedal Christianity" with the classic formulations of Christian doctrine that emerged in the course of the Christological controversies of the fourth and fifth centuries and resulted in the formulation of the Nicene and Chalcedonian statements of faith.

find the real Jesus—the Jesus whom some claim has been hidden and distorted by the early Christian church—has led to a series of scholarly "quests" to discover who Jesus really was. On a more popular level, the suspicion that the real Jesus was different from the Jesus of the Gospels has found expression in the widely popular book and film *The Da Vinci Code*.

Where does one turn, then, for answers? If the ancient creeds are irrelevant and if the Gospel accounts cannot be trusted—as both Jesus scholars and a skeptical, secular culture seem to insist—what is an ordinary believer to do? One response has been to allow one's devotional life to become privatized and individualized—insulation, after all, can be comforting. As long as one remains within one's private devotional life or that of a small group of like-minded people, images or claims about Jesus can remain largely unexamined. Yet, the desire to bridge this gap between faith and understanding has focused the work of theologians in recent years, and these attempts define the landscape of contemporary Christology.

Changing Paradigms and Shifting Terrain

In the past, Christology was a rather straightforward theological discipline. A course on Christology had a mathematical precision to it—one investigated how God became human in Christ, what powers Christ had, and how the death and resurrection of Christ saved humanity. As the reader can probably tell already, the account of Christology offered in these pages will not be so straightforward, for contemporary Christology in general is not straightforward. In fact, most theologians now would begin by discussing how modern times really shifted the terrain or the paradigm for doing Christology (and all theology).

This paradigm shift in the way Christology is done and taught was championed by, among others, the great Roman Catholic theologian Karl Rahner (1904–1984). Rahner was particularly concerned with how modern Christians had all but forgotten their own Christological teaching, which emphasized both the full humanity and full divinity of Jesus.[2] Although established at the Council of Chalcedon in 451, by Rahner's day most Christians paid only lip service to this doctrine, which to the average lay person seemed essentially irrelevant. Rahner believed that the teaching of Chalcedon, and indeed all the classic formulations on Christ, represented both obstacle and opportunity for the renewal of Christology.

The Council of Chalcedon had emphasized the full humanity of Christ along with his full divinity. Nevertheless, all of the early Christological proclamations, Chalcedon included, tended to enshrine a "high descending" approach

---

2. Karl Rahner, "Current Problems in Christology," *Theological Investigations*, vol. 1 (Baltimore: Helicon, 1961), 149–200.

to Christology. The prologue to John's Gospel best illustrates this approach: the Word of God descends from heaven, becomes flesh, is glorified in death, and returns to the Father in heaven. In Christian art, we often see images of the Annunciation represented as a tiny person (often carrying a cross, as in Robert Campin's *Annunciation Triptych*) who flies down from heaven and occupies the womb of the Blessed Mother. Such an approach to Christology tends toward a crude literalism—which may have made perfect sense in the worldview of ancient peoples, but as Rahner argued, it has become perilously out of date and theologically dangerous today.

A high-descending approach has burdened many Christians with a warped and unorthodox Christology that Rahner termed crypto-monophysitism. That is, he accused people of being closet "monophysites"; monophysites—from the Greek words *monos* (one) and *physis* (nature)—were early Christian heretics who believed that Jesus had only one (divine) nature. In effect, Rahner was saying that modern Christians, although verbally affirming the full humanity and full divinity of Christ, actually downplay or forget that Christ was also fully human. This neglect of Jesus' humanity is entirely understandable given the high-descending approach that dominated Christological discourse and popular piety for centuries. Such an approach tended to produce a mythical understanding of Jesus that disconnects him from human experience and history alike—which is not at all what those who framed the creed of Chalcedon had in mind.

Rahner argued for a shift in Christological thinking, away from the high-descending approach to an emphasis on Christ's humanity—a low-ascending approach—as the path to recovery of authentic Christology. Some theologians, however, objected to this move, arguing that a low-ascending approach would diminish the divinity of Christ. Anticipating such an objection, Rahner asserted, "Anyone who takes seriously the historicity [authenticity] of human truth (in which God's truth too has become incarnate in Revelation) must see that neither the abandonment of a [theological] formula nor its preservation in a petrified form does justice to human understanding."[3] Just because one states a doctrine correctly does not mean that one really believes it—i.e., one doesn't necessarily act according to one's stated belief. The mere repetition of Christological doctrines and formulae does not mean that they have been properly understood or adequately appropriated.

When talking about God, something more is always possible, Rahner argued. Therefore, the shift to a low-ascending Christology is not really a challenge to traditional Christology; rather, it is the means by which contemporary Christians do homage to the tradition and renew it.

This book will follow a low-ascending approach. Such an approach will inevitably raise issues that can prove both helpful and problematic for

---

3. Ibid., 150.

articulating a contemporary Christology that is faithful to the tradition. However, in the end, this approach also positions the discipline of Christology to address the questions and issues raised within the broader culture so that the Christological tradition may be better understood beyond the boundaries of the Christian church.

Interest in a low-ascending Christology has been responsible, in part, for the wave of books, films, and documentaries on Jesus we have seen over the past two decades. Christians have found some of these images of Jesus disconcerting: Jesus as a violent revolutionary, a confused and naïve religious reformer, a magician, and a philosopher. The diverse depictions all purport to offer a view of the person behind the canonical Gospels, the historical human rather than the religious figure proclaimed by the Christian church—which brings us back to the question of "the real Jesus" behind the Gospel accounts. In scholarly terms, this is the question of "the historical Jesus"; the remainder of this chapter will be devoted to it.

The Old Quest: The Challenge of the Enlightenment

The Enlightenment provides the basic backdrop against which the so-called old or original quest for the historical Jesus is best understood. In the sixteenth and seventeenth centuries, "wars of religion," sparked by the Reformation and the Catholic Counter-Reformation, had swept across Europe; allegedly Christian rulers busily tried to kill one another in the name of Jesus (the wars of religion were, in many ways, not about religion but about political power).[4] These wars helped to discredit religion and religious authority in Europe. If Christian authorities on either side of a conflict could cite divine sanction for their violent aggression, the logic behind their respective rationale had to be highly selective and self-serving, to say the least.

The discrediting of religion and religious authority prompted many thinkers to look outside religion for answers to questions of reason, truth, and morality. The era of the Enlightenment, which followed, was characterized by a pervasive suspicion of religious claims and religious authority. Instead, the Enlightenment celebrated the work of the individual mind that was free from irrational beliefs and unconstrained by religious authority. The Enlightenment set the stage for the old quest for the historical Jesus that emerged in the nineteenth century by discrediting traditional Christianity and its scriptures.

However, the Enlightenment's hostility to organized religion provides only one piece of the background necessary for understanding the old quest. The

---

4. For a provocative and insightful account of these conflicts, see William T. Cavanaugh, *The Myth of Religious Violence: Secular Ideology and the Roots of Modern Conflict* (Oxford University Press, 2011), 123–80.

other piece involves the Enlightenment's successor, Romanticism. Whereas the Enlightenment emphasized the cool logic of scientific reason as the sole criterion of truth and value, Romanticism emphasized the emotional, mystical, and more natural aspects of human existence. Like the Enlightenment, Romanticism prized individual experience and was suspicious of organized religion and religious authority. However, Romanticism was much more comfortable creatively engaging traditional Christianity than was the Enlightenment, albeit in a subversive way. Together Romanticism and the Enlightenment, to varying degrees, fueled the major efforts of the old quest.

Looking for Jesus amid Social and Cultural Revolution

The French Revolution (1789) was a watershed in the political, social, and religious life of Europe. The insights and challenges posed by Enlightenment thinkers came to fruition in the French Revolution, with its wholesale rejection of the old order of Europe, including the cultural and political influence of the Christianity. At this time the father of historical Jesus research, Hermann Samuel Reimarus (1694–1768), inaugurated what has come to be known as the old quest for the historical Jesus.

The general indictment of the church that accompanied the French Revolution seems to have played a role in Reimarus's description of the origins of Christianity and the place of Jesus therein. Reimarus suggested that Jesus' proclamation of the kingdom of God stood in contrast to the disciples' emphasis on the person of Jesus and the church. Jesus' ministry, according to Reimarus, was primarily a nationalist religious and political reform movement (much like the French Revolution), while Jesus' disciples, through their preaching and writing, misrepresented Jesus' message for their own purposes. Reimarus concluded that traditional Christianity was, simply stated, a fraud, a deception that an investigation into the life of Jesus behind the Gospels helps to unmask. Such an account of Jesus and the origins of the church further eroded the power of the church while affirming those who sought political and social reform.

The attack on the Christian church as a fraud resonated within many quarters in nineteenth-century Europe, but the profound religious and philosophical sensibilities of the culture also admitted a more nuanced revision of the origins of Christianity, such as that offered by David Friedrich Strauss (1808–1874). His major work, *The Life of Jesus Critically Examined* (1836), went through several editions during Strauss's lifetime. An admirer of the German philosopher G. F. Hegel (1770–1831), Strauss argued that the Gospels were myth and attempted to communicate a reality that Hegel designated the ideal of "God-manhood." Stated simply, this ideal describes human life lived toward the goal of actualizing the great spiritual orientation of human existence: a union with God. Jesus, therefore, is not the incarnation of God but a sign, or an example, of what humans might become if they are awakened to the spiritual foundations of their existence. For Strauss, the disciples' desire to communicate the dynamics of a personal encounter with Jesus could only be effective if that communication were evocative—it had to invite people to respond or react in a certain way, rather than merely describe or report the events of Jesus' life. Myth, Strauss argued, was the literary and religious convention early Christian writers used to bring the encounter with Jesus alive and make the realization of God-manhood possible in a way that mere description could not. For Strauss, Christianity was not a fraud but a mistake or a misunderstanding of this basic dynamic, a mistake that could be corrected. This correction, however, required the demise of traditional Christianity but at the same time would create a new, more authentic, and non-dogmatic religion. Around the time of Strauss, a movement emerged within theological circles that sought to find middle ground between the principles of the Enlightenment and traditional Christianity. This position came to be known as liberal theology, and one of its most popular exponents at the turn of the twentieth century was the great historian Adolf von Harnack (1851–1930).

Liberal theology sought to accommodate the principles of the Enlightenment and Christianity—usually by adopting a thoroughly modern outlook, retaining aspects of traditional Christianity that seemed to fit, and abandoning elements that did not. For example, the miracle stories were given naturalistic and moral interpretations. Jesus' healings had natural explanations, and so-called nature miracles like the feeding of the multitude had moral but not literal significance, e.g., when we share, we find that there is more than enough to go around. In his famous book *What Is Christianity?* (1900), Harnack depicted Jesus as an eminently reasonable human and did away with any hint of the supernatural. The resultant portrait of Jesus and his mission revolved around three central ideas: (1) the kingdom of God as a present interior reality, (2) the infinite value of the human soul, and (3) the law of love as the supreme religious and moral value. For Harnack, Jesus did not point to himself; rather, he directed all people to God as a loving Father. Harnack, like Strauss, rejected the doctrines of traditional Christianity but not on the grounds that the church had misunderstood Jesus. Rather, he argued, Christian doctrines, even those in Scripture, are historically and culturally determined—the product of Greek and other influences—and only of passing value.

Harnack was an important and serious church historian, and he was closely connected to many of the Romantic and "liberal" approaches to the historical Jesus that emerged in the middle and latter part of the nineteenth century. These approaches imaginatively narrated the life and ministry of Jesus so that the worldview of Jesus was made to fit with that of modern European intellectuals. Around the turn of the nineteenth century, many began to wonder whether the quest for the historical Jesus was sufficiently self-critical.

The End of the Old Quest:
The Limits of Historical Investigations

The old quest was brought to a close through the development of a better understanding of the formation and purpose of the Gospels, and a better (though still imperfect) understanding of first-century Palestinian Judaism and its theology.

For the better part of Christian history, the Gospels were thought to present eyewitness accounts of the life and death of Jesus (particularly the Gospel of Matthew, the "first Gospel"). Beginning in the middle of the nineteenth century, Mark came to be regarded as the first Gospel, a kind of bare-bones account of Jesus' life and ministry with few theological accretions. Some circles confidently regarded Mark as a basic, historically reliable account of Jesus' life, whereas the other Gospels were thought to have comparatively little historical value.

At the close of the nineteenth century, the historicity of Mark came under fire in the work of William Wrede (1859–1906), who suggested that even Mark's Gospel was suffused with the theology of the early church. Wrede claimed that one example of this was the so-called messianic secret material in Mark. The messianic secret refers to passages in Mark in which those who have witnessed Jesus' divine power (e.g., in a healing or exorcism) are instructed not to tell others of Jesus' identity as the divine agent (Mark 1:40–45; 5:21–24, 35–43; 7:31–37; 8:22–26). Wrede claimed that early Christians had come to believe that Jesus became the Messiah after his death (the development of New Testament Christologies will be discussed in chapter 4). As beliefs regarding Jesus' divinity developed, Jesus' identity as Messiah was read back into the stories about his ministry, but this created a tension—was Jesus the Messiah before or only after his death? According to Wrede, Mark's community resolved this tension by creating the messianic secret: Jesus was the Messiah during his life, but he hid his identity and revealed it only after his resurrection. This feature of Mark's Gospel was but one example of how later concerns and developments within early Christianity came to dominate the proclamation of the gospel. For Wrede, the Gospels were excellent sources for the study of earliest Christianity but poor sources for the reconstruction of the historical Jesus.

Criticism of the actual history of the Gospels was also fueled by the emergence of a more sophisticated account of first-century Judaism and its theology. Johannes Weiss (1863–1914) put another nail in the coffin of the uncritical assumptions of the old quest with his book *Jesus' Proclamation of the Kingdom of God* (1892). Weiss argued that one may indeed gain some knowledge of the historical Jesus by reading the Gospels, but the picture that emerges makes Jesus irrelevant to modern humans because his message and his actions all revolve around an ancient understanding of the world and God. Weiss claimed that Jesus' preaching and ministry was informed by first-century Jewish apocalypticism, or more precisely, apocalyptic eschatology.

Apocalyptic eschatology, which flourished from the second century BCE to the second century CE, expressed particularly Jewish and Christian perspectives about the coming of the end of the world. The term refers to a theological genre of literature as well as a theological movement. This eschatology (from the Greek *eschaton*, "end") was blended with ideas from Persia and Greece and came to focus on the idea that God would shortly intervene in history, raise the dead, give both the wicked and righteous their just rewards, and reestablish Israel as an independent kingdom ruled by God. Apocalyptic eschatology usually involved the communication of this message or "revelation" (Greek, *apocalypsis*) of hope to a persecuted community through the work of an intermediary—an angel or a famous figure from the history of Israel. Needless to say, if Weiss was correct about the basic content and meaning of Jesus' ministry and self-understanding, then the entire project of liberal theology would be undercut. In fact, the entire historical Jesus quest would be irrelevant, because the resulting picture of Jesus would not be useful for modern people.

Albert Schweitzer (1875–1965), notable composer, physician, medical doctor, winner of the Nobel Peace Prize, and theologian, brought the old quest for the historical Jesus to a halt in 1906 with the publication of *The Quest of the Historical Jesus: A Critical Study of Its Progress from Reimarus to Wrede*. In this book, Schweitzer traced the progress and aberrations of the various attempts to discover the historical Jesus in the nineteenth century. Schweitzer seconded George Tyrrell's famous image of historical Jesus research at the time: such research is like looking down a dark well—one sees only one's reflection. In other words, the political philosopher and revolutionary see Jesus as a revolutionary, the Hegelian philosopher sees Jesus as a Hegelian philosopher, and the humanist sees Jesus as a humanist. Schweitzer's position was similar to the thoroughgoing eschatology of Johannes Weiss. Schweitzer contended that the Jesus of history was so thoroughly immersed in the situation of first-century Palestine and its concern with eschatology that any attempt to bring him into the modern period does so only through violence and distortion. The historical Jesus is alien to modern ways of thinking.

In his account of the progress of the old quest for the historical Jesus, William Loewe identified four major positions at the end of the nineteenth century:[5] (1) the historical Jesus is the Jesus of the Gospels (the position of fundamentalists or reactionaries), (2) the historical Jesus is the Jesus of philosophers and humanists (liberal theologians), (3) the historical Jesus cannot be reconstructed from the Gospels (Wrede), and (4) the historical Jesus is freakish and irrelevant to our time (Weiss and Schweitzer). Within academic circles in Europe, positions three and four carry the day, but positions one and two enjoy significant popularity. The result of this division between academics and the broader culture

---

5. William P. Loewe, *The College Student's Introduction to Christology* (Collegeville, MN: Liturgical, 1996), 31–32.

was the general acceptance of the position outlined in Martin Kähler's book *The So-Called Historical Jesus and the Historic Biblical Christ* (actually published before Schweitzer's book). For Kähler, the "historical" (*geschichtlich* in German) Jesus cannot be identified as the object of faith; rather, it is the Christ proclaimed at Easter that is the object of proclamation and belief, and it is this "historic" (*historisch* in German) Jesus who makes a difference in history. Kähler's distinction between the historical person and the Christ of the faith community would be influential over the next several decades.

Person of Interest: Albert Schweitzer

Albert Schweitzer

© dpa / Corbis

Albert Schweitzer (1875–1965) was one of the most important figures within twentieth-century Western culture. His family was deeply religious as well as musically and academically inclined, which helped to chart Albert's future. His greatness first manifested itself in Albert's musical abilities: he was nine when he first performed at his father's church in Strasbourg. Schweitzer's musical interest continued unabated to the end of his life—he wasn't just good; he was internationally renowned. His performances and musical publications made him wealthy, and as a young man, he used his financial resources to further his education. Initially, Schweitzer studied theology at the University of Strasbourg where he completed his doctorate in philosophy (1899). He also received a licentiate in theology a year later. He served as a pastor and professor over the next decade, during which he wrote several important books, including his celebrated account of the old quest for the historical Jesus (*The Quest of the Historical Jesus*, 1906). Around the same time, Schweitzer decided to go to Africa as a medical missionary and proceeded to earn a medical degree in 1913. He founded a hospital at Lambaréné in French Equatorial Africa, which he would operate until his death in 1965. The hospital could serve as many as five hundred patients at its height, and Schweitzer had multiple roles there: physician, surgeon, pastor, administrator, and janitor. He was awarded the Nobel Peace Prize in 1952.

Beyond the Question of the Historical Jesus

Few figures have dominated theological debates as did Rudolf Bultmann (1884–1976) in the middle decades of the twentieth century. Bultmann, a Lutheran, helped to move theology away from the seemingly intractable situation created by the demise of liberal theology and the old quest to locate an authentic religious expression of Christianity within a modern context. The movement became known as *dialectical theology*. Dialectical theology did not share with liberal theology its optimism regarding human history and progress; rather, God was understood as entirely "other"—apart from the world—and such a position carries some important implications for the study of the historical Jesus. Bultmann denied the theological significance of the historical Jesus beyond the mere fact of his existence (*das Dass*). The fact of Jesus' existence was simply the precondition for the proclamation of the early church. Bultmann was concerned instead with historical issues surrounding the formation of the Gospels, in particular a method known as form criticism. He and other form critics (especially Martin Debelius) sought to deconstruct the Gospels into individual units to determine the original life setting of the early church in which these units took shape. By doing this Bultmann hoped to discern the manner in which the early church came to understand and communicate its faith in Christ. Armed with this knowledge, the contingencies that formed much of the New Testament could be relativized or dismissed in a project of demythologizing. For Bultmann, as for Kähler, it is the proclamation of Jesus risen and now living (i.e., the Jesus of the kerygma) that has import for believers. Bultmann outlined the main features of his theology and his approach to historical Jesus research in his famous essay on demythologizing the New Testament.[6]

For Bultmann, the New Testament presents a mythical worldview and a corresponding mythical view of salvation. The New Testament assumes that the world is a three-story structure (heaven is "up there," earth is "here," and hell is "down there"); the course of human history is governed by spiritual powers; salvation occurs as a result of the God-man's atoning sacrifice and the victory this gives him over the powers of evil; anyone who belongs to the Christian community is guaranteed resurrection. For Bultmann, a modern person cannot appropriate this primitive, unscientific worldview, which has its roots in the mythology of either first-century Judaism or that of the Greco-Roman world. Christians cannot accept this worldview because (1) there is nothing specifically Christian about this worldview, and (2) no one can appropriate this worldview today in light of modern culture and science. More important for Bultmann, however, is the way self-understanding helps to shape the modern worldview, and this has great implications for a contemporary understanding of salvation.

---

6. Rudolf Bultmann, "New Testament and Mythology," in *New Testament and Mythology and Other Basic Writings*, ed. Schubert Ogden (Philadelphia: Fortress, 1984; German original published in 1941).

Demythologizing does not imply a cafeteria approach to Christianity—taking what fits with our modern worldview and leaving behind ideas or doctrines that do not conform to modern sensibilities. Rather, Bultmann insists, "We can only accept the mythical world picture or completely reject it."[7] He contends that the mythic picture of the New Testament will be done away with as one uncovers the real intention of the New Testament and its use of myth. For Bultmann, myth is to be understood not in cosmological terms but in anthropological terms. It gives expression to the "beyond" or the limit of human existence that lies beyond the familiar disposable world that one takes for granted. In other words, myth must be understood as disclosing the mystery of human existence (what it means to be human).

This approach to the Christian gospel is not altogether novel, according to Bultmann; rather, the task of demythologizing is already undertaken in the New Testament itself.[8] Earlier attempts at demythologizing the New Testament were offered in the nineteenth century, most notably by Strauss and by some within liberal theology. These attempts, however, failed to understand the kerygma (the faith proclamation of the church). The modern world requires an existential interpretation of the New Testament myths, an interpretation that will speak to the difficulties of human existence in the modern world.

The understanding of "being" that underlies the Christian kerygma contrasts existence (or "human being") *with* faith and *without* faith. The human being outside faith—one who lives "according to the flesh"—is subject to the impermanence and decay associated with the world. However, in faith, humans live "according to the Spirit" because their lives are based on what cannot be seen and what is not disposable. For Bultmann, the eschatology usually associated with Jewish apocalypticism is now to be read as the new life of the believer, a new creation, free from the trouble of this transitory and disposable world.

Bultmann contends that this discovery is dependent upon the New Testament. The revelation that takes place in Christ is the revelation of the love of God. This love frees one from one's self and opens one to freedom and future possibility. Christian faith recognizes the act of God in Christ as the condition for the possibility of human love and authenticity. That is why, for Bultmann, the significance of the Christ occurrence rests not in historical questions but in discerning what God wants to say to humanity in the proclamation of Christ.

---

7. Ibid., 9.

8. Ibid., 11. "The New Testament itself invites this kind of criticism. Not only are there rough edges in its mythology, but some of its features are actually contradictory. For example, the death of Christ is sometimes a sacrifice and sometimes a cosmic event. Sometimes his person is interpreted as the Messiah and sometimes as the Second Adam. The *kenōsis* of the preexistent Son (Philippians 2:6ff.) is incompatible with the miracle narratives as proofs of his messianic claims. The virgin birth is inconsistent with the assertion of his preexistence. The doctrine of the Creation is incompatible with the conception of the 'rulers of this world' (1 Corinthians 2:6ff.), the 'god of this world' (2 Corinthians 4:4) and the 'elements of this world' (Galatians 4:3). It is impossible to square the belief that the law was given by God with the theory that it comes from the angels (Galatians 3:19f.)."

The cross of Christ is to be understood not as an occurrence outside of oneself and one's world; rather, the meaning of the cross is found in the lives of believers who commit to the suffering that authentic freedom demands.

The project of demythologizing the New Testament preserves the paradox (apparent contradiction) of the Christian faith: the transcendent God—the God that is totally beyond us—becomes present in the concrete history and lives of people. Bultmann's project, though criticized during his lifetime, was eminently pastoral (rather than simply academic) as it tried to outline how Christians are to believe.

The Historical Jesus at the Turn of the Last Century

At the close of the nineteenth century, the quest for the historical Jesus had all but come to an end in one of four major positions on the historical Jesus.

The Historical Jesus Is the Jesus of the Gospels

For many Christians, the rise of biblical criticism in the wake of the Enlightenment seemed obviously contrary to the spirit of Christianity; they responded by rejecting any separation between Jesus in the Gospels and accounts of the historical Jesus. Many Christians today continue to find such distinctions troubling because they seem to cast doubt on the truthfulness of the Gospels.

The Historical Jesus Is the Jesus of Philosophers and Humanists

Not all Christians viewed the contributions of the Enlightenment, and the modern world in general, as destructive. Liberal theology saw the Enlightenment as an opportunity to formulate a new understanding of Christianity. Liberal theology worked tirelessly to construct a positive account of Jesus as the ultimate humanist and philosopher rather than the incarnate Son of God.

The Historical Jesus Cannot Be Reconstructed from the Gospels

William Wrede denied that the Gospels could serve as a source for uncovering the life and ministry of Jesus. Wrede saw the Gospels as good resources for understanding the early church, which created the Gospels to help it deal with its own particular situation. Christians, therefore, are left without any sure historical resource for their faith.

The Historical Jesus Is Freakish and Irrelevant

Weiss and Schweitzer both attacked the supposition of liberal theology that Jesus could best be understood through an appeal to modern ideas. Rather, Weiss and Schweitzer emphasized that Jesus was a unique individual who was a product of a first-century Jewish worldview: Jesus thought that the world was coming to an end in the fiery and dramatic advent of God. His crucifixion was, therefore, a failure, a last desperate attempt to force God to act.

The Quest Gets Baptized

The dismissal of the historical Jesus from the scope of theology was difficult for many to accept, even some of those who closely supported Bultmann's overall project. Ernst Käsemann (1906–1998), one of Bultmann's former students, launched the new quest for the historical Jesus when he challenged Bultmann's position on the historical Jesus.

Käsemann respected the basic theological insights of Bultmann and sympathized with Bultmann's dissatisfaction with liberal theology and the old quest. Though Bultmann's concern to present a thoroughly modern yet Lutheran approach to the gospel succeeded in many ways for Käsemann, his denial of the theological significance of historical Jesus research came dangerously close to embracing the early heresy known as Docetism. Docetism (from the Greek verb *dokeō*, meaning "to think" or "to seem") denied the reality of the Incarnation, saying instead that Jesus only "seemed" or appeared to be human, but because he was divine, he could never be a real (material) human. Käsemann argued that the denial of the theological significance of historical Jesus research in favor of the kerygma was almost the same as denying the Incarnation.

The second and third points on which Käsemann criticized Bultmann are directly related. First, Käsemann argued, Bultmann fails to deal with the fact that the kerygma of the early church developed into the narratives of Jesus' life and ministry today called the Gospels. This happened, Käsemann argued (his third point), because the earliest Christians wanted to make the explicit connection between the faith to which the kerygma calls Christians and the life of the human Jesus that was the basis for the kerygma. These points combine to argue that the quest for the historical Jesus, contrary to Bultmann's assertion, was not only possible but also theologically necessary.

From Bultmann's students, few full-length works on the life and ministry of Jesus emerged, with the notable exception of Günther Bornkam's *Jesus of Nazareth*, which was widely read and influential for almost two decades. Among Roman Catholics, however, historical Jesus research quickly became a focal point of Christological reflection. One of the most prominent and influential books released was *Jesus: An Experiment in Christology* and *Christ: The Experience of Jesus as Lord*, a two-volume study by the Dutch Dominican Edward Schillebeeckx (1914–2009). Schillebeeckx offered readers an outline of what historians can reasonably assert about Jesus, a critically assured minimum of information on this historical figure. This initial sketch focused on the words of Jesus and his association with the marginalized and suffering. From this point, Schillebeeckx reflected upon the development of Christology in the New Testament. The "experience" (an important concept in Schillebeeckx's theology) of the early disciples provides the basis for their subsequent proclamations about Jesus' identity as Messiah. Because of this, Schillebeeckx has been accused of blending his historical reconstruction of Jesus with his own theology, the theology of experience. This is a common accusation raised against the entire new quest: it aims to uncover the unique personality of Jesus and, thereby, gain an understanding of how Christian faith emerged from the personal encounter with Jesus. In other words, there seems to be a theological agenda that controls the historical reconstruction of Jesus. Taking due note of these criticisms, the new quest, nonetheless, rescued historical Jesus research as an integral part of contemporary Christian faith, while failing to define precisely the place of historical Jesus research within contemporary Christology.

The British scholar and Anglican bishop N. T. Wright coined the expression "third quest" to describe the wave of Jesus research that took place from the mid-1980s to today. Generally, several new features distinguish this wave of Jesus research from the earlier quests, but some of the concerns of a previous generation of scholarship persist. For example, the Jesus Seminar, a group of scholars and other interested individuals, have produced a series of works that seem, in many ways, to continue the old quest's objective of using historical Jesus research to attack traditional forms of Christianity. John P. Meier, however, argues that the third quest for the historical Jesus represents a significant departure from previous quests. He identifies seven notable gains that define the third quest:[9]

1. The third quest has an ecumenical and international character (whereas earlier quests were almost exclusively male, German, and Protestant).
2. It clarifies the question of reliable sources (the New Testament is viewed as the primary source for research, and other texts and artifacts like the apocryphal gospels or the Dead Sea Scrolls are only secondary sources).
3. It draws upon a more accurate picture of first-century Judaism (as opposed to the tendency in previous quests simply to contrast Jesus and first-century Judaism).
4. It employs new insights from archeology, philology, and sociology.
5. It clarifies the application of criteria of historicity (i.e., unlike previous quests it consistently and carefully applies certain criteria for sifting the New Testament and other sources for historically reliable material).
6. It gives proper attention to the miracle tradition (as opposed to the previous quests, which relegated the miracle tradition to the status of legend or myth).
7. It takes the Jewishness of Jesus with utter seriousness (Jesus is understood as a first-century Jew).

The two most important of these unique features of the third quest—the Jewish background of Jesus (items 3 and 7) and the use of criteria (5)—deserve further comment.

---

9. John P. Meier, "The Present State of the 'Third Quest' for the Historical Jesus: Loss and Gain," *Biblica* 80 (1999): 459–87.

Following World War II and the Holocaust, Christians have come to acknowledge that their understanding of Judaism, especially the Judaism of the first century, has been slanted and incomplete. For example, in the old and new quests, and in Bultmann's theology, Judaism served as a foil for the presentation of Jesus. First-century Judaism was portrayed as petty, materialistic, and oriented toward earning salvation from God through good works. This is a caricature of Judaism rather than a historically and theologically responsible portrait. The work of E. P. Sanders in the 1970s revolutionized Christian scholarly descriptions of first-century Judaism, which subsequently became much more sophisticated and sympathetic. Additionally, the discovery of the Dead Sea Scrolls, a collection of first-century Jewish sectarian texts, underscored the picture of first-century Judaism as diverse and, therefore, less authoritarian. These factors help to situate Jesus within Judaism as a faithful or perhaps prophetic critic, someone on the margins but nonetheless recognizable as a first-century Palestinian Jew.

Meier also zealously defends the use of criteria in historical Jesus research. In his voluminous treatment of the historical Jesus, *A Marginal Jew*, Meier often insists that whether we affirm or deny the historicity of a particular story from the New Testament, we must know why we do so. In fact, for Meier the greatest contribution of the third quest may be its historical autonomy. History guides the quest, not theology:

> It is only in the light of this rigorous application of historical standards that one comes to see what was wrong with so much of the first and second quests. All too often, the first and second quests were theological projects masquerading as historical projects. Now, there is nothing wrong with a historically informed theology or Christology; indeed, they are to be welcomed and fostered. But a Christology that seeks to profit from historical research into Jesus is not the same thing and must be carefully distinguished from a purely empirical, historical quest for Jesus that prescinds from or brackets what is known by faith. This is not to betray faith. . . . Let the *historical* Jesus be a truly and solely *historical* reconstruction, with all the lacunae and truncations of the total reality that a purely historical inquiry into a marginal figure of ancient history will inevitably involve. After the purely historical project is finished, there will be more than enough time to ask about correlations with Christian faith and academic Christology. ("The Present State of the 'Third Quest' for the Historical Jesus: Loss and Gain," *Biblica* 80 [1999]: 459–87, 463)

In short, Meier's concern is to defend the idea, rooted in the goals of the new quest, that historical Jesus research is primarily an academic project that can defend the reasonableness of Christian faith. Yet Meier's concerns about the historical integrity of Jesus research emanates from his frustration with the way liberation theologians in particular (including both Latin American and feminist theologians) have understood the nature of historical inquiry and the use of historical Jesus research.[10] Meier suggests that liberation theologians have traveled down a "primrose path" that equates the historical Jesus with the real Jesus "and then elevates *that* Jesus to the canon within the canon."[11] In doing so, Meier claims that liberation theologians neglect the complexity and limitations of historical Jesus research and confuse historical Jesus research with Christology.

Christianity and Existentialism

Existentialism is a philosophical movement that flourished in the middle part of the twentieth century and that rejected classical philosophy and its insistence upon abstractions such as "essence." The famous existentialist philosopher Jean-Paul Sartre defined *existentialism* in the following maxim: "existence precedes essence." In other words, humans are thrown into the world, "thrown towards death" to use Martin Heidegger's expression, without any definition or foundation to guide them. According to existentialism, one is forced to wrestle with one's own existence and through the exercise of will, responsibly create one's essence. Such a project no doubt explains why humans are so anxious—consumed by the desire to possess and control, under the illusion that the one who controls or owns the most "wins."

While some of the most famous existentialists were atheists (Sartre, de Beuavoir, Camus) the movement had its roots in the work of the Danish theologian and philosopher Søren Kierkegaard († 1855). Kirkegaard, deeply dissatisfied with the modern emphasis on science and a corresponding concern with universals in accounts of human existence, emphasized the problems of individual existence. Gabriel Marcel, a twentieth-century existentialist philosopher, framed the issue simply: the primary task of human life is not to have or control but to be or become. Such an outlook transcends the scientific emphasis of the modern world without rejecting its advances. Thus, the modern world is neither vilified nor glorified.

Both founders of dialectical theology (Karl Barth and Rudolf Bultmann) appealed to the thought of Kierkegaard, though Bultmann was well acquainted with the thought of the German philosopher Martin Heidegger as well. For dialectical theology, existentialism helped to move Christianity away from liberal theology's problematic embrace of modernity and the dangerous idea of "progress." Existentialism helped to emphasize the precarious position of the human person and the need to abandon oneself to God in an outrageous leap of faith. As such, existentialism helped to reinforce the Reformation's emphasis on salvation as a gift that cannot be earned.

---

10. See, John P. Meier, "The Bible as a Source for Theology," *Proceedings of the Catholic Theological Society of America* 43 (1988): 1–14.

11. Ibid., 13–14.

The Problem of History: Understanding the Limits and Value of History

In the mid-1980s, Elizabeth Johnson, then at the Catholic University of America, and David Tracy, a professor at the University of Chicago, debated the question of the theological relevance of historical Jesus research.[12] Johnson maintains that a critically assured minimum of knowledge about the historical Jesus can be obtained through historical research. This basic set of data can then be cast into a particular interpretive mold or framework, and can yield multiple Christologies given the particular sets of concerns or locations of the theologian. Johnson also emphasized the theological necessity of the historical Jesus as "the memory image" by which the church and the tradition have always referred to a reality that predates the church. Even though the historical Jesus is the product of modern historical research—no one was asking questions about the historical Jesus in the Middle Ages—it still functions as the symbol that mediates the reality of God's saving activity. A sketch of the historical Jesus can provide necessary content for Christian faith and can also test competing representations of Jesus. For example, if one's historical sketch of Jesus conclusively proved that Jesus prohibited violence, then images of Christ, or Christologies, that portray Christ as a warrior could be rightly criticized as inconsistent with the historical Jesus.

Johnson also asserted that historical Jesus research functions as a norm or foundation for Christology—a claim that has proven contentious. In 2000, William Loewe challenged those who would argue for the normative value of historical Jesus research.[13] He concluded that while there has been a shift to historical Jesus studies in contemporary Christology, this shift has significant limits, perhaps the most obvious being its provisional character—such research is always open to revision. What historians and biblical scholars affirm about Jesus in one decade may have to be revised significantly in the next decade in light of a new archaeological find, a previously neglected piece of data, or a more precise and encompassing theory. Additionally, there seems to be less and less consensus concerning what one can affirm of the historical Jesus. For instance, while John Meier concludes that "the Twelve" (the twelve disciples) was a feature of Jesus' own ministry, John Dominic Crossan contends that it is a creation of the early church and runs counter to Jesus' practice of inclusive discipleship: Jesus treated everyone as equals and would not have privileged one group over others. This lack of consensus among scholars, therefore, challenges the naïve assumption that there is one established account of *the* historical Jesus and compromises any talk of historical Jesus research as normative.

---

12. See Elizabeth Johnson, "The Theological Relevance of the Historical Jesus: A Debate and a Thesis," *Thomist* 48 (1984): 1–43. Johnson's position has developed considerably in the past twenty years.

13. William P. Loewe, "From the Humanity of Christ to the Historical Jesus," *Theological Studies* 61 (2000): 314–31.

Modernism among Catholics and Protestants

The panic that had taken hold of the Christian church in the nineteenth century amid the spirit of revolution and the rise of secularism peaked at the dawn of the twentieth century. In Roman Catholic circles, Pope Pius X (1903–1914) led the fight against modern culture. Under his leadership, the social, political, and philosophical spirit of the nineteenth century were condemned under the term *Modernism*. Although there was no official movement that labeled itself *Modernism*, Pius X, in essence, created a "heresy" out of a pastiche of the cultural and intellectual tendencies of the day that included the following:

- A critical view of Scripture based on history and comparative literature
- A rejection of scholasticism (i.e., medieval theology) and its account of the harmony between faith and reason in favor of emphasizing religious feeling or sentiment
- Emphasis on the complete autonomy of the natural and human sciences
- A teleological view of history that privileges the revelatory character of an event in its consequences rather than in its origins

According to officials in Rome, Modernism had infiltrated the Catholic Church, and several prominent intellectuals were accused of supporting the movement (e.g., Alfred Loisy and George Tyrrell). In his 1907 encyclical letter, "On the Doctrines of the Modernists" (*Pascendi dominici gregis*), Pius X helped to establish some of the most rigid controls on theological activity in Church history. Censorship, monitoring, and reporting of suspected Modernists were encouraged and even demanded in the encyclical. Supplementing it was "The Oath against Modernism" that was required of all clergy, religious, and seminary professors.

Yet, at the same time, a theological renaissance was emerging in the wake of the cultivation of a distinctively Christian philosophy emerging from a renewed interest in medieval theologian Thomas Aquinas. This revival, though sponsored by Rome to combat secularized education and secularized accounts of reason, would eventually promote a historical consciousness about theology as well as scripture study, culminating in the critical embrace of modern culture and an historical critical approach to the Bible at the Second Vatican Council (1962–1965).

In the early twentieth century, many Protestant Christians reacted similarly to challenges to biblical authority. Across confessional lines, conservatives began to impose limits on seminary faculty and to cultivate suspicion. The Presbyterian Church particularly showed this tension, as rivals at the conservative Princeton Theological Seminary and the modernist Union Theological Seminary helped to divide the denomination, a divide mirrored in American Protestant churches and culminating in the divide between "mainline" and "evangelical" churches. Many Protestant Christians in the United States began to articulate the plenary (i.e., full or complete) inerrancy of the Bible in all matters as a way of insulating it against the claims of historical scholarship, an affirmation that became the hallmark of evangelical churches.

Loewe concluded that the historical Jesus cannot be the ground of either Christian faith or Christology. Rather, historical Jesus research helps Christology to move away from an ahistorical, metaphysical approach, characteristic of those who would simply take the Scriptures at face value or repeat the formulas of church councils and old catechisms. Instead, historical Jesus research enables one, in part, to focus on a historical and genetic account of the Christological tradition. By enabling one to get a sense of Jesus as a historical figure, one can more fully appreciate the dynamics of his ministry. In turn, a historical sketch of Jesus' ministry may help one to understand why and how the earliest Christians came to believe that this human being, Jesus, was God's own self-expression to the world, God's agent for conquering sin and evil. In this way, historical Jesus research helps one to offer constructive statements on Christology and its contemporary significance. However, this importance must not be overestimated, for historical Jesus research is not the foundation or norm of Christian faith.

The third quest has opened up the possibility for more fruitful historical research through its attentiveness to more precise criteria, its concern for the Jewish background of Jesus, and its ecumenical or interdenominational character (Catholic, Protestant, Jewish, and non-religious scholars working together). Yet these improvements in methodology and in the diversity of scholars engaged in the field have not yielded more stable results. In fact, the results are arguably more confused than ever. Perhaps the third quest's lasting contribution is a sense of humility, regarding both the results of this research and its theological significance.

Some theologians have gone so far as to question the validity of any so-called quest for the historical Jesus. Instead, they argue for the fundamental reliability of the canonical Gospels for understanding Jesus, and they eschew the criteria and formulae proffered by scholars. One notable example of this approach has been Pope Benedict XVI, who authored a three-volume work on the life of Jesus. Although the work takes advantage of the work of scholars such as John Meier and Joachim Gnilka among others, the pope offers something more in the nature of a Christological treatise, unconcerned with recent developments in historical Jesus research.

Conclusion

The quest for the historical Jesus has consumed vast amounts of ink, paper, and bytes over the last two centuries. Those who want to attack traditional forms of Christianity have appealed to the historical Jesus for vindication, while defenders of the faith have also appealed to these historical reconstructions to support their cause. It would appear, however, that both sides in the debate are asking too much of historical Jesus research. Bultmann was indeed correct when he warned against pursuing historical Jesus research in order to prove Christian faith, but his abandonment of the quest was problematic for the Christian understanding of the Incarnation—"the Word became flesh and made his dwelling among us" (John 1:14). William Loewe, along with much of the theological community, concludes that historical Jesus research has value in that it provides contemporary theology with important insights and moves away from mythological understandings of the New Testament, but it is limited in that Christian faith does not rest on a historical reconstruction. In other words, Christians do not put their faith into a critical sketch offered by historians. Historical research on Jesus is legitimate and constructive, but its results are not normative. As the great churchman and theologian John Henry Cardinal Newman said, "History is not a creed or a catechism; it gives lessons rather than rules. . . . Bold outlines and broad masses of color rise out of the records of the past. They may be dim, they may be incomplete; but they are definite."[14]

Questions for Understanding

1. What were the defining concerns of the old quest?
2. Why did the old quest end?
3. What was the major contribution of Albert Schweitzer to the quest for the historical Jesus?
4. Why did Rudolf Bultmann reject the quest for the historical Jesus? What place does his project of demythologizing have in his theology?
5. On what grounds did Ernst Käsemann challenge Bultmann on the historical Jesus?
6. Describe three defining characteristics of the third quest.
7. Contrast the positions of Elizabeth Johnson and William Loewe on the theological significance of historical Jesus research.

Questions for Reflection

1. Can we overcome George Tyrrell's parable about historical Jesus research? If so, how?
2. What do you think about the notion of "myth" used in this chapter? Given that David Friedrich Strauss used myth positively and Rudolf Bultmann used it negatively, what is the place of the concept in the study of the New Testament?

---

14. John Henry Newman, *An Essay on the Development of Doctrine* (various editions), Introduction, n. 5.

3. If historians reached a consensus and determined that Jesus offered a definitive teaching, would this teaching be binding for contemporary Christians? Why or why not? What is the connection between the history of Jesus and the Christian faith?

For Further Reading

Allison, Dale C. *The Historical Christ and the Theological Jesus*. Grand Rapids, MI: Eerdmans, 2009.

Johnson, Luke Timothy. *The Real Jesus: The Misguided Quest for the Historical Jesus and the Truth of the Traditional Gospels*. San Francisco, CA: HarperOne, 1997.

Powell, Mark Allan. *Jesus as a Figure in History: How Modern Historians View the Man from Galilee*. Louisville, KY: Westminster John Knox, 1998.

Schweitzer, Albert. *The Quest of the Historical Jesus: A Critical Study of Its Progress from Reimarus to Wrede*. Baltimore, MD: Johns Hopkins University Press, 1998.

A Tentative Historical Portrait of Jesus

Chapter 1 described how the shift from a "high descending" to a "low ascending" Christology related to the ongoing quest for the historical Jesus. The story of that quest demonstrates that any attempt to sketch a picture of Jesus "behind the Gospels" will be fraught with difficulties, flawed by inconsistent judgment and selective or idiosyncratic methodology. Nevertheless, a brief sketch or outline of Jesus' historical life and ministry—however tentatively drawn—seems a necessary prelude to the study of the earliest accounts of Christology. Chapter 2 will offer such an outline. Although admittedly selective, the picture presented generally represents the state of scholarship on the historical Jesus in the early twenty-first century.

Historical Jesus and the Criteria of Historicity

A distinct merit of contemporary historical Jesus research is its emphasis on methodology (the set of operations or tasks one uses to produce results, in this case, how one reconstructs "Jesus behind the Gospels"). While such an emphasis cannot produce an objective account of the historical Jesus, it can promote discussion and debate by providing common points of reference for those who disagree about particular matters. Moreover, by concentrating on objective criteria, scholars from diverse backgrounds (Catholic, Protestant, Jewish, agnostic) can and must participate. As a result, no one set of theological assumptions is allowed to color the reconstruction of the historical Jesus.

Meier outlines five primary criteria for historical Jesus research.[1] Scholars use these criteria, or principles, to judge whether a given biblical story, or part of a story, is historical. Before proceeding, it is well to remember that all such

---

1. John P. Meier, *A Marginal Jew: Rethinking the Historical Jesus*, 4 vols. ABRL (Garden City, NJ/ New Haven, CT: Doubleday/Yale, 1991–2009), 1:297; hereafter *AMJ*.

Selectively Sketching Jesus

As noted in chapter 1, any account or sketch of the historical Jesus will reflect the perspective of the one who is doing the sketching of "Jesus behind the Gospels." Every account of the historical Jesus can be criticized as self-serving. Listed here are four of the most respected and popular scholars who have written on the historical Jesus. These four are not unique in their "selectivity" or the idiosyncratic nature of their approach; to the contrary, any scholar, regardless of how responsible, is necessarily selective in portraying the historical Jesus.

Four Sketches of the Historical Jesus

Scholar	Background	Sketch of Jesus
J. D. Crossan	Crossan is former chair of the Jesus Seminar, a nonorthodox, somewhat post-Christian community of scholars.	Jesus was a social critic and not an apocalyptic prophet. He was a social reformer who threatened those who were entrenched in the current system, and they killed him for it.
J. P. Meier	Meier has taught at major Catholic seminaries in the United States and is now at the University of Notre Dame.	Jesus was a prophet in the tradition of Elijah and Elisha who instituted an organized community around him. He understood himself to be intimately related to God and understood his mission, including his death, as redemptive.
E. P. Sanders	A progressive mainline Protestant scholar, Sanders is most noted for his work on overcoming popular readings of Paul and Jesus that pit them against Judaism.	Jesus was a reform-minded Jew, interested in recovering and affirming Judaism in his ministry.
E. Schüssler Fiorenza	Schüssler Fiorenza is a Harvard professor and perhaps the preeminent Catholic feminist scholar of Jesus.	Jesus was an egalitarian preacher who cut through distinctions of gender and religious difference to institute a new kind of community.

Stages and Sources in the Gospel Tradition

Stage One (before 30 CE)	Jesus teaches about the coming of the kingdom of God.	No written material exists from this stage, but the criteria help to sift later material to determine which portions of the New Testament can be assigned to stage one.
Stage Two (c. 30–68 CE)	Following the death of Jesus, his followers make a proclamation that focuses on their experience of the resurrection of Jesus and his presence within the community of believers.	Paul's authentic letters, portions of Acts, and the Gospels also contain examples of the primitive apostolic kerygma, the proclamation of the risen Jesus.
Stage Three (c. 68–100 CE)	The memories of Jesus' life and ministry are incorporated into the kerygma along with other material from various sources to create the Gospels.	The Gospels

judgments are tentative because they are open to revision given further evidence. Moreover, not all scholars agree about how to use any set of criteria. In fact, some scholars of the historical Jesus, such as the noted Anglican bishop and theologian N. T. Wright, believe that using a set of criteria is ineffective and ignores larger questions of historical interpretation that are at the heart of any historical reconstruction. Nonetheless, a substantial number of New Testament scholars find value in the use of these criteria.

The criteria presuppose an understanding of how the early traditions (or stories) about Jesus developed. This general consensus affirms that the actual life and ministry Jesus of Nazareth forms the basis of these traditions: this is stage one. With the death of Jesus (and belief in his resurrection), the tradition took a distinct turn in that the one who had made the proclamation (Jesus) became the object of the early church's preaching, or kerygma: this is stage two. For example, Jesus proclaimed the advent of the kingdom of God in stage one, while Paul in his letters (stage two) proclaims the resurrected Christ and his presence in the believing community, the church. Finally, in stage three, the canonical Gospels emerge, and these Gospels combine elements of stage one in the form of the memory tradition of the earliest Christian communities with the experience of the risen Jesus believed to be alive and present in those communities.

Therefore, for the earliest Christians there was not always a neat and clean separation between stages one and two. Moreover, the creation of the Gospels themselves raises some questions about their genre and purpose. The Gospels were created not simply as records of what Jesus said and did; but also to preserve the memory tradition of the earliest church and as faith proclamations addressed to a community of believers at a particular place and time. Given this understanding, one would expect to find much material in the Gospels that does not come from stage one. The following five criteria are meant to help distinguish what material indeed comes from stage one and what material is the product of stage two or three.

Criterion 1: Embarrassment

One basic indicator of historicity is the criterion of embarrassment. According to this criterion, one begins with the assumption that the New Testament—and the Gospels in particular—were created to promote faith in Jesus as God's definitive agent of salvation and reconciliation and even God's self-expression. The New Testament would, therefore, quite naturally try to present Jesus in the best possible light. The authors of the New Testament, if they were going to add, clarify, or embellish the material they were presenting, would naturally choose material that would inspire rather than detract from faith in Jesus. Therefore, the criterion of embarrassment decrees: if there is a story or saying of Jesus in the New Testament that might compromise or embarrass the early church and its proclamation regarding Jesus, it stands to reason that it is probably not an embellishment or fabrication of the early church. Rather, the material in question should be attributed to a memory about what Jesus actually said or did.

One example of material that would satisfy the criterion of embarrassment is Jesus' baptism by John: it is not easy to explain why Jesus undergoes a baptism "for the remission of sins" (how this episode might be consistent with traditional Christological claims is discussed later). Another example is Jesus' crucifixion as a criminal by the Roman authorities and at the urging of the Jewish leadership in Jerusalem. It's hard to imagine a scenario less likely to support the claim that Jesus was the Son of God and Israel's Messiah. This aspect of the gospel message was no doubt a hard sell for those earliest Christian missionaries trying to evangelize the Roman world (see 1 Corinthians 1:23–24). The point of the criterion of embarrassment is that the early church would not likely have gone out of its way to create material that weakened its own tenuous position in the plethora of religious movements of the first century. Thus, difficult or potentially embarrassing stories in the New Testament may be attributed to Jesus' life and ministry (stage one: see sidebar) rather than to the concerns and theology of the early post-resurrectional church (stage two or three).

Criterion 2: Multiple Attestation

Multiple attestation of forms and sources is perhaps the most objective criterion of historicity, though still not without controversy. This criterion focuses on the principle that material found in more than one independent source or in several different literary forms is more likely to be rooted in stage one. For example, it is now widely assumed that Mark's Gospel was the source for both Matthew and Luke, along with another source that has been designated Q (see sidebar on the Markan hypothesis). If indeed this two-source hypothesis is correct, if we were to find a story or saying attributed to Jesus in Mark and Q, then that material stands a better chance of going back to the earliest traditions about Jesus than if it occurred only in Mark; it probably comes from stage one and was not created by the early church. Additionally, if one finds two different literary forms (e.g., a parable and a miracle story) both claiming that Jesus acted in a certain way or used a certain pattern of speech, then that also may be judged historical. For example, we find in the Gospels many stories of Jesus healing people, but we also have a conflict story (e.g., Mark 3:20–30) or a saying in which Jesus talks about the significance of his healings (e.g., Matthew 11:4–6). Because we have two different types of stories or different literary forms that report that Jesus healed people, one can be relatively confident that Jesus at least had the reputation of a healer during his lifetime.

The Markan Hypothesis, the Two-Source Theory, and Q

Read the Gospels of Matthew, Mark, and Luke together. You will probably notice that there are a number of passages that are almost identical—word for word—while other passages could not be more different. These three Gospels (John's is a very different Gospel) are called the Synoptic Gospels (*synoptic* means, "to see together"). Their similarities and differences suggest a literary relationship among them (i.e., one copied from another). The problem of accounting for the relationship among the Synoptic Gospels is what is called the Synoptic Problem. For centuries, most Christians assumed that Matthew's Gospel was written first, especially because Matthew was thought to have been one of the Twelve, and that the Gospels of Mark and Luke were adaptations of Matthew's Gospel. In the nineteenth century, many scholars (e.g., K. Lachmann, C. Weisse, and C. Wilke) began to question this approach and to argue for the priority of Mark—this is the Markan hypothesis. Their reasoning included that Mark leaves out many important stories, including the birth of Jesus, resurrection appearances,

Continued

The Markan Hypothesis, the Two-Source Theory, and Q *Continued*

and the Sermon on the Mount); it is easier to suppose that Matthew, working from Mark, inserted these stories than that Mark, working from Matthew, deleted them. Additionally, when Matthew and Luke agree with each other, they agree with Mark, and when they depart from Mark, they also do not agree with each other. It appeared, then, to many scholars in the nineteenth century that Mark represented the most basic form of the Gospel story, and that Matthew and Luke both borrowed from Mark.

There remained the problem of accounting for the material that Matthew and Luke had in common with each other but was not found in Mark. C. Weisse, J. Holzmann, and later, B. H. Streeter theorized that Matthew and Luke both utilized some form of a document that contained many sayings of Jesus. He designated this source Q. Thus was born the two-source hypothesis: two sources, Mark and Q, account for the differences and similarities among the three Synoptic Gospels. In addition, it is assumed that material unique to Matthew came from a source only he used (*M*), and that Luke's unique material also came from a special source (*L*).

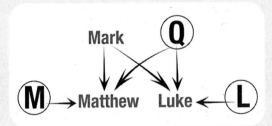

Criterion 3: Rejection and Execution

The criterion of rejection and execution stems from the historically indisputable fact that Jesus died on a Roman cross. Jesus was executed at the behest of the Roman government and their collaborators among the political and religious leadership of Jerusalem with the support of at least some segment of the populace. It stands to reason that Jesus must have done something to disturb or threaten those in power; otherwise, they would merely have mocked or ignored him, not tortured him to death in public. This criterion seeks to isolate material in the Gospels that might help to explain why Jesus caused people in power to become upset or threatened (e.g., he claimed a kind of sweeping authority, he spoke or acted against the Temple, or he questioned social norms that carried political overtones). If Jesus was just a philosopher who preached love of neighbor, he would probably have been ignored, not executed.

Criterion 4: Discontinuity or Dissimilarity

The criterion of discontinuity or dissimilarity is perhaps the most controversial of all the primary criteria in historical Jesus research. The criterion originally sought to isolate sayings and deeds of Jesus that could not be derived from the various forms of Judaism that existed in the first century or from the practice of the early church at the time of the Gospels' composition. For example, the Gospels depict Jesus as including women (without their husbands) among his close friends and associates, which was unusual for a first-century Jew (e.g., Luke 8:2–3 and Mark 15:41). It is unlikely that the early church would have created such stories given that it was moving in the direction of reaffirming sex-role distinctions (e.g., Ephesians 5 and various passages in the Pastoral Epistles). Jesus' practice of inviting women into his closest circle of friends and disciples stood in contrast, or was dissimilar, to the practices of early Judaism and the early Christian church.

For Bultmann, as well as for those involved in the new quest, dissimilarity was the defining criterion of historical Jesus research, the surest test for isolating material from stage one. However, the use of this criterion has rightly been tempered in recent years. Critics point out that if all materials that fail this criterion are rejected as inauthentic, the Jesus that emerges is a freak, totally at odds with both his Jewish contemporaries and his subsequent followers.[2]

Criterion 5: Coherence

The criterion of coherence rounds out the five primary criteria for historical Jesus research. This criterion looks for material that strongly echoes patterns of speech or behavior identified by the other criteria. For example, if the use of other criteria establishes that Jesus exercised special concern for the marginalized in his ministry (the poor, the sick, and the women), and we have another passage that depicts Jesus reacting favorably when he was approached by a woman with a public reputation as a sinner (e.g., Luke 7:36–50), then the story is probably historical even though it does not satisfy any of the other four criteria. It is considered authentic because it coheres well with the pattern of behavior exercised by Jesus during his lifetime; it is the kind of thing Jesus said and did. Materials that meet this criterion are considered particularly reliable when they involve both sayings and corresponding actions that were characteristic of Jesus.

These five primary criteria represent an important advance in historical Jesus research. Although not all scholars would agree on the use or importance of the individual criteria, most scholars have recognized the significance of these five in helping to introduce some rigor and consistency in the attempt

---

2. See Morna Hooker, "On Using the Wrong Tool," *Theology* 75 (1970): 570–81, at 580–81.

to reconstruct the life and ministry of Jesus. Meier has fondly pointed out that whether someone affirms or denies that a particular New Testament story comes from stage one, we can at least understand the basis for that judgment. The so-called third quest, therefore, represents a significant development in historical Jesus research insofar as the methodological rigor it has introduced should create more consensus and move historical Jesus research away from the proverbial dark well in which every scholar simply sees his or her own reflection.

Primary Criteria for Historical Jesus Research

Embarrassment

The criterion of embarrassment focuses on the sayings or deeds of Jesus that would have created difficulty for the early church's efforts to promote faith in Jesus. Because the early church would not likely have gone out of its way to create material that weakened its own tenuous position, the criterion identifies as authentic sayings or deeds of Jesus that the church continued to hand down even though they were inconvenient or embarrassing. Some examples of material affirmed as historical by this criterion include Jesus' baptism by John and his execution by the authorities as a criminal.

Discontinuity or Dissimilarity

Some sayings and deeds attributed to Jesus could have been mistakenly inserted into the tradition simply because they were commonplace of either the Judaism of the time or of the early church. This criterion asserts, therefore, that sayings and deeds of Jesus that seem "out of step" with both first-century Judaism and the early church are likely to be authentic. It is a controversial criterion because, on the one hand, it seems to vilify early Judaism—suggesting that what is important about Jesus are the ways in which he is least Jewish. On the other hand, the criterion tends to exaggerate the gap between Jesus and the very movement that cherished and preserved traditions about him, the Christian church. One example of this criterion is Jesus' celibacy, as celibacy is discontinuous with both first-century Judaism and earliest Christianity.

Multiple Attestation of Forms and Sources

As in a courtroom where the testimony of witnesses who have no connection to one another is stronger than the testimony of witnesses who are in collusion with one another, the criterion of multiple attestation looks for sayings or deeds of Jesus that are reported in multiple independent sources (e.g., Paul and Mark, but not necessarily Matthew and Mark) as well as more than one form (i.e., parable and miracle story). One example of multiple attestation of sources is the Last Supper, which is reported in Mark 14:22–25 and in 1 Corinthians 11:23–26.

Continued

Rejection and Execution

That Jesus died on a Roman cross with the support of at least some of the Jewish leaders suggests that something within Jesus' ministry was seen as a threat to those in power. This criterion seeks to isolate those sayings and deeds of Jesus that would help to explain why some people in power found Jesus to be worthy of public execution. One example of the criterion is the story of Jesus' triumphant or messianic entry into Jerusalem—such a demonstration helps to explain why people in power thought Jesus was dangerous.

Coherence

This criterion supplements the rest. It operates by examining material that otherwise would not enjoy historical credibility (i.e., material that does not satisfy the other criteria listed previously) and suggests that such material may be admitted as historically plausible if it coheres well with other material that has been judged historically authentic. For example, if through the use of the other criteria we determine that Jesus expressed an openness toward outsiders, strangers, and foreigners and also enjoyed offering parables and example stories regularly, then the story of the "Good Samaritan," which does not satisfy any other criterion of historicity, may be judged authentic, albeit tentatively, because it coheres well with what we already know about Jesus. The story of the Good Samaritan is typical of the kind of story Jesus would have told.

Applying the Criteria: A Tentative Sketch of the Historical Jesus

Applying the criteria just discussed is not as simple as it might first appear. One might suppose that once the sources are defined and the criteria delineated, the "historical Jesus machine" can go to work and produce a definitive portrait of Jesus. However, the criteria do not work apart from the intelligence, reasonableness, and responsibility of those who are engaged in historical research. In other words, criteria do not make the historical Jesus, people do.[3] The following scholarly claims about Jesus of Nazareth are not set in stone but are substantiated by rigorous research and argumentation and can be revised only through new insights, further research, and refined argumentation.

---

3. For a good discussion of this issue in relation to John Meier's work see the following essays: Tony Kelly, "The Historical Jesus and Human Subjectivity: A Response to John Meier," *Pacifica* 4 (1991): 202–28; Ben Meyer, "The Relevance of 'Horizon'," *Downside Review* 386 (1994): 1–15; Christopher McMahon, "The Historical Jesus and Frankenstein's Monster: The Historical Jesus According to John P. Meier," *New Blackfriars* 83 (2002): 505–13.

Birth and Lineage

The Christian tradition speculated about the family and background of Jesus since the first centuries of the Common Era. The canonical Gospels suggest that Jesus' contemporaries questioned his parentage (John 7:41), and Jesus' attitude toward his family does not always seem positive. (e.g., Mark 3:21; John 7:5). By the second century, an anti-Christian apologist named Celsus retold a story about the mother of Jesus and her rape by a Roman soldier.

Our earliest sources of information on the birth and lineage of Jesus are the first two chapters of Matthew and Luke. Based on the criteria mentioned previously, scholars find the stories of Jesus' family and genealogy to be historically problematic, as both infancy narratives are examples of an established literary genre of the ancient world that dealt with events surrounding the birth of a great man (compare stories about Sargon the Great, Augustus, Moses, and Samuel).

The name *Jesus* (*Yeshu* in Hebrew), an abbreviated form of the name Joshua or *Yehoshua*, as well as the names of other family members (Joseph, Mary, James, Joses, and Simon), are all names of important figures in the Pentateuch.[4] Meier believes this suggests that the family was caught up in the reawakening of Jewish nationalism in Galilee in the first century. Many Galileans were fed up with Roman domination. Hope simmered just beneath the surface that God would soon intervene in Israel's history to bring about deliverance from Gentile oppression and the restoration of the Davidic monarchy. This may help to explain the tradition of Jesus' Davidic descent recorded throughout the Gospels and even in Paul (Romans 1:3–4). According to Meier, such emphasis is not necessarily the product of the early church, as it dates from the mid-50s CE and needs to be taken seriously as part of a very early tradition about Jesus. The criterion of multiple attestation, while not necessarily establishing the descent of Jesus from David as a biological fact, does suggest that Davidic descent is clearly a staple within the Christology of the earliest community of Christians, and perhaps goes back to the ministry of Jesus.

Scholars generally agree that the formative years of Jesus are virtually unknowable, though some reasonable general conclusions about these years may be inferred. For instance, it is most probable that Jesus spoke Aramaic. Perhaps he knew some Hebrew in order to read the sacred texts, but not being a scholar, he would not have had the opportunity or the necessity to study Hebrew in any depth. In Mark 6:3 Jesus is called a *tektōn* or "woodworker," so Jesus was not among the many destitute in Galilee but was a craftsman. While he was not the poorest of the poor, he surely knew what it meant to struggle for one's existence.

Like the issue of the virgin birth, the issue of Jesus' brothers and sisters touches upon significant theological issues in the history of the Christian

---

4. The Pentateuch consists of the first five books of the Bible: Genesis, Exodus, Leviticus, Numbers, and Deuteronomy.

tradition, with Catholic and Orthodox Christians asserting that Jesus had only step-brothers or sisters, and many other Christians (including most Protestants) arguing that the plain sense of Scripture means that Jesus did have brothers and sisters.[5] The fourth-century theologian, Jerome, suggested that the brothers and sisters of Jesus mentioned in the Gospels are really cousins.[6] Meier insists that Jerome's position carries little exegetical or philological weight, especially because first-century Jewish and Christian writers (e.g., Josephus, Paul, and the evangelists) regularly distinguish *anepsioi* (cousins) from *adelphoi* (brothers). The more common explanation is that Joseph was a widower when he married Mary; thus, Jesus' "brothers and sisters" were Joseph's children by his first wife, not children of Mary. This explanation can be found as early as an apocryphal second-century work, the *Protoevangelium of James*. It is sometimes called the Epiphanean solution, after a fourth-century bishop who championed this interpretation.

Clearly the early church, concerned with safeguarding the perpetual virginity of Mary, was troubled about the identity of these brothers and sisters and their precise relationship to Jesus. This concern, however, is not evident in the pages of the New Testament in which the criterion of multiple attestation (the Synoptics and John as well as Paul mention the brothers of Jesus) and perhaps even embarrassment (the tension between Jesus and his siblings in many passages) are satisfied. Rather, the linguistic evidence and the text of the New Testament seem to favor the position developed by the ancient Christian writer Helvidius, who asserted that Jesus' brothers and sisters mentioned in the Gospels were his true brothers and sisters born after Jesus.[7] However, this evidence does not necessarily exclude the Epiphanean solution. The vast majority of Christians accept the Epiphanean solution, albeit not because the evidence demands it, but because of belief in the perpetual virginity of Mary.

Questions about Jesus' family of origin lead quite naturally to questions about whether Jesus had a family of his own—a question popularized by books such as *The Da Vinci Code*. Some argue that the silence of the New Testament regarding Jesus' marital status should lead one to conclude that Jesus in fact was married because marriage was a standard and an all but universal practice within first-century Palestinian Judaism. These scholars argue that without any evidence to the contrary, we must assume that Jesus

---

5. It is interesting to note that both Martin Luther and John Calvin, great champions of the Reformation who opposed Marian devotions in the church, nonetheless supported the doctrine of the perpetual virginity of Mary (see Martin Luther, *Sermons on John*, chaps. 1–4, *LW* 22: 23, 214–15 and John Calvin, *Harmony of Matthew, Mark & Luke*, vols. 1–3, Calvin's Commentaries, 1:107 and 2:215).

6. *Against Helvidius*.

7. Meier, *AMJ* 1, 318–32; *idem.*, "The Brothers and Sisters of Jesus in Ecumenical Perspective," *Catholic Biblical Quarterly* 54 (1992): 1–28; *idem.*, "On Retrojecting Later Questions from Later Texts: A Reply to Richard Bauckham," *Catholic Biblical Quarterly* 59 (1997): 511–27.

thought and behaved like the vast majority of other Palestinian Jews in the matter of marriage.

This position fails on three points. First, the context of the New Testament is much more biographical than some want to admit. The silence of

Person of Interest: Josephus

Josephus

Josephus (c. 37–100 CE) was a Galilean, the son of a priest who also claimed to be a Pharisee.[8] During the first revolt against Rome, Josephus became a leader of the Jewish army in Galilee, but his forces were destroyed quickly by the Roman legions. After the destruction of his army, Josephus tried to "save his skin" and ingratiated himself with his Roman captors by presenting himself as a prophet. He even went so far as to predict that the Roman general, Vespasian, would become emperor and that he was the "messiah" whom Israel had long awaited. Remarkably, Vespasian did indeed become emperor amid the chaos that surrounded Rome in 68 and 69 CE. Josephus' star was on the rise, and he was well rewarded when the Flavians adopted him. Josephus, thus, became known as "Flavius Josephus." In the last years of the Jewish war, Josephus assisted the Roman general Titus, the son of Vespasian, and even translated for him in negotiations over the siege of Jerusalem. His fellow Jews derided him as a traitor, and the Romans forced him to watch as they breached the walls of the city and eventually destroyed it along with the Temple. Following the war, Josephus went to Rome and began to write a history of the Jewish rebellion against Rome (*The Jewish War*). It appears to be an evenhanded account of events, but it had a moral to it—don't mess with Rome (after all he knew who was "signing his checks"). After improving his Greek, he began writing a massive work explaining the history of the Jews to the general non-Jewish audience of Rome (*Jewish Antiquities*); most of the book is a paraphrase of the Bible. Both works, but particularly his account of the war, are important sources for our knowledge about first-century Judaism.

---

8. See *AMJ* 3:302–305.

the Gospels on the question of Jesus' wife and children cannot necessarily be regarded as evidence in favor of marriage. The names of women with whom Jesus associated have been preserved in the New Testament texts. It would be very odd for the New Testament to eliminate any reference to Jesus' wife and children while at the same time giving frequent mention of his other family members. Second, Josephus and Philo, two prominent first-century Jewish authors, both contend that at least some of the Essene community remained celibate.[9] Third, the prophet Jeremiah is a good biblical example of the celibate life for the sake of a vocation. Political events dominated Jeremiah's prophetic career, creating an atmosphere of tension and desperation, and Jeremiah's own celibacy seems to have been a sign to his fellow Jews that any idea of "business as usual" (i.e., making plans to marry and start a family) were out of place given the events that were beginning to transpire—God's judgment was falling upon Judah in the form of the Babylonian army and its conquest of Jerusalem. It is possible Jesus could have modeled his life and ministry on this important figure; and in the context of his eschatological ministry, celibacy seems an appropriate symbol in the first century. This is further supported by evidence that Jesus' predecessor and associate, John the Baptist, was celibate, not to mention the apostle Paul.[10]

Jesus and John the Baptist

Like the evidence for the existence of Jesus, the evidence for the existence of the Baptist is overwhelming in many ways. Corroborating texts from the third-century theologian Origen and the fourth-century Christian historian Eusebius help to buttress the historical credibility of the testimony offered by the first-century Jewish historian Josephus in *The Jewish Antiquities*.[11] In this text, Josephus says nothing of any relationship between John and Jesus (cf. Luke's portrayal of John and Jesus as distant relatives) and portrays John not as an eschatological prophet but as a moralizing philosopher. In the end, questions remain as to the content of John's message and his relationship to Jesus.

The Gospels portray the Baptist as an antiestablishment figure who ministered in the wilderness of Judea near the Jordan (Luke 1:80), near the Essene settlement at Qumran. The literature discovered at Qumran appears to have some relevance for understanding John. In particular, John's baptizing activity resembles Essene water purification rituals and poses interesting questions about how much John focused on the corruption of the ruling classes in Jerusalem—a favorite topic for the Essenes.[12] Yet important differences between John and the

---

9. See, Flavius Josephus, *Jewish War* 2. 8. 2. and *Every Good Man is Free* 12–13.

10. On the celibacy of John the Baptist, see *AMJ* 1:339–340; on Paul, see 1 Corinthians 7:8.

11. *Antiquities* 18.3.3.

12. E.g., see 1QpHab, the commentary or "*pesher*" on Habakkuk from Qumran.

Essenes remain, including that John's ministry was public and oriented to the repentance of the nation, whereas the Essenes tended to be reclusive and sectarian. Whatever the precise relationship between John the Baptist and the Essene community, John's career seems to echo many of the characteristic concerns and practices of the Essenes, thereby helping historians ground an account of both Jesus and John within the religious and social context of first-century Judaism.

In the initial part of the first block of material on the Baptist from the sayings source *Q* (i.e., that source common to both Matthew and Luke; see Matthew 3:7–10 par.), John does not refer to Jesus. He is a fiery eschatological prophet calling those who have come to him for baptism "a brood of vipers." Like the prophets of the Old Testament, he calls upon them not simply to run in fear of God's coming judgment but also to repent. John is also in line with the Old Testament prophets in saying "already the axe is laid to the root of the tree" (cf., Isaiah 10: 33:34; 32:19). What is striking about the quote is that John preached this message to those who had come out to the desert to be baptized by him. The Baptist appears to have commanded more than simple curiosity; rather, he demanded a swift decision to be baptized and a radical reformation of "both inner attitudes and external conduct."[13] In Matthew 3:11–12, John looks to the future when someone "stronger than me" will come and exercise judgment. The phrase is interesting because it has no specific Christological content, but this "stronger one" cannot be the God of Israel because the image of "untying his sandal" would be excessively anthropomorphic (i.e., an image of God as a human). The question then arises as to the identity of the "stronger one." John Meier argues that John was deliberately ambiguous; this "stronger one" functions as a judge, while the actual destruction of the wicked is left to God. The righteous ones, those who repent, can be spared this judgment if their repentance is sincere, and John's baptism was the appropriate sign of this repentance.

According to Meier, John's baptism shared some common traits with other Jewish rituals of water purification performed by those who dwelt in the Judean desert: (1) there was the belief that "all Israel" had gone astray, (2) purification was offered to those who sought it through repentance, (3) this repentance offered hope for salvation on the day of reckoning.[14] John was unlike other figures who practiced rituals of water baptism in the first century in that his baptism was a one-time action, and John performed the ritual, thereby, accentuating his role in the eschatological drama. John saw his ministry of baptism as an act that anticipated the final pouring out of the Spirit onto the repentant for their salvation and not as a rite of initiation into some new group or "church" (although in the first century the Essenes at Qumran used baptism as a ritual of initiation as well as for those who have "converted" to Judaism).[15]

---

13. *AMJ* 2:30.14. *AMJ*, 2:50

14. *AMJ* 2:50.

15. See *AMJ* 2:49–56.

The question of the meaning of John's baptism is complicated by the phrase "for the remission of sins" in Mark 1:4. The issue is whether this phrase in Mark reflects early Christian practice or John's (i.e., a pre-Christian) understanding of baptism. The case against a Christian interpretation is twofold: (1) while the New Testament associates Christian baptism with forgiveness, it never applies this entire phrase to Christian baptism; (2) it is highly unlikely that the early church would attribute such power to John's baptism and retell the story of the sinless Jesus receiving this baptism (criterion of embarrassment; see further explanation in next paragraph). When one avoids the anachronistic sacramental questions it is best to interpret the phrase in line with the rest of the data on John. John understood his baptism as a dramatic acting out of the candidate's repentance while anticipating and announcing the definitive action of God in the outpouring of the Holy Spirit by "the one who is more powerful than I" (Mark 1:7).

The question of John's baptism of Jesus (Mark 1:9–11 pars.) is significant for any attempt to piece together the relationship between John and Jesus. The criterion of embarrassment suggests that it is a piece of historical data. Why would Christians who claim that Jesus was sinless invent a story in which he participates in a ritual that Christians associated with the forgiveness of sins? It would seem more likely that the Gospel authors in this case retain authentic tradition, however problematic they may have found it. The criterion of multiple attestation also suggests authenticity, as both Mark and *Q* give witness to Jesus' baptism by John, as well as 1 John 1:5–6. Additionally, the criterion of discontinuity authenticates this material given that elsewhere in the New Testament Christian baptism is understood and legitimated in light of Jesus' death and resurrection (e.g., Romans 6:3–11) and not through an appeal to Jesus' own experience of baptism. The meaning of Jesus' baptism is a matter distinct from the theology of Christian baptism.

Meier draws from this episode four inferences regarding the religious mindset of Jesus at the start of his ministry. First, like John, Jesus believed that the end of Israel's history was approaching. Second, he believed Israel had gone astray and was in need of repentance. Third, the only way to escape the coming wrath was not to claim descent from Abraham but to undergo conversion and repentance—a change in mind and heart. Fourth, his baptism was a way for him to acknowledge John's role as eschatological prophet.[16] So, Meier contends that Jesus submitted to John's charismatic ritual because he believed that it was necessary for salvation from God's judgment. However, this seems to attribute to Jesus consciousness of sin—a real problem for Christian theology, which states that Jesus is like every human "in all things except sin" (Hebrews 4:15). As Meier points out, however, Jesus' consciousness of sin does not equal "personal sin" in first-century Judaism.[17] Ezra and Nehemiah may be cited to

---

16. Ibid., 109.
17. Ibid., 113.

offer examples of how Jews of the Second Temple period could identify themselves as sinners without necessarily identifying sin with personal transgressions (Ezra 9:6–7; Nehemiah 9:36–37; also 1QS 1:18–2:2). In the example of Ezra

Qumran and the Dead Sea Scrolls

In 1947, a young shepherd was wandering in the wilderness near the shores of the Dead Sea in Palestine at a place called Qumran. As he threw stones into some caves located above him he heard a sound of breaking pottery, and so signaled one of the most sensational archeological discoveries of the twentieth century. The caves contained dozens of clay jars filled with ancient manuscripts of both biblical and non-biblical books. A group or sect within early Judaism known as the Essenes had deposited these manuscripts in the caves at Qumran. The Essenes had copied and preserved both biblical manuscripts as well as many sectarian documents, i.e., documents that reflected the group's distinctive theology. When their monastic community came under threat from the advancing Roman legions at the end of the first century, they hid their sacred texts in caves. Their community was destroyed, and the documents remained hidden and undisturbed for almost two thousand years.

For Christians, the scrolls are important for several reasons. The scrolls are some of the oldest biblical manuscripts ever discovered. The oldest complete text of any portion of the Old Testament previously obtained was from the early Middle Ages. The commentaries, translations, and expansions of biblical books are also helpful for exegesis (i.e., biblical interpretation) and textual criticism (i.e., determining the original text of the Bible). Perhaps most importantly, the scrolls demonstrate the theological diversity of Palestinian Judaism around the time of Jesus, particularly as it pertains to eschatology (i.e., discourse about the culmination of human history). Before the discovery of the scrolls at Qumran, many scholars believed that certain eschatological beliefs of early Christianity were alien to Judaism and were, therefore, borrowed from the Greek world. However, the scrolls reveal that Christian eschatology—apocalyptic eschatology—had its roots within Judaism. The sectarian documents found at Qumran envisioned a community of purified believers ("the sons of light") who awaited a final cosmic battle to bring about the defeat of their enemies ("the sons of darkness") and the victory of God. Central in this battle is an enigmatic figure named the Teacher of Righteousness. Before that battle, the Essenes believed they were called upon to live as a holy people—a people set apart from the rest of the world. This separation was certainly geographical at Qumran—they were in a desert far outside Jerusalem—but it was also spiritual and ideological. Those who were to become members of the community dedicated themselves to rituals of water immersion (baptism) and communal eating that set them apart from the rest of the world.[18]

18. See, *The Dead Sea Scrolls in English*, rev. ed., ed. G. Vermes (New York: Penguin, 2004).

and Nehemiah, they associate themselves with the generations that had brought about the destruction of the nation two hundred years earlier, in addition to their contemporaries who are unrepentant.

There is the possibility, and even the likelihood, that Jesus envisioned his baptism "for the remission of sins" as part of a corporate act of penance: it would be like American antiwar activists fasting as an act of penance for a war. Though the activists have never been guilty of supporting the war, they, nonetheless, recognize that, as Americans, they too must do penance for what they see as a "national sin."

So what was the nature of the relationship between John and Jesus? Much of the evidence (e.g., Matthew 11:2–3 and Luke 7:18–19) suggests it was rather ambiguous. Meier argues that Jesus was a disciple of John the Baptist. It is apparent from the Gospels that John the Baptist did in fact have some followers, although not all who were baptized were "disciples" (i.e., not all those who were baptized left their families and work to live with John and join in his ministry).

The Fourth Gospel offers some evidence regarding Jesus' direct association with John. In John 1:28–45, Jesus appears with the Baptist in the desert near the area by the Jordan where John was engaged in a ministry of baptism. In John 3:22 ff., Jesus spends some time with his disciples baptizing, while John continues to baptize nearby. In John 4:1, the Pharisees learn that Jesus' disciples are baptizing and gaining more followers than the Baptist is. The criterion of embarrassment helps to substantiate that Jesus and his first disciples came from John's circle as there is a tendency within the Fourth Gospel to suppress any direct connection between the ministry of John and the ministry of Jesus. This same material also seems to cohere with what has already been established, i.e., that John baptized Jesus and that Jesus interpreted this baptism as an important event in his own ministry.

The so-called second Baptist block in *Q* (Matthew 11:2–19; Luke 7:18–35) offers some evidence of what Jesus thought of John. In Matthew 11:2–6, John sends disciples to ask if Jesus is "the one who is to come." There is no indication that this phrase functioned as any kind of messianic title in the Judaism of the first century; rather, like "the stronger one," "the one who is to come" is deliberately ambiguous. Jesus' response is thoughtful in that it focuses on the point at which Jesus' ministry diverges from John's; it sounds a note of hope and joy not prominent elsewhere in the sayings of the Baptist. In the Old Testament images he cites (Isaiah 35:4; 29:20; 61:2), Jesus basically tells John that the *eschaton*, or "end," has arrived. The lack of any response of faith or acknowledgment on the part of the Baptist argues, through the criterion of embarrassment, in favor of the historicity of the episode as if it were a creation of the early church (i.e., part of stage two or three) then it would most likely contain some sort of affirmation from John about Jesus. The absence of that affirmation on John's part does not help the Christian cause as well as a bold affirmation would.

The thin sketch historians offer of Jesus' background contrasts sharply with the wild stories that have circulated over the centuries and that have become popular in recent years. There is no evidence that Jesus went to India or Britain. Neither is there any evidence that Jesus was married or had a family. What can be affirmed about Jesus' background squares well with the material available from Jesus' life and ministry. It seems that Jesus' entire life was directed toward his ministry—a ministry that would lead him to a brutal death. The formation of that ministry and the formation of Jesus' self-identity took place in the context of great ferment and unrest in Galilee and Judea, at the feet of his family, and in relationship to the fiery message of John the Baptist.

The Kingdom of God

It is now thought that the New Testament phrase usually translated as "the kingdom of God" (*he basileia tou theou*), demands a translation and an interpretation that moves away from any spatial or temporal interpretation. Rather than use "kingdom of God" many insist on a translation like "reign of God" because the phrase envisions a state of affairs or relationship rather than any geopolitical entity. However, others have insisted that the image of the kingdom was meant to refer to the empire of Rome as it was oppressing the poor of the region. These scholars argue that translating *basileia* as *empire* best brings out the politically and socially subversive character of Jesus' ministry.

Scholars unanimously assign this phrase to stage one (through an appeal to the criterion of multiple attestation of forms and sources) and interpret it against the backdrop of first-century Palestinian Judaism.[19] In the first century, most Jews would have understood the phrase as evoking Israel's story and its hope for God's decisive intervention in history. Cultic (i.e., priestly) and prophetic proclamations of God's kingship as past, present, and future reality are found throughout the Old Testament. In fact, the most common image of God in the Old Testament is not that of a father but that of a king (e.g., Exodus 15:18; Isaiah 6:5; Psalm 145:15).[20] The human who held the title of king in Jerusalem was understood to be acting in God's place as God's agent. As such, the king, while a sign of hope for Israel, was also answerable to God through the prophets, and when that human kingship ultimately failed with the Babylonian destruction of Jerusalem (leading to the Babylonian Exile, c. 586–532 BCE), this hope for God's kingship became bound with Israel's hope for liberation from Gentile

---

19. That Jesus proclaimed the kingdom of God is supported by the criteria of multiple attestation and of discontinuity. The criterion of embarrassment might also be invoked, as Jesus did not, in fact, bring about the kingdom of God in any overt or obvious way.

20. See, e.g., Marc Zvi Brettler, *God Is King: Understanding an Israelite Metaphor* (Sheffield: JSOT Press, 1989).

(i.e., Greek or Roman) oppression. The phrase, "kingdom of God," therefore, brought together religious, political, and social ideas and was tied to the hope that persisted among many first-century Jews, namely, the hope for a new king to restore God's rule. This is the root of the hope for a messiah in Israel, but that hope was polymorphous and often vague. There was, therefore, a close connection between Jesus' proclamation of the in-breaking kingdom of God and the implications of this announcement for understanding Jesus' identity as messiah, a topic treated more extensively later in this chapter and in chapter 4.

Debates have raged for decades concerning the best understanding of what Jesus meant by "kingdom of God." At issue is the relevance of apocalyptic eschatology (sometimes called "futurist" or "consistent eschatology") for understanding the kingdom of God. Since the late nineteenth century, the place of the phrase "kingdom of God" in the teaching of Jesus has been understood in terms of a future reality that would obliterate the present world order through a demonstrable and terrible act of divine intervention. New Testament scholars in the middle part of the twentieth century began to formulate the idea of a realized eschatology, particularly in light of a close reading of the Fourth Gospel. In realized eschatology, the kingdom is something that happens, or is realized, in the person of Jesus as he confronts people and elicits the response of conversion and faith. The kingdom is an interior and spiritual reality more than an extrinsic dramatic reality.

Yet another position understands the kingdom in terms of a proleptic or inaugurated eschatology—an "already and not yet" eschatology. According to this position, the kingdom is present in the person of Jesus and in the response of conversion and faith made by those who encountered him, but the definitive, cosmic arrival of the kingdom in which all opposition of God would be destroyed is yet to come. One may identify yet another position emerging in the 1980s that sought to understand the kingdom of God as a social reality and not a religious reality. The kingdom of God was the reversal of oppression and an undoing of the patronage system that kept the poor oppressed and marginalized. This position, advocated by groups like the Jesus Seminar, is difficult to label, but perhaps it is best termed *social eschatology*.

These competing interpretations of the kingdom, as well as how best to understand when it may arrive, are not necessarily mutually exclusive. Scholars generally agree that there is a temporal tension in Jesus' proclamation of the kingdom—an already but not yet, proleptic kingdom that has spiritual as well as social and even political implications. In other words, the social and political dimensions of Jesus' proclamation need not be sacrificed for a more "religious" interpretation (the latter being a genuine temptation given the desire of contemporary readers to separate the spiritual and the political realms, a temptation alien to the first century). Additionally, the kingdom seems to be both present and future realities in Jesus' ministry, though some sayings and deeds of Jesus seem to emphasize one over the other. William Loewe has taken a functional rather than a temporal approach to the interpretation of this symbol. For Loewe, a functional definition of the kingdom cuts to the heart of the matter because it addresses the question, what does the kingdom accomplish, or what is it for? The answer: the kingdom of God is meant to bring human and cosmic fulfillment and an answer to the problem of

Some Modern Approaches to New Testament Eschatology

Name	Description
Consistent Eschatology)	The known world will soon end. God will intervene in history to bring this end about, and at that time, also bring about the defeat of evil—this is what Jesus meant when he announced the impending arrival of the "kingdom" or "reign of God."
Realized Eschatology	The kingdom of which Jesus spoke is an interior reality. The arrival of the kingdom occurs when one encounters Jesus and responds with conversion and faith. The believer, thus renewed, has experienced the arrival of God's *basileia* (*reign*) as Jesus described it.
Proleptic Eschatology	Many sayings of Jesus point to a future in-breaking of the kingdom, while at other times it appears as though God's reign is present in Jesus. According to this view, the kingdom is in the process of arriving in the person of Jesus, but it still awaits its definitive realization in the future.
Social Eschatology	Jesus used religious symbols and religious language to unmask the unjust and dehumanizing conditions of first-century Palestine. His proclamation of the kingdom is primarily about social transformation and the creation of a countercultural and counter-imperial community.
Functional Eschatology	Rather than attempting to figure out when the kingdom is to arrive, this approach seeks to understand how the kingdom functions, what it is supposed to accomplish. For William Loewe, the reign of God brings about the solution to the problem of sin as well as brings about cosmic fulfillment. Such an approach affirms the insights of all four approaches listed previously in this chart.

evil.[21] The solution to the problem of evil is not a cosmic, mythical battle but a response to God's love and mercy uniquely present in Jesus as he summoned his contemporaries to "be converted and believe."[22]

Several related questions come to mind at this point: How does Jesus make this transformation possible? Is it merely an exhortation—a rhetorical flourish? Bernard Lonergan has written at length about the response Jesus sought from those he encountered, and characterizes it as "religious conversion." In religious conversion, one's vision of the world and self-understanding in that world is radically transformed. For Lonergan, this happens as humans perceive themselves as being loved and accepted, or to use the biblical language favored by Lonergan, one experiences the overwhelming power of God's love flooding one's heart (Romans 5:5). As a result, Lonergan contends, one then need not feel threatened by forces or power; one views one's life as a gift and no longer must pile up possessions or condemn others to protect oneself. One finds in this experience a power by which forgiveness of others is radically made possible. The experience of religious conversion is made available through Jesus' words, actions, and his very person. An exploration of how Jesus proclaimed the kingdom and empowered religious conversion may yield a fuller understanding of Jesus' ministry, a proclamation very much rooted in the religious experience and tradition of Israel.

At this point, historical scholarship enters theological territory. However, such an entry remains entirely justified; Jesus is a historical figure, but his historical significance comes from his religious mission.

The Parables

Jesus' parables have long intrigued interpreters. C. H. Dodd defined a parable as "a metaphor or simile drawn from nature or common life, arresting the hearer by its vividness or strangeness, and leaving the mind in sufficient doubt about its precise application to tease it into active thought."[23] For Dodd, parables included a manner of "play" between the image and the audience, a play that required the audience to respond to the parable. Dodd's agenda was limited, i.e., he simply wanted to show that Jesus inaugurated the kingdom through these parabolic invitations to faith. Yet Dodd did see the dialogical character of the parables, recognizing that parables required something from the respondent.

21. William P. Loewe, *A College Student's Introduction to Christology* (Collegeville, MN: Liturgical, 1996), 47–48.

22. See Mark 1:15. The Greek verb *metanoeō* means "to be converted" and is translated in the NRSV as *repent*.

23. C. H. Dodd, *Parables of the Kingdom* (New York: Scribners, 1936), 5.

Recent research has also tried to understand Jesus' parables in their Jewish literary context.[24] For example, David Stern notes that the rabbis often employed *meshalim* (Hebrew for *parables*; singular *mashal*) as playful encounters with the audience.[25] In the *mashal*, individuals in the audience were roughly connected to the agents (i.e., characters) in the *mashal* itself so that there was always a powerful and even dangerous edge to each story—one cannot be sure how the audience will react once they see themselves in a story! Stern also rejects the distinction between metaphor and allegory, arguing that such a distinction is blurred in rabbinic *meshalim*. The explanation of a parable was quite often a necessary part of the *mashalim*, so the allegorical interpretations of parables may well originate with Jesus—contrary to the assertion of a number of scholars that the interpretations of parables date to a later stage of transmission.

There is room for both disclosure and concealment in parables—this is part of the "play" that is so important to the interpretation of parables as well as an understanding of their role in the ministry of Jesus. This role perhaps differentiates Jesus' use of parables from the rabbinic *meshalim*—the parables are not merely tools to communicate information; rather, they necessarily conceal their meaning in order to provoke a dynamic response from the hearer. Jesus' parables in the Synoptics call for a radical reversal of societal roles and expectations. The social challenge in Jesus' parables is evident and is at the heart of his summons to conversion. Additionally, N. T. Wright and other scholars have argued that Jesus, as the central feature of his ministry, retold Israel's story through the parables in ways that subverted Israel's temptation to embrace violent nationalism, the desire to solve Israel's problems through an armed struggle against Rome.

An example from the Gospels may serve to illustrate the formal aspects of Jesus' parables just described. To be sure, identifying individual parables as stage-one material is immensely difficult. Meier in particular is convinced that the parables were thoroughly reworked by the early church so that attributing a parable to stage one is tenuous at best. However, that Jesus spoke in parables seems clear.

Some scholars regard the parable of the lost sheep (Matthew 18:12–14; Luke 15:3–7) as authentic.[26] This parable, though put in different contexts by each of the evangelists, was originally meant to vindicate Jesus' association with sinners and other marginalized figures and seems to have been addressed to those who objected to the fellowship Jesus offered. The dynamic of the parable is pretty straightforward: those who listen to it would immediately identify with ninety-nine sheep rather than the lost one. After all, who would leave the

---

24. That Jesus taught in parables is supported by the criterion of multiple attestation.

25. David Stern, *Parables in Midrash* (Cambridge, MA: Harvard, 1994).

26. The criterion of coherence would apply in this case; the criteria of authenticity substantiate many examples of Jesus' concern to reach out to marginal members of the community, the "lost." This parable is consistent with that theme.

rest of the flock in the wilderness to be ravaged by animals and thieves while he went to look for the lost sheep? Those who have worked in retail situations will recognize this as "shrinkage"—a certain percentage of merchandise will be damaged or stolen, which will cut into profits; and this is factored into the pricing of the merchandise. However, Jesus startlingly reverses his audience's expectations and describes the shepherd's joy at finding the lost sheep and his lack of concern for those he left in the wilderness! Those who have identified themselves as the ninety-nine obedient sheep are now identified as lost. The only solution for Jesus' audience is then to self-identify with the one who was lost and then found. Such identification opens the door for recognizing God's love and mercy but also removes the barriers between the righteous and the sinners that had occasioned the parable in the first place. The parable provokes the audience; it invites Jesus' opponents to understand themselves as "found" and their lives as God's gift.

The Kingdom in Action

Jesus' proclamation of the kingdom also includes provocative actions. The most obvious actions are often referred to as miracles in the Christian church. In Christian parlance today, a miracle is an event that cannot be explained according to the laws of nature but must be attributed to the direct activity of God..[27] How one would determine whether a miracle took place—given this definition—seems troublesome, even with the elaborate structures that exist for defining miracles in some circles (e.g., the Roman Catholic Church actually has a system in place for such verification).

From a historical perspective, things are more complex because there was no formal definition of miracle. First, one must come to grips with the fact that there were many people in the ancient world who claimed to exercise and were recognized as having extraordinary power. History can neither affirm nor deny that they had such powers, but that others believed they had the power is unquestioned. For example, some regarded Apollonius of Tyana, a remarkable contemporary of Jesus, as a "divine man." A later admirer even penned a popular narrative of Apollonius's life and healing (Philastratus, *Life of Apollonius*). While there are many features of Jesus' ministry that differentiate him from Apollonius, relevant here is that for the ancients, the works or miracles of both men were accepted by all. In Mark 3:22, for example, the opponents of Jesus do not claim that he cannot exorcise demons; rather, they claim that this power of exorcism is a sign of Jesus' own demonic possession ("He is possessed by Beelzebul, and it is by the power of the prince of demons that he casts out demons").[28] So for the

---

27. Thomas Aquinas in *Contra Gent.*, 3.102, defines a miracle as those events "done by divine agency outside the commonly observed order of things."

28. The criterion of multiple attestation assures that Jesus' reputation for performing miracles dates from stage one of the tradition.

Person of Interest: Apollonius of Tyana

Apollonius of Tyana

Apollonius of Tyana was a contemporary of Jesus and engaged in a ministry/career similar in some ways to that of Jesus. A countercultural critic, an ascetic, a philosopher, and a miracle worker, Apollonius established himself as an important religious figure in the first century. The Greek writer Philostratus, with his biography (*Life of Apollonius*) sealed Apollonius's legacy in the third century and, in the minds of some people (e.g., the French philosopher Voltaire), created a rival for Jesus. Philostratus was commissioned to write the biography by the Roman empress Julia Domna, wife of the emperor Septimius Severus (reigned 194–211 CE). The empress was a lover of religious traditions and was busy collecting the teachings and accounts of various religious figures. She came into possession of the diary of a man named Damis, a disciple of Apollonius. Intrigued by what she read, she commissioned Philostratus to write a full biography based on the account of Damis. Philostratus's *Life of Apollonius* contains several stories that echo biblical accounts, particularly when it comes to exorcisms and healings. Some have suggested that the example of Apollonius marginalizes Christian claims about the uniqueness of Jesus' miracles, while others suggest that Philostratus simply relied upon Gospel stories to create his account of Apollonius' career and present him as an alternative to Christ.

contemporaries of Jesus, the question concerning his miracles was not whether he could do amazing things, but what was the meaning of the things he did.

The New Testament uses Greek words such as *dynamis* (*power*), *ergon* (*work*), or *sēmeion* (*sign*) to describe what today are called miracles. These signs or works function on a variety of levels to differentiate Jesus from his contemporaries—including Apollonius. According to Meier, the ideal type of miracle in the Gospels has seven characteristics:[29]

---

29. *AMJ* 2, 548–49.

1. A relationship of faith and love exists between the human and the deity/divine agent.
2. The person in need is a disciple or worshipper.
3. The miracle is performed with a brief but intelligible set of words.
4. There is no indication that the deity is coerced into acting on behalf of the human.
5. The miracle is performed in obedience to Jesus' Father and in the context of his mission.
6. The miracle is understood as a symbolic representation of the kingdom.
7. The miracle does not directly punish or hurt anyone.

The uniqueness of Jesus' *miracles*, for lack of a better term, rests in the way these actions supported his claim to authority in announcing the in-breaking of the kingdom.

Like the parables, Jesus' miracles offer his audience an opportunity to see God's mercy and love in the lives of people who are marginalized. In the first century, disease, infirmity, and demonic possession were all often considered signs of God's absence in the life of those who suffered. The possessed, the poor, the suffering, and even those written off as dead were all excluded from the common life and from common meals. However, Jesus' ministry reincorporates these people into the life of the community—bringing about a dramatic reconciliation or reconstitution of a humanity that is whole, complete, and without exclusion. It must be remembered, however, that this is all done in the service of Jesus' proclamation of the kingdom—a reign that comes about through the experience of conversion to God. Jesus' dramatic actions are, in essence, parables in action; they empower a kind of love that is possible when people understand and experience being loved unrestrictedly. However, this conversion is never quite complete, for people are always looking for ways to exclude others or to protect themselves from perceived threats.

A New Community

Jesus announced an inclusive kingdom, a new community, a new fellowship made possible by the experience of conversion. He then gathered a group of followers, an apparent echo of the tradition of the Old Testament prophet Elijah (1 Kings 19:20).[30] A wide range of people were attracted to Jesus, and the Gospels depict

---

30. *AMJ* 3, 48, 50–54; see also Günther Bornkamm, *Jesus of Nazareth*, trans. Irene and Fraser McLuskey with James M. Robinson (New York: Harper, 1960), 145. Note that Jesus assembled a group of twelve disciples is supported by the criteria of multiple attestation and discontinuity; as later followers of Jesus did not perpetuate a central group of twelve, it is unlikely that they would have invented stories of Jesus that involve such a group.

large crowds following after him, but only a small portion of these admirers are called disciples.

Discipleship, or following Jesus, was the special place of a group of people who met certain criteria. First, disciples did not choose their status; rather, Jesus called them. He initiated and established the parameters of the relationship. Jesus' invitation cut across social divides and included a wide swath of first-century Jewish society—including both the impoverished, public sinners, as well as more "respectable" members of society. This inclusiveness may also be inferred from other figures closely associated with Jesus but who are not called disciples. The Gospels cite a number of these well-to-do individuals, including Zacchaeus the publican, Lazarus and his sisters, and the anonymous host of the Last Supper. Although the Gospels do not call the many women who followed Jesus disciples— because there was no feminine form of the word in Aramaic—there can be little doubt that they were in fact disciples.[31]

Second, Jesus' call to discipleship required a radical break with personal and social ties that defined one—including family, friends, and livelihood. Disciples also needed to be prepared to endure danger and hostility. Jesus gave his disciples several distinguishing practices: the practice of baptism, special instructions about simplicity in prayer, and the practice of feasting rather than fasting. The practices, along with the commands to imitate Jesus and participate in his ministry, created among Jesus' followers a new kind of family. This phenomenon is sometimes called "fictive kinship," i.e., the process of granting someone who is not a member of a family the title, the rights, and the obligations normally given to family.[32] This family and the people it included posed problems for some first-century Jews.

First-century Jews were concerned about maintaining the covenantal identity of the nation—the identity of Israel was that of God's chosen people, a people set apart. In order to do this the Law of Moses had to be observed and the cult of the Temple maintained. Those who did not consistently and appropriately observe the Law and utilize the system of sacrifices in the Temple jeopardized not only their own relationship to God but also the national identity, the Jewish people's relationship with God. Scripture often associated Israel and Judah's ethical failures with their willingness to adopt the customs, religious practices, and lifestyles of their neighbors (e.g., 2 Kings 17:7–18)—in effect, the Israelites went astray when they failed to distance themselves from sinners. Seen from the perspective of inclusive, twenty-first-century Western society, those who condemned Jesus' association with public sinners appear small-minded and

---

31. See, Joachim Gnilka, *Jesus of Nazareth: Message and History* (Peabody, MA: Hendrickson, 1997), 179. For a fuller discussion of the place of women in the ministry of Jesus see, Elisabeth Schüssler Fiorenza, *In Memory of Her: A Feminist Theological Reconstruction of Christian Origins* (New York: Crossroad, 1983).

32. N. T. Wright, *Jesus and the Victory of God* (Minneapolis, Fortress, 1996), 430–32.

prejudiced. However, seen in context, it becomes apparent that they believed that they were heeding the lessons of the history of Israel and the admonitions of the prophets. Jesus' actions in this area certainly caused controversy and disturbed many of his contemporaries. What was Jesus' purpose in these actions? Did Jesus intend to call into question Israel's status as God's chosen people?

One may cite Jesus' designation of a group known as "the twelve" as evidence that he did not call into question Israel's chosen status; rather, through this symbolic act, Jesus sought to renew or reconstitute Israel. These twelve, though we know little about most of them (note that even the lists of the twelve in the Gospels differ somewhat), symbolized a reconstituted Israel around the ministry of Jesus as they embodied what it meant to be a disciple. For Jesus and his Jewish contemporaries, any understanding of God's rule over the world—the kingdom—is unthinkable without the fulfillment of the hopes of Israel. Although Jesus radically redefined these hopes and expectations, he nonetheless acted within the framework of first-century Judaism.

Major Sects in First-Century Palestinian Judaism

Sect	Composition	Theology	Politics
Sadducees	mostly priestly aristocracy	The strict observance of the written Torah and the operation of the Temple cult were the necessary and sufficient grounds for maintaining Israel's relationship, its covenant, with God.	The Sadducees sought to make accommodations with the Romans in order to ensure that the Temple could function and the Torah could be observed.
Pharisees	mostly laymen, though with support from among some priests	For the Pharisees, the Torah and its demands for purity had to be at the heart of all Jewish life, not just the cultic life of the Temple. They were the great democratizers of Judaism and introduced the importance of Torah study for all laypeople.	The Pharisees, or "separate ones," objected to the accommodations made by the Sadducees and generally resented Roman rule.

Continued

Major Sects in First-Century Palestinian Judaism *Continued*

Sect	Composition	Theology	Politics
Pharisees (*cont.*)		In addition to the written Torah, the Pharisees adopted oral traditions connected to the Torah that they insisted were equally valid. At least some Pharisees held apocalyptic beliefs such as resurrection and final judgment that were not held by the Sadducees.	
Essenes	mostly disenfranchised priests	These priestly figures separated themselves from the Temple when illegitimate priests and corruption had despoiled it. They retreated to the desert, though they had members/supporters who lived in towns and villages. In the desert, they prepared for the apocalyptic battle that would bring an end to the Temple and its corrupt priesthood.	The Essenes were separatists and did not form political alliances.
Armed Resistance Groups	laypeople—such groups were strong in Galilee	The armed resistance groups, of which the Zealots are best known, believed that foreign domination had to end in order for Israel to be faithful to God. They adopted the tactics of modern terrorists—assassinations, insurrections, theft. They did not proliferate until the middle part of the first century—well after the death of Jesus.	Armed resistance groups tended to be highly suspect in the eyes of other Jews, and they formed no alliances.

Within that framework, however, Jesus also stretched some social and religious boundaries, particularly in his practice of eating with outsiders, or table fellowship. In first-century Judaism, the company one kept at mealtime was of no small consequence. One either shared a blessing or a curse depending upon the company one kept at the dinner table. The fact that Jesus chose to eat with outsiders (i.e., public sinners and tax collectors) raised eyebrows and caused consternation among his coreligionists. Yet the practice of table fellowship is more than just an example of Jesus keeping dangerous company or his propensity to shock and annoy "the establishment"; rather, through table fellowship Jesus extended an offer of fellowship, forgiveness, and community. It is instructive that Jesus' ministry is characterized by an offer of fellowship to tax collectors and sinners before he demanded a change of life. In other words, the offer of forgiveness and fellowship precedes the call for repentance and conversion. One might even say that it is the fellowship that makes such conversion possible. Jesus' practice of table fellowship, thus, signaled the in-breaking of the kingdom in ways that many in Israel would have found familiar as well as challenging and threatening.

Jesus and Judaism

It is a mischaracterization of early Judaism to suggest that there is a dichotomy between the Torah and love/mercy. The idea of "covenantal love" is at the heart of Judaism. The relationship between covenantal love and "righteousness" can be problematic for Christians as they attempt to discern the attitude of Jesus toward the practices of early Judaism. The ideal of love and mercy tends to stand in tension with the pursuit of righteousness in practical religion—just think about Christian history, or Islamic history. The ideal of covenantal love as the origin and end of the pursuit of righteousness often does not meet with the reality of religious living; many voices have called for reform in this regard throughout the history of Israel and the church: Amos, Hosea, and the rest of the Old Testament prophets; Francis of Assisi, Catherine of Sienna, and Mother Theresa of Calcutta. One should see Jesus' teaching not as an abrogation of Mosaic Law but as a prophetic critique of religious practice.

First and foremost, the ministry of Jesus must be understood as a ministry to Israel. Jesus was a Jew and his ministry is intelligible as a religious renewal or reform movement. Some scholars have registered concern regarding this interpretation of Jesus' sayings, that portraying Jesus as a reformer or renewer of Judaism implies something was amiss with Judaism in the first century. While concerns over Christian misinterpretations of Judaism are generally well founded, to say that Jesus was concerned about religious reform does not imply anti-Semitism or a dismissal of Judaism.

The Battle to Understand Judaism in the New Testament

Christian faith has long presented itself as a religion of grace and contrasted itself with Judaism as a religion of "works" or personal achievement—in Judaism one has to work hard to earn God's favor and blessing. Such an attitude is especially apparent in the way Christians tend to read the letters of Paul, especially to the Romans and Galatians. From the earliest centuries of the Common Era, Christian writers and preachers attacked Judaism and the Jewish people as corrupt and petty. Such charges became engrained in Christian consciousness and provided the soil from which sprang anti-Semitism. Even the great theologians of the twentieth century were largely complicit in the anti-Judaism (bigotry oriented toward the religion) if not the anti-Semitism (racial bigotry) so prevalent in Europe and the United States at that time.

George F. Moore was perhaps one of the first modern scholars to identify the problem of Christian interpretations of Judaism in the New Testament. In an essay titled "Christian Writers on Judaism,"[33] Moore documented how late-nineteenth-century writers portrayed Judaism as the antithesis of Christianity: Judaism was a legalistic religion; God was inaccessible; one must earn salvation by good works/merit. This view dominated much New Testament scholarship, though Moore began to poke some holes into this interpretation. A drastic reappraisal of Judaism finally began with the work of the Canadian scholar E. P. Sanders. While some may disagree with his reading of Paul's letters—the so-called new perspective on Paul—his contribution to an understanding of Judaism in the first century has been revolutionary. His two major works are *Paul and Palestinian Judaism: a Comparison of Patterns of Religion* (London: SCM, 1977) and *Jesus and Judaism* (Minneapolis: Fortress, 1985). In the former, Sanders outlines his understanding of the concept that ties first-century Palestinian Judaism together: covenantal nomism (the Greek word *nomos* means "law"). Sanders' point was this:

(1) God has chosen Israel and (2) given the law. The law implies both (3) God's promise to maintain election and (4) the requirement to obey. (5) God rewards obedience and punishes transgression. (6) The law provides for means of atonement, and atonement results in (7) maintenance or re-establishment of the covenantal relationship. (8) All those who are maintained in the covenant by obedience, atonement and God's mercy belong to the group which will be saved. An important interpretation of the first and last points is that election and ultimately salvation are considered to be by God's mercy rather than human achievement. . . .

Continued

---

33. *Harvard Theological Review* 14 (1921): 197–254.

By consistently maintaining the basic framework of covenantal nomism, the gift and demand of God were kept in a healthy relationship with each other, the minutiae of the law were observed on the basis of the large principles of religion and because of commitment to God, and humility before God who chose and would ultimately redeem Israel was encouraged. (*Paul and Palestinian Judaism*, 422 and 427)

Rather, traditions are vital to the extent that they can inspire reformers: decadent, late-medieval Catholicism produced Martin Luther. Though Roman Catholicism does not agree with everything Luther taught, he is rightly viewed in Catholic circles as someone interested in reforming the church precisely because he valued the Christian church, not because he hated it or wanted it destroyed. While the comparison between Christ and Luther is limited, it may help demonstrate that Jesus' disputes with religious authorities revolved around important principles on which there was general agreement.

The Torah, the first five books of the Bible, formed the heart of Jewish life in the Second Temple Period. These books narrate the story of Israel's ancestors (*haggadah*, Hebrew for "telling" or "narrating") and offer instruction for responding to Israel's God (*halakah*, Hebrew for *walking*; it refers to principles, guidelines, or instruction). The stories provide Israel with its self-understanding as God's beloved, chosen, and redeemed people. This election was gratuitous, there was nothing that Israel did to deserve it, and, in fact, the Old Testament points out time and again the way Israel turns away from God's election. The instruction, the Law, provided Israel with the appropriate response to God's gracious election.[34] Divorced from the narratives, the instruction could take on a life of its own and be used to brutalize and marginalize people. One can interpret many of Jesus' disputes with Jewish officials (often stereotyped with the expression "scribes and Pharisees," or "chief priests and Pharisees") as stemming from Jesus' desire to protect the traditions of Israel by connecting them with the story of God's mercy and love. A good example is the story of the woman caught in adultery (John 7:53–8:11). Though the story is not likely to date to stage one (it even appears to be a later addition to John's Gospel), it illustrates how Jesus, in the midst of what appears to be a legal dispute, appeals to the story of Israel to call for an expanded and deeper interpretation of the demands of *halakah*. In the story, a woman caught in the act of adultery is brought before Jesus (one may

---

34. This is at the heart of E. P. Sanders' notion of "covenantal nomism."

fairly wonder what happened to her partner). The Pharisees ask Jesus whether they should stone her as the Torah seemed to require. In response, Jesus writes with his finger on the ground, and invites anyone who is without sin to cast a stone at her. Jesus then bends down to write a second time. John Paul Heil has rightly pointed to Jesus' writing as the *crux interpretum* of the passage. For Heil, this act recalls God's giving of the commandments on Sinai. The tablets that are given to Moses were inscribed with letters that came from God's finger (Exodus 31:18; Deuteronomy 9:10; 10:2), but these tablets had to be rewritten because when Moses descended the mountain he found the people of Israel, who had just sworn loyalty to God, in a drunken orgy around the golden calf. The Old Testament tells us that despite Israel's sin, disobedience, and failure, God gave them another chance. The commandments were rewritten, and Israel remained chosen, even though they deserved to be forsaken by God.[35] Thus, when Jesus writes with his finger on the ground, and particularly when he writes the second time, he is reminding the Jewish community of their own story. They, the entire people of Israel, like the adulterous woman, have sinned. Jesus, thus, challenges those who would use the commandments to play a game of "gotcha" apart from the story of God's love, mercy, and fidelity.

Though the historical accuracy of the story is open to question, it has a resonance within the life of Jesus, and a case can be made through the criterion of coherence. Jesus, faithful to the prophetic and best rabbinic traditions, sees the story of God's love and the value of the human (made in God's image) as the determining factor for the interpretation and application of any commandments. Jesus' summons to conversion, however, did not make Jesus a libertine; rather, the demands of the covenant are properly understood and lived when interpreted as part of the story of God's love for Israel.

The Death of Jesus

Mel Gibson's controversial film, *The Passion of the Christ*, raised several important issues surrounding the execution of Jesus. Many scholars and theologians believe that Gibson erroneously portrayed the Jewish authorities as primarily responsible for the death of Jesus and placed them in an exceedingly negative light. The controversy surrounding the film has highlighted the historical question of who was responsible for the death of Jesus. One point of agreement that has emerged among scholars is that Jesus provoked opposition, yet the identity of his opponents is harder to pin down. That he is often portrayed in the Gospels as fighting with "the scribes and the Pharisees" or even "the Jews" does not clarify the matter, for the Gospels also contend that the

---

35. John Paul Heil, "The Story of Jesus and the Adulteress (John 7:53–8:11) Reconsidered," *Biblica* 72 (1991): 182–91.

Jewish Sanhedrin, led by the Sadducees at the time, was responsible for "hand-ing over" Jesus to the Romans. The Sanhedrin was a group of clerics who were responsible for the administration of the Temple and ensuring the obser-vance of Jewish Law. Since 6 CE, when Herod's son Archelaeus was deposed and a Roman prefecture was instituted in Judea, the Sanhedrin had to work under the prefect's watchful eye. It is apparent that some arrangement existed between the Roman governor, Pontius Pilate, and the Sanhedrin. The Roman governor confirmed the leader of the Sanhedrin, who was allowed to exercise his office only with the support of Rome. It is interesting to note that Joseph Caiaphas, the High Priest (the head of the Sanhedrin) at the time of Jesus, was elevated to that office shortly before Pilate became governor and stayed in that office until Pilate was recalled to Rome in 36 CE. This is remarkable given that rapid turnover was normal in the high priesthood up to the time of Caiaphas. It seems likely that Caiaphas managed to hold onto his office by cooperating with the Roman authorities.

Cooperation between Pilate and Caiaphas does not explain who was responsible for Jesus' death; neither does it address the irregularities one finds in the Gospel accounts of Jesus' "trial": there could not have been a trial at night, for such a thing was forbidden by law and good sense, and a charge of sedition, or any change calling for the death penalty, could not have involved the Sanhe-drin as it did not have the power to execute.[36] Perhaps the hearing before Caia-phas was not a trial but merely a kind of interview that provided a transition to the real trial before Pilate that took place in the morning. However, what could have caused the Sanhedrin, controlled by the Sadducees and not the Pharisees at this time, to see Jesus as a threat? In Mark 14:64, the Sanhedrin charged Jesus with blasphemy (i.e., speaking against God). What could Jesus have said or done that could be construed as blasphemous?

In the Gospels, the hearing before Caiaphas centers on Jesus' activ-ity in the Temple[37] and the question of Jesus' self-understanding it seemed to raise. Jesus' stay in Jerusalem, and particularly his symbolic activity in the Temple (Mark 11:15–19), presents a crucial piece of data for grasping Jesus' self-understanding. Jesus' driving the money changers and vendors out of the Temple is to be viewed in the context of the prophetic literature—particularly Zechariah, whom Jesus evokes with his messianic entry into Jerusalem (Mark 11:1–10; cf. Zechariah 9:9). Jesus answers the high priest's charges by appealing

---

36. The only exception appears to be the following concession: if a Gentile were to enter the Temple he would be subject to stoning. There are at least two inscriptions from the Temple area that attest to this (e.g., see Josephus, *Antiquities*, 15. 427).

37. That Jesus performed some action against the Temple similar to that described in the Gos-pels should be judged reliable on the criterion of discontinuity. It was unusual for first-century Jews to oppose the Temple (apart from the Essenes, whose reasons for doing so were very different from Jesus'), and such opposition is alien to the early Christian tradition as well.

to Daniel 7 ("the Son of Man") and Psalm 110 ("seated at the right hand" [of God]) and tells the high priest that he will be a witness to the events that will vindicate Jesus' claim to be Messiah (even though he uses the phrase "Son of Man"; Mark 14:62 pars.).[38] Although the response Jesus gives in the Gospels is suffused with later Christology, the basics of the dispute seem plausible: if Jesus spoke against the Temple and offered a form of reconciliation to sinners apart from the Temple, he was implicitly claiming an authority for himself that rivaled the authority of the ruling elite.

Jesus' entry into Jerusalem and his prophetic action in the Temple both evidence an authoritative self-understanding, i.e., Jesus understood himself as having divine authority. Many New Testament scholars are reasonably hesitant to identify Jesus' self-understanding as it smacks of historical psychology (a highly suspect "discipline"). After all, it is difficult to psychoanalyze the self-understanding of even a well-known, contemporary figure (or, indeed, oneself), much less a shadowy figure from the distant past! Other scholars insist that one can infer the basic contours of Jesus' self-understanding from his actions. N. T. Wright argues that Jesus understood himself to be Israel's Messiah—with the caveat that the messiah, in first-century Judaism, was a highly complex idea.[39] Wright offers some basic ideas and tasks associated with the Messiah that cut across the sectarian literature of the time, including the belief that the Messiah was to defeat Israel's enemies in battle, and the Messiah would rebuild, restore, or cleanse the Temple.[40] Based upon Jesus' actions in the Temple, Wright contends that Jesus envisioned himself as the king, the Messiah, God's anointed, through whom God was at last restoring his people.[41] This definition, or redefinition, of *messiah* emerges within the context of Wright's presentation of Jesus' prophetic "kingdom praxis," i.e., the stories Jesus told, and the worldview created by these stories as well as the actions he performed.

Jesus' announcement of the kingdom was meant to embody and enact the hope that God would visit and restore the people of Israel. This is apparent in the Synoptic Gospels (stage three of the tradition), in which Jesus is consistently portrayed as conscious of his status as Messiah and never misses an opportunity to express that self-understanding.[42] Yet, one must also reckon that

---

38. For Wright, Psalm 110 plays a significant role in Jesus' self-understanding in Mark 12:35–37 pars. On the use of Psalm 110 in early Christianity, see David Hay, *Glory at the Right Hand: Psalm 110 in Early Christianity*, Society of Biblical Literature Monograph Series, n. 18 (Nashville: Abingdon, 1973).

39. N. T. Wright, *The New Testament and the People of God* (Minneapolis: Fortress, 1992), 307–20; hereafter, *NTPG*.

40. N. T. Wright, *Jesus and the Victory of God* (Minneapolis: Fortress, 1996), 481–86; hereafter, *JVG*.

41. *JVG*, 481–86.

42. *JVG*, 487–88. Wright cites Wrede and Bultmann as two influential figures who advocated the identification of Jesus as Messiah as a post-resurrectional event.

the Gospels present a clear gap between the authority Jesus seems to claim through his actions and his reticence to accept the *designation* of messiah. It is Jesus' reluctance to use the title *messiah* that may account, in part, for his use of the self-designation Son of Man. In the hearing before Caiaphas, Jesus' use of this self-designation causes dismay within the Sanhedrin because the Son of Man figure is best situated and understood within the context of Israel's nationalistic hope for restoration. From the perspective of Jesus' contemporaries, Jesus' subversion of Israel's story and symbols were the heart of the matter. Both the Pharisees and the Sadducees believed Jesus was a "false prophet" who led the people away from the true worship of God. For the Sadducees, Jesus was also troublesome because he stirred up sentiment against those who controlled access to God through the Temple. Though Jesus did not lead an army, his messianic pretensions could become the focus of a real revolution, for which Rome would hold the entire nation responsible. Additionally, Wright contends, Jesus was understood as having committed blasphemy by placing himself beside God. Quite simply, from the Jewish perspective, Jesus was a false prophet and deserved death (Deuteronomy 13:1–11).

Jesus' attitude toward his death is best grasped through a reading of his last supper with his disciples. Through this last supper, Jesus blends the story of his life with the story of Israel so that Jesus' life is understood as the climax of Israel's story.[43] Wright believes that the symbolic activity in the Temple makes it clear that Jesus is replacing the system of sacrifice with himself; his death was to bring about a new Exodus, or an end to Israel's oppression.[44] This interpretation fits in well with Jesus' prophetic ministry—reinterpreting the nationalistic and violent symbols of Israel with nonviolent resistance. Jesus' life would be the symbol of the "new people of God," a people defined by their suffering and the suffering of their Messiah. Wright also contends that Jesus understood his approaching death as vicarious substitution—Jesus would suffer in place of the people of Israel. In doing so, Jesus was utilizing the tradition established in the stories of Maccabean martyrs as well as the theology articulated in Isaiah's suffering servant.[45] Jesus' death would bring about a victory:

> Jesus believed it was his [G]od-given vocation to identify with the rebel cause, the kingdom cause, when at last that identification could not be understood as [an] endorsement [of violent nationalism]. . . . He would go ahead of his people, to take upon himself both the fate that they had suffered one way or another for half a millennium at the

---

43. *JVG*, 553–63.

44. *JVG*, 558.

45. *JVG*, 576–92. In early Judaism there were stories that envisioned salvation from the present evil age through the sufferings of certain figures who embodied the sufferings of Israel.

hands of pagan empires and the fate that [many of] his contemporaries were apparently hell-bent upon pulling down on their heads once for all. The martyr tradition [as embodied in the Maccabean literature in particular] suggested that this was the way in which Israel would at last be brought through suffering to vindication (N. T. Wright, *Jesus and the Victory of God*, 596).

In Wright's analysis, this victory and vindication was to be accomplished in Jesus' mind through the two central tasks of the Messiah: purification of the Temple and victory in battle. The purification of the Temple and Jesus' interpretation of his death have been shown as sacrificial in the Last Supper. Jesus' messianic task was completed with the victory in battle over Israel's enemies—yet these enemies were not those defined by violent nationalists in Jerusalem or Galilee. Rather, Jesus' proclamation of the kingdom and his call to conversion redefined Israel's enemy as Satan rather than Rome—as sin rather than as the presence of a Gentile government in Israel. His confrontation with power, particularly Roman power, and the love he demonstrated in the face of that power, were evident in the story of his life and his death.[46]

Wright's convictions about how Jesus understood himself and his death remain controversial. Many of his critics believe his position seems to be born of religious convictions rather than by historical research. Wright nonetheless stands out as offering an integrative approach that moves historical Jesus research in the direction of theology while remaining robustly historical. Such a move seems to be the natural outgrowth of a low-ascending approach to Christology and the embrace of the historical Jesus. Meier's characterization of history as a discrete discipline, separate from theology, while well founded, has its own critics. Meier's use of history belies this segregation inasmuch as he seems to generate theological conclusions in his picture of Jesus. Theologians and historians are, in many instances, either left with the frustrations that have characterized historical Jesus research for two centuries or, like Wright, they push beyond those frustrations despite the inevitable criticisms that come from such a move.

Conclusion

A historically reconstructed portrait of Jesus, no matter how intriguing or provocative, is not the norm or foundation for Christian faith. Yet, such a sketch, like the one provided in this chapter, is useful for gaining an account of the way Christian faith developed in relationship to the life and ministry of Jesus. It forces one to wrestle with the historical particularities of Jesus' ministry and

---

46. *JVG*, 606–9.

self-understanding. Additionally, this sketch highlights the importance of Jesus' call to conversion in response to his proclamation of the kingdom. It is apparent from the brief sketch offered here that this conversion and the kingdom are complex realities that can only be sketched partially from the historical point of view. The experience of religious conversion, anticipated in the initial faith of Jesus' followers during his lifetime, nonetheless, cannot substitute for the centerpiece of the Christian faith—the resurrection of Christ. Yet, the experience of the resurrection is deeply connected to the life and ministry of Jesus and is unintelligible without it.

Questions for Understanding

1. Which of the five primary criteria discussed at the beginning of the chapter is perhaps most controversial? Why? Which is, perhaps, the most "objective"? Why?

2. What are some of the major features of Jesus' background, family, and life before his public ministry?

3. Describe the relationship between John the Baptist and Jesus.

4. How should one understand the expression "the kingdom of God"? Describe the issues inherent in any interpretation of this expression.

5. What is a parable, and how does it relate to Jesus' proclamation of the kingdom? How do the miracles tie in to the proclamation of the kingdom?

6. Who was Apollonius of Tyana, and why is he important for understanding Jesus' miracles?

7. Did Jesus do away with the Mosaic or Jewish Law? Did he seek to establish a new religion? Explain.

8. Why was Jesus executed? How does N. T. Wright suggest that Jesus understood his death?

Questions for Reflection and Action

1. Identify two important areas of historical Jesus research that show evidence of anti-Semitism. Is Christianity inherently anti-Semitic? Explain.

2. Did Jesus' message have political implications? Explain.

3. Historians generally believe that Jesus included women among his closest disciples. Should this claim have any bearing on the role of women in the Christian church today? Explain.

For Further Reading

Gnilka, Joachim. *Jesus of Nazareth: Message and History.* Translated by Siegfried
    S. Schatzman. Peabody, MA: Henrickson, 1997.

Lohfink, Gerhard. *Jesus of Nazareth: What He Wanted, Who He Was.* Translated by
    Linda M. Maloney. Collegeville, MN: Liturgical, 2012.

Thiessen, Gerd and Annette Mertz. *The Historical Jesus: A Comprehensive Guide.*
    Translated by John Bowden. London: SCM, 1998.

3

The Resurrection

Chapters 1 and 2 concluded with some provocative ideas about how Jesus lived his life and understood his death, pursued from a historian's perspective. Chapter 3 turns to the question of the origins of Christian faith, the religious experience of the followers of Jesus, and the genesis of the Christian church. Specifically, the focus will move to the accounts and theology of the resurrection of Jesus. This theology is so central to the Christian expression of faith that in 1 Corinthians 15:14 Paul writes, "and if Christ has not been raised, then our proclamation has been vain and your faith has been in vain." Such a sharp statement helps to delineate the importance of the present chapter and puts into perspective those scholars who find discussion of the resurrection narratives so challenging.

The Old Testament Period

The Afterlife in the Deuteronomistic Tradition

The Old Testament holds no uniform belief concerning an afterlife. In fact, for most of the Old Testament, an afterlife is never acknowledged. Many modern students wonder why one would believe in God if there is no heaven? One of the most stirring responses to this question is found in Deuteronomy 30. Here Moses speaks to the Hebrew people at the end of their long journey out of slavery in Egypt and just before they cross the Jordan River to occupy the land promised to Abraham in Genesis 15. He gathers the people together and challenges them to embrace the covenant—to bind themselves to God who brought them out of Egypt and slavery. Moses spells out the terms of the covenant:

> If you obey the commandments of the Lord, your God that I am commanding you today, by loving the Lord your God, walking in his ways, and observing his commandments, decrees, and ordinances, then you shall live and become numerous, and the Lord your God, will bless you in the land you are entering to possess. But if your heart turns away and you do not hear, but are led astray to bow down to other gods and serve

them, I declare to you today that you shall perish; you shall not live long in the land that you are crossing the Jordan to enter and possess. I call heaven and earth to witness against you today that I have set before you life and death, blessings and curses. Choose life so that you and your descendants may live, loving the Lord your God, obeying him, and holding fast to him; for that will mean life to you so that you may live in the land that the Lord swore to give to your ancestors, to Abraham, to Isaac and to Jacob. (Deuteronomy 30:16–20)

For the Deuteronomist (i.e., the author[s] of Deuteronomy and the Deuteronomistic History that runs from Joshua to 2 Kings), the rewards for covenantal obedience and fidelity are life, prosperity, and security in the land. Breaking covenantal fidelity brings with it famine, war, and death. So the choice is just that straightforward: life versus death, blessings, or curses. This outlook is shared by most of the authors in the Old Testament; for them, there is no discernible afterlife. To the extent that an afterlife is envisioned at all, it is described by the Hebrew word *Sheol*, the abode of the dead. In *Sheol* the dead sleep; they forget life and do not praise God (e.g., Isaiah 38:18; Psalm 88:10–12; Job 7:9; 31:3–19).

This picture of earthly blessing for the righteous faithful and curses for the wicked often ran up against the experience of the suffering righteous and the prospering wicked. Jeremiah, who was closely associated with the Deuteronomic outlook, wondered how God would address the apparent inconsistencies in this theology (Jeremiah 12:1–4). In the prophets, a pervasive pessimism about an afterlife appears, bracketed by deep questions and concerns about how to understand God's covenantal love and fidelity beyond death, beyond the destruction that befell the nation in the eighth and sixth centuries BCE.

The Babylonian Exile and the Afterlife

Perhaps the most dramatic event in the history of Judah was the destruction of Solomon's Temple and the exile of the leading citizens of Jerusalem in 587 BCE by the Babylonian king Nebuchadnezzar. The Hebrew prophet Ezekiel heard of these events while he was in Babylon and offered prophetic messages that sought to reassure the people of God's fidelity. Perhaps his most dramatic image is the famous passage in which Ezekiel is instructed to prophesy over the dry bones.

The hand of the Lord came upon me, and he brought me out in the spirit of the Lord and set me down in the middle of a valley; it was full of bones. . . . He said to me, Mortal, can these bones live? I answered, "O Lord God, you know." Then he said to me, "Prophesy to these bones, and say to them: O dry bones, hear the word of the Lord. Thus says the Lord God to these bones: I will cause breath to enter you, and you shall live. . . . So I prophesied as I had been commanded; and as

I prophesied, suddenly there was a noise, a rattling, and the bones came together, bone to its bone. I looked, and there were sinews on them, and flesh had come upon them, and skin had covered them; but there was no breath in them. Then he said to me, "Prophesy to the breath, prophesy, mortal, and say to the breath: Thus says the Lord God: Come from the four winds, O breath, and breathe upon these slain that they may live." I prophesied as he commanded me, and the breath came into them, and they lived, and stood on their feet, a vast multitude. Then he said to me, Mortal, these bones are the whole house of Israel. They say, "Our bones are dried up, and our hope is lost; we are cut off completely." Therefore prophesy, and say to them: Thus says the Lord God: I am going to open your graves and bring you up from your graves, O my people; and I will bring you back to the land of Israel. And you shall know that I am the Lord, when I open your graves, and bring you up from your graves, O my people. I will put my spirit within you, and you shall live, and I will place you on your own soil; then you shall know that I, the Lord, have spoken and will act, says the Lord. (Ezekiel 37:1–14)

This passage is undoubtedly from the sixth century BCE and, thus, earlier than similar biblical passages that are actually later additions to the biblical books (e.g., Isaiah 26). However, the question remains, does Ezekiel envision an actual "resurrection from the dead" as a hope for Judah? Or is this passage symbolic, a vivid way of consoling the exiles from Jerusalem and promising that God will return the people to their land? Most scholars would argue for a symbolic interpretation. However, this passage and the events that gave rise to it are decisive for the development of Jewish belief in an afterlife and particularly in resurrection.

The Afterlife in History and Tradition

Judaism and Christianity, of course, are not the only religious traditions with beliefs on the afterlife. Following is a highly simplified sampling of historical beliefs on the afterlife.

Ancient Egypt

Egyptian attitudes toward death and what follows can be gleaned from the practice of mummification. Egyptian burial practices such as the inclusion of household goods and servants in the tombs of the nobility suggest an expectation of life continuing after death in much the same manner as before death. There seems to have been no expectation of corporate judgment or cosmic battles.

Continued

Ancient Greece and Rome

In ancient Greece and Rome, the dead were confined to Hades or Pluto, where three judges would rule on their fate. The heroes, i.e., those who had shown virtue in battle, could earn a place in the Elysian Fields, while those who had offended the gods were relegated to Tartarus. Originally seen as a place of confinement for those who endangered the gods, Tartarus later became a place for punishment. The vast majority of the dead, who were neither virtuous nor evil, were consigned to the Fields of Asphodel where they existed as shadows or ghosts.

Hinduism

In Hinduism, human existence is defined by *samsara* or the cycle of rebirth. According to the *Code of Manu*, for instance, one's rebirth is determined by the degree to which one abides by the caste system (i.e., the hierarchical system by which families are given certain roles within society). Certain duties define castes; to the extent one remains faithful to those duties, he or she can be released from that caste. Yet the cycle of rebirth is not permanent; rather, one seeks union with the divine and liberation from *samsara*.

Buddhism

Like Hinduism, Buddhism envisions a cycle of rebirth, also called *samsara*. One can be reborn into a heavenly, godlike existence, but that existence is still within *samsara*, as is rebirth into a region of "hell." Within Buddhism, the goal of afterlife is not union with the divine but liberation from *samsara* through recognizing the nature of reality and its inherent emptiness (*anatman* and *sunyata*). *Nirvana* is the name given to the state of perfect rest and nothingness that one finds with enlightenment and the practice of the Noble Eightfold Path. Some forms of Buddhism (e.g., Pure Land) envision a "western land" of bliss into which devotees of Buddha will be reborn, but this is merely an intermediary stage in which one practices the Noble Eightfold Path—the only path to Nirvana.

Islam

Unlike the other traditions mentioned previously, Islam emerged after both Judaism and Christianity, in the seventh century CE. Islam's vision of the afterlife roughly mirrors apocalyptic visions within Judaism and Christianity. Within Islam, the afterlife is divided into two abodes—*Jannah* or *Firdous* (the "garden" or "paradise"; see Qur'an 18:107; 23:11) for those who have done good deeds and followed God's commands, *Jahannam* for those who have done evil. There is some uncertainty as to whether *Jahannam* is a place of eternal punishment or remedial punishment, i.e., temporary punishment meant to bring about repentance.

The Afterlife and the Maccabean Crisis

The crucial event for the development of an afterlife tradition was the Maccabean Rebellion in the second century BCE. Following the return from the Babylonian Exile and the rebuilding of the Temple in Jerusalem by Joshua and Zerubbabel in 515 BCE, the Jewish people enjoyed relative peace. They were no longer an independent and autonomous nation as they had been from the time of David through Zedekiah, having been incorporated into the great Persian Empire. However, the Persians generally allowed the Jewish people to worship Yahweh as they saw fit, so long as good order was preserved.

With the demise of the Persian Empire under pressure from Alexander the Great and his Greek armies in the fourth century (around 332 BCE), the situation began to change. Though Alexander and his immediate successors who controlled Judah and Jerusalem (these successors were part of what came to be known as the Ptolemaic Kingdom) generally allowed the Jews to worship in peace, Alexander's wars had a number of goals, and prominent among those goals was a form of cultural imperialism. Alexander was convinced that Greek culture and the Greek way of life were far superior to all others, and wherever he went he established Greek cities (usually bearing his name—Alexandria). Among his successors this became an increasingly important goal, i.e., assimilating the local populace into a Greek lifestyle and worldview. When control of Jerusalem shifted to the Seleucid Kingdom, also founded by Alexander's successors, the Jewish people were put under great duress.

The Seleucid king Antiochus IV Epiphanes outlawed the Jewish religion (1 Maccabees 1:41–64 and 2 Maccabees 6:1–11) and erected an altar to (and perhaps even an image of) the Greek god Zeus in the Jerusalem Temple (2 Maccabees 6:2). Antiochus's goal was the full assimilation of Jews into the dominant Greek culture. His plan received support from many prominent priestly families, and even some of the high priests, but the majority rose up in rebellion led by a family known as the Maccabees. The books that bear the name "Maccabees"—which are found in Catholic and Orthodox Bibles but are considered "apocryphal" (noncanonical) by Protestants—relate harrowing accounts of devout Jews who were willing to suffer torture and die rather than forsake the covenant and its obligations.

This turn of events sharply raised the question of God's fidelity: if faithfulness was supposed to bring peace and prosperity, why are the righteous suffering and dying for their faithfulness to God? When are they going to see the rewards promised them in Deuteronomy 30? It is in the midst of this crisis that an important conviction began to form in Jewish theology: God hears the cries of his suffering people and will come soon to vindicate the righteous and punish the wicked. Until then, God asks his people to be patient and endure faithfully. But what will this vindication look like?

The Canon, the Apocrypha, and the Deuterocanonicals

The word *canon* (from the Greek *kanōn,* meaning "rule" or "measure") has come to designate the collection of books recognized as sacred Scripture, the rule or measure of the Christian faith.

The Old Testament

The Hebrew Bible—which Christians call the Old Testament—is made up of three sections. The first section consists of the Torah (meaning "law" or "instruction"), also called the Pentateuch (five scrolls). The next section is the Nevi'im (Prophets), which consists of writings by or about prophets. Last is the Kethuvim (Writings), a fairly eclectic collection of books that include histories, legends, psalms, and wisdom writings. In Jewish tradition, the Bible is called the "Tanak," which is an acronym formed from the first letter of each major division (Torah, Nevi'im, Kethuvim = TNK). The exact number of books that make up the Tanak was agreed upon at least by the end of the second century CE.

The picture was rather more complicated in the first century, for it seems that some Jewish groups were using scriptures that eventually would be excluded from the Tanak—the Dead Sea Scrolls community, for one. By the time of Jesus, large numbers of Jews were living outside Palestine and were speaking Greek. Consequently, a more-or-less standard Greek translation of the Hebrew Scriptures evolved, known as the Septuagint (abbreviated LXX). It appears to have originated in the large Jewish community in Alexandria, Egypt, in the second century BCE. The Septuagint included a number of books that would eventually be rejected from the Hebrew canon—for example, the several books of Maccabees.

As the followers of Jesus spread their movement throughout the Greek-speaking world, naturally they made use of the Septuagint—most of the Old Testament quotations found in the New Testament are based upon it. In effect, the Septuagint became the Christian Bible. While all Christians accepted the books now found in the Tanak, they never agreed as a whole as to which of the additional books should or should not be accepted in their Old Testament: Western Christians accepted one group (which became the Roman Catholic canon), Eastern Christians another (which became the Greek Orthodox canon), with some smaller groups accepting further variations (e.g., the Ethiopic Church). The books accepted in the West consisted of Judith, Tobit, Wisdom, Sirach, Baruch, 1 and 2 Maccabees, as well as Greek additions to Daniel and Esther. These books are called "deuterocanonical" in Catholic circles (meaning "second canon"). A number of books that were written during the same period as the deuterocanonicals never became part of anyone's canon but, nonetheless, exercised considerable influence. Some examples include the sectarian documents from Qumran, *Jubilees, Enoch,* and *The Testaments of the Twelve Patriarchs.*

Continued

The Canon, the Apocrypha, and the Deuterocanonicals *Continued*

Over the centuries, a number of theologians questioned whether the deuterocanonical works ought to be accepted as Scripture (including Jerome, Cyril of Jerusalem, Athanasius, and Gregory Nazianzen), but by and large, the situation remained static until the sixteenth century. Then the Protestant Reformers rejected the deuterocanonicals because, among other things, some passages (e.g., 2 Maccabees 12:46) seemed to support the practice of buying and selling indulgences. Consequently, Protestant denominations do not accept these works, which they call the Apocrypha, as canonical. The Protestant Old Testament is identical to the Jewish Tanak.

The New Testament

Most of the books that now make up the canon of the New Testament were accepted without question almost from the first—e.g., the four Gospels and the epistles of Paul. Others, such as 2 Peter and Revelation, only gradually gained in popularity. There were also a large number of works that were deliberately rejected.

Some Christian (or quasi-Christian) groups produced writings in the late first and second centuries, and a number of these were being used, for a time, as Scripture. Many of these works, known collectively as New Testament Apocrypha, were orthodox in outlook, but quite a few were written from the perspective of one or another of the early Christian heresies, the most important being Gnosticism. Gnosticism was a religious movement that blended elements of Hellenistic philosophy with parts of the Jesus story. Many of these apocryphal works were examples of pseudepigrapha, i.e., writings that had been falsely attributed to some important figure, e.g., *The Gospel of Thomas*.

Irenaeus, second-century bishop of Lyons, attacked in a work called *Against Heresies* what he saw as Gnostic distortions of Christian teaching. In it, he laid out several criteria by which books might be judged authentic or spurious. These criteria were (1) usage in important Christian communities/churches, (2) apostolic origin, and (3) conformity with "the rule of faith." By the time Athanasius listed the books of the New Testament in his thirty-ninth festal letter (367 CE), there was wide agreement among Christians that those twenty-seven books and only those books should be accepted as canonical.

At this time (i.e., in the second century BCE), a genre of literature and theology emerged that sought to address the crisis many Jews were facing: apocalyptic eschatology (discussed in chapter 1). Apocalyptic eschatology attempted to answer more directly the questions about God's fidelity and justice. A comprehensive definition of apocalyptic eschatology has proved somewhat elusive, but the following reflects a general consensus on the subject in current scholarship.

Apocalyptic eschatology is as a genre of revelatory literature with a narrative framework, in which a revelation from God is given to a human being, usually through an intermediary, making known a transcendent reality which envisages eschatological salvation and the existence of another, supernatural world, and usually intended for a group in crisis with the purpose of exhortation and/or consolation by means of divine authority.[1]

Additional characteristics include dualistic views, signs of the coming end (*eschaton* means "end" or "culmination"), emphasis on the "end of the world," and final judgment.

An early and important example of apocalyptic is the book of Daniel. Though it purports to be an account of events and visions during the Babylonian Exile (i.e., 587–539 BCE), it is really a product of the Maccabean crisis (around 167–164 BCE) and should be read as such. It tells the story of Israel suffering at the hands of an unjust king and the heroic acts of a young man named Daniel who receives special visions and messages from heaven that give him and others consolation amid their great suffering. One of the most important consolations described in Daniel is the expectation that those who die will be raised up to receive the rewards or punishments merited by their behavior. The following is a classical statement of Jewish apocalyptic hope for resurrection.

"At that time, Michael, the great prince, the protector of your people, shall rise. There shall be a time of anguish, such as never occurred since nations first came into existence. But at that time your people shall be delivered, everyone who is found written in the book. Many of those who sleep in the dust of the earth shall awake, some to everlasting life, and some to shame and everlasting contempt. Those who are wise shall shine like the brightness of the sky, and those who lead many to the righteousness, like the stars forever and ever." (Daniel 12:1–3)

For Daniel, God's fidelity and love for Israel will be definitively vindicated when, at the end of time evil will be defeated, the wicked will be punished, and the faithful will rise from their graves and be transformed and taken into a new heavenly existence.

---

1. Society of Biblical Literature (SBL) definition emended by David Hellholm, "The Problem of Apocalyptic Genre and the Apocalypse of John," in A. Y. Collins, ed., *Early Christian Apocalypticism: Genre and Social Setting* (Semeia 36; Decatur, GA: Scholars Press, 1986), 27.

The Afterlife in the Intertestamental Period

In the intertestamental period, i.e., from the close of the Old Testament period to the beginning of the Christian writings (around 150 BCE–50 CE), Judaism entertained a range of opinions about the afterlife. Prominent among these was belief in resurrection, but other options included the denial of any afterlife or a disembodied afterlife. One finds a denial of the afterlife behind the controversy between Jesus and the Sadducees in Mark 12:18–27. The Sadducees mockingly ask Jesus about a woman who has been widowed several times, whose wife would she be at the resurrection? Some commentators, such as Alan Segal, believe that the Sadducees denied an afterlife because they enjoyed power and privilege in this life.[2] While Segal may be guilty of reducing the Sadducees' theology to a materialist principle, these principles probably did play a role in their denial of the afterlife.

Philo of Alexandria, an Egyptian Jewish philosopher who lived around the same time as Jesus, provides the best example of hope for an afterlife in the form of a disembodied existence with God in first-century Judaism. Philo's ideas of the afterlife derive largely from the Greek philosopher Plato. The righteous dead, "who deserves so high a title, does not surely die, but has his life prolonged, and so attains to an eternal end" (*Questions and Answers on Genesis* 1. 16). A similar position is found in the nonbiblical book *Jubilees*:

And at that time the Lord will heal His servants,
And they shall rise up and see great peace,
And drive out their adversaries.
And the righteous shall see and be thankful,
And rejoice with joy for ever and ever,
And shall see all their judgments and all their curses on their enemies.
And their bones shall rest in the earth,
And their spirits shall have much joy,
And they shall know that it is the Lord who executes judgment,
And shows mercy to hundreds and thousands and to all that love Him.

(*Jubilees* 23:30–31)[3]

This passage does not hope for the transformation of the body after death; rather, hope is expressed in terms of a disembodied happiness, a spiritual joy with God.

---

2. Alan Segal, *Life After Death: A History of the Afterlife in Western Religion* (New York: Doubleday, 2004), 378.

3. Translation taken from R. H. Charles, *The Apocrypha and Pseudepigrapha of the Old Testament* (Oxford: Clarendon, 1913).

Person of Interest: Philo

Philo

Philo (c. 25 BCE–45 CE) was a contemporary of Jesus. A Greek-speaking Jew, Philo was born and lived in the ancient center of Hellenistic culture, Alexandria. As an admirer of Greek philosophy, he used it to interpret Judaism. Although he was viewed with suspicion by his own tradition, he became highly influential within early Christianity through his allegorical interpretation of scripture and his appropriation of the notion of the divine Logos or Word.

Philo embraced a dualistic understanding of reality, particularly the duality of God and the world, the infinite and the finite. This dualism had been rooted in Greek philosophy for centuries and informed his reading of scripture. The materialism of scripture, its earthy narrative, needed to be unlocked through allegorical interpretation, i.e., by interpreting each element in scripture as referring to a spiritual reality. For example, Philo interpreted Genesis, particularly the early chapters, as describing the soul's relationship to God rather than as a literal account of the origins of the universe. Additionally, his interpretation of Jewish law (Torah) centered on the moral life and the union of the soul with God so that the value of the scriptures rests in their capacity to promote spiritual union with God and not in their power to describe "events" in history.

Philo's dualism also influenced his account of God. Although he did not go as far as many of the Greek philosophers who separated God from humans, he did adopt the notion that God related to the created order and to humans through the Logos—the divine Word of God. Philo's understanding of the divine Logos would appeal to the early Christians in their attempts to articulate an understanding of the relationship between Jesus and God (see chapter 4).

As noted previously, the third option, resurrection from the dead, originated with apocalyptic eschatology. For the Jews of the first century, resurrection was not simply a form of life after death. Resurrection was an event for which people hoped. When loved ones died they were not assumed to have immediately been resurrected; rather, they were thought to endure an "in-between," waiting for the resurrection and God's definitive breakthrough in history. So resurrection was not simply "life after death," it was "life after life after death."[4]

The Jewish people developed a variety of ways to describe the "in-between" state of the righteous ones who had died: the Persian word *paradise* was borrowed to describe this state—a garden in which the righteous existed before the resurrection (e.g. *1 Enoch* 37–70). Others described the righteous resting in God's hands (Wisdom 3:1–8), and still others described them as angelic beings or spirits. But this "in-between" state was not the goal; resurrection was not merely a pious way Jews described the way one endures after death. Resurrection was the reversal of death; it involved the transformation of the dead body. For example, the Maccabean martyrs of the second century BCE taunted their executioners and boldly declared their confidence that God would restore their tongues when they were cut out, their hands when they were cut off, etc.[5]

While a number of striking examples of belief in the resurrection of the dead can be cited, it should be noted that there was no uniformity of expectation on this issue. Note the contrast between Daniel 12, which describes the resurrected body as "star-like," and the much more mundanely physical body envisioned by the Maccabean martyrs.

While the details of how resurrection was understood differed among the Jews of the first-century, what was important about the resurrection concerned not primarily the individual, but also the people of God. Resurrection was a primary way many Jews envisioned the vindication of God's covenantal faithfulness because this was how God intended to restore Israel and punish the wicked (usually Gentiles and their Jewish collaborators). So the resurrection was a cosmic event, bringing the righteous and the wicked together so that the great reversal could take place: the oppressed would find prosperity, while the powerful would be cast out and despised. Resurrection was for all people.

At least a segment of the Jewish population also accepted an important corollary to belief in the eschaton and resurrection: the messiah. As noted in chapter 2, Jewish expectations concerning the messiah were hardly uniform, so it is not surprising that the precise relationship between the messiah and resurrection is neither clear nor consistent. Generally, the messiah would establish God's kingdom by defeating God's enemies and rebuilding or cleansing the Temple. So belief in the messiah, like belief in the resurrection, was necessarily social and political as well as religious, because God's kingdom and the great reversal of the eschaton meant that those in power now would be thrown out.

---

4. N. T. Wright, *The Resurrection of the Son of God* (Minneapolis: Fortress, 2003), 201.

5. 2 Maccabees 7:11.

Some Messianic Figures in Judaism

The term *messiah* means "anointed one" in Hebrew (the Greek translation is *christos*). The word is deeply rooted in the history of the kings of Israel, especially David and his descendants in the southern kingdom of Judah. Among the prophets of the southern kingdom, a particular type of theology of the monarchy emerged in which the king, or a new king, would be the means by which the covenant with God would be renewed and evil would be banished. However, with the collapse of the monarchy, this Davidic theology was transposed so as to focus on the coming of a new king, a new ruler "anointed" by God to renew the covenant and defeat evil. The term has been applied to several figures over time.

Cyrus the Great (576 BCE–529 BCE)

The great Persian king defeated the Babylonians, sent the Jews back to Jerusalem from their exile in Babylon, and gave them funds to rebuild the Temple. For this reason, scripture hails Cyrus as "the Lord's anointed," i.e., "messiah." He is the only Gentile to be given that title (Isaiah 45:1).

Zerubbabel (sixth century BCE)

He was the grandson of King Jehoiachin (also Jeconiah). When the Babylonian king Nebuchadnezzar took hostages after his first conquest of Jerusalem in 598 BCE, Jehoiachin was among his most prized captives. He quickly won respect among his Babylonian captors. When the Jews returned to Jerusalem to rebuild their Temple, Jehoiachin's grandson, Zerubbabel, became a prominent leader of the efforts to restore the nation after the exile. As the political ruler of the city, many hoped that he would reestablish the Davidic monarchy—thus, many began to recognize him as God's anointed one, or messiah. Possibly for political reasons, his Persian overlords removed Zerubbabel from his position; and Joshua, the high priest, became the new symbol of national rule. As the Second Temple period unfolded, the high priest rather than a descendant of David ruled the affairs of the Jews in Jerusalem, yet many continued to expect that God would raise up one of David's descendants to restore the kingdom.

Simon ben Kosibah († 135 CE)

Also known as Simon bar Kokhba (or "Son of a Star" referring to Numbers 24:17, which was viewed as a messianic prophecy), he was the last independent Jewish ruler of Judea. Following the first revolt against Rome (66–73 CE), the people of Judea, the territory around Jerusalem, continued to chafe under Roman rule. When the emperor Hadrian attempted to erect an altar on the site of the Temple in Jerusalem and curtailed the practice of circumcision, the Jews

Continued

revolted again. Simon became the military and political leader of the revolt and was designated by several rabbis as "messiah."[6] Through the use of guerilla tactics he was able to defeat the Roman soldiers garrisoned in the region in 132 CE and succeeded in establishing an independent Jewish state. By 135 CE, the Romans sent more troops and put down the revolt. Following the Roman victory, the emperor decreed that Jews were not to be admitted to the region or even look upon Jerusalem from a distance. Hadrian renamed the province "Syria Palestine"—Palestine being the name of Israel's much despised enemy the Philistines—and built a Roman city (Aelia Capitolina) on the remains of Jerusalem.

The New Testament Period

The Language of Resurrection

Among those Jews of the first century who held an apocalyptic outlook, such as the Pharisees, talk of resurrection would have resonated nicely. The resurrection was intelligible; it made sense within the context of Jesus' life and ministry— especially his proclamation of the kingdom (see chapter 2)—as well as within the larger context of Israel's history. Yet when one turns to the narratives of Jesus' resurrection, one finds a lack of clarity and consistency.

The apostle Paul, a self-described Pharisee and someone who was predisposed to the theological importance of resurrection, reported the earliest proclamation of Jesus' resurrection. This is some of the oldest material in the New Testament, hearkening back to the period of Paul's conversion and association with the Jerusalem community (late 30s CE).

> For I handed on to you as of first importance what I in turn received: that Christ died for our sins in accordance with the scriptures, and that he was buried, and that he was raised on the third day in accordance with the scriptures; that he appeared to Cephas, then to the twelve. Then, he appeared to more than five hundred brothers and sisters at one time, most of whom are still alive, though some have died. Then he appeared to James, then to all the apostles. Last of all, as to one untimely born, he appeared also to me. (1 Corinthians 15:3–8)

Notice that there is no narrative of the empty tomb in Paul's account, only a list of those to whom the risen Christ appeared. Moreover, Paul includes his

---

6. *Midrash Rabbah Lamentations* 2.2.4.

own experience of the risen Christ some years after Jesus' crucifixion. Was Paul's experience of the risen Christ the same as that of the women at the tomb, as Peter's and the others?

Two phrases key to an understanding of the resurrection appear in this passage: "He was raised" and "He appeared." These two phrases provide us with a direction for exploring the New Testament proclamation of Jesus' resurrection.

"He was raised" places the verb in the passive voice: Jesus is the recipient of the action and God is the actor (cf. 1 Thessalonians 5:14). Additionally, the action is metaphorical. While the word *resurrection* has a particular religious meaning in English, in the Greek of the New Testament *resurrection* and cognate expressions are common terms from everyday life; they are not specifically religious but refer to the quite normal activity of standing up or waking someone out of their sleep. Neither of these meanings describes *resurrection* in a literal sense. Rather, the description of God's activity is metaphorical or analogical. Paul also offers something positive in being raised from the dead, namely that in the resurrection all that is negative about one's current condition will be removed. He contrasts the "natural body" of current life with the "spiritual body" of the resurrection. The resurrection is not the resuscitation of a corpse but a final or eschatological transformation of a human life (including the body) as it encounters God.

The second phrase from First Corinthians that demands attention is "He appeared." What does Paul mean by this? The verb employed here (a passive form of the verb *to see*) is used throughout Scripture to describe ecstatic and visionary experiences. These experiences have several components: (1) the initiative rests with the revealer, i.e., the one who discloses; (2) the recipient of the revelation has a prior involvement with the one who does the disclosing; and (3) the recipient usually emerges from the encounter with some sort of mission.[7] In light of the metaphorical character of the "appearance" language in the New Testament one might also question the objectivity of the experience of the resurrection. In other words, is the risen Christ physically visible to the casual observer, or is an encounter with the risen Christ a privileged revelatory event, visible only to the chosen recipients?

Paul's early testimony regarding the Easter proclamation reaffirms that resurrection language utilizes analogy and metaphor—clearly, he is not describing a zombie coming out of the grave. Rather, the resurrection of Jesus is a transcendent event that is only accessible or describable through metaphor, i.e., by comparing the experience of the resurrection to more common experiences. Yet the Gospels do not suggest that the resurrection is a metaphor.

---

7. N. T. Wright challenges this by appealing to the case of James and Paul, both of whom were not among Jesus' followers and both of whom "saw" the risen Christ (1 Corinthinans 15:7–8).

The Gospel Accounts of the Resurrection

The accounts of Jesus' resurrection and appearances in the Gospels utilize metaphor, but the Gospels also strongly emphasize the relational and revelatory character of the resurrection. The basic account of Jesus' resurrection is found in Mark 16:1–8. The original ending of Mark's Gospel in 16:8 gives no account of Jesus appearing to the disciples.[8] It simply says that Mary Magdalene, Mary the mother of James, and Salome discover the empty tomb and receive notice from a messenger that "He is risen!" They are told to instruct the other disciples to go to Galilee, where Jesus will appear. It is, in many ways, a strange ending. Yet for Mark, the story of the women at the tomb directs the reader to the experience of Jesus' resurrection common to most Christians. Such an experience is accompanied by misgivings, doubt, and even fear.

Matthew 28:1–20 reports the discovery of the empty tomb, but it also includes an appearance of the risen Christ to the women in Jerusalem and an appearance to the Eleven (what was the Twelve, after the departure and death of Judas) in Galilee. Some remarkable scenes, including the story of the guards at the tomb, who are subsequently bribed to spread a rumor that Jesus' disciples had taken him from the tomb, accompanied the account of the resurrection in Matthew. Even more remarkable in Matthew is the inclusion of other resurrections at the time of Jesus' resurrection. Matthew 27:51–53 states that at the moment of Jesus' death, "the curtain of the temple was torn in two, from top to bottom. The earth shook, and the rocks were split. The tombs also were opened, and many bodies of the saints who had fallen asleep were raised. After his resurrection, they came out of the tombs and entered the holy city and appeared to many." The scene evokes both Isaiah 26 and Daniel 12, but if this is a historical recollection, it is strange that it would not make its way into the other Gospel accounts. This detail in Matthew helps to situate the resurrection of Jesus within the expectation of a general resurrection from the dead. In other words, the resurrection of an individual was difficult to make sense of in first-century Judaism, and Matthew's reference to other resurrections is an overt attempt to address such questions. Even so, Matthew is still not claiming a general resurrection occurred, only a foretaste or anticipation of the resurrection.

Luke, uniquely, records the appearance of the risen Christ in and around Jerusalem and not in Galilee. Perhaps most distinctive, however, is Luke's account of the encounter between the risen Christ and two disciples on the road to Emmaus. These disciples know full well the story of Jesus and the reports of

---

8. Mark contains three different conclusions. The first ending (Mark 16:1–8) is found in the oldest and in this instance most reliable manuscripts of Mark's Gospel. The other two endings, the so-called shorter ending, added in the fourth century CE, and the longer ending in 16:9–20, added in the second century CE, are secondary.

The Variant Accounts of Jesus' Resurrection in the Gospels[9]

	Mark 16:1–8	Matthew 28:1–20	Luke 24	Mark 16:9–20	John 20
Time of Day	very early; first day of the week	first day of week; growing light	first day of week at dawn	early first day of the week	still dark on first day of the week
Women Present at the Tomb	Mary Magdalene, Mary the mother of James, and Salome	Mary Magdalene and "the other Mary"	Mary Magdalene, Mary the mother of James; Joanna; others	Mary Magdalene	Mary Magdalene and another
Purpose for the Women's Visit	brought oils / spices to anoint the body	came to see tomb	brought spices they had prepared on Friday	none	none
What about the Stone Seal on the Tomb?	the women find the stone rolled back and a youth sitting inside the tomb	there is an earthquake; an angel descends, rolls back the stone, and sits on it while the guards sleep	the women find the stone rolled back; two men in dazzling robes appear and speak to them	none	the women find the stone rolled away; later two angels appear sitting inside the tomb
Conversation at the Tomb	youth says not to fear; Jesus is risen; go tell disciples that he is going to Galilee	angel says not to fear; Jesus is risen; go tell disciples that he is going to Galilee	men ask question; recalled prophesy made in Galilee	none	angels ask: "Why do you weep?" thought body was stolen
Reaction of the Women at the Tomb	fear and trembling; told no one	went away quickly with fear to tell disciples	returned and told the Eleven and the rest	went and told followers	went and told Peter and "other disciple"

Continued

9. Adapted from Raymond Brown, *The Virginal Conception and Bodily Resurrection of Jesus* (New York: Paulist, 1973), 11.

The Variant Accounts *Continued*

	Mark 16:1–8	Matthew 28:1–20	Luke 24	Mark 16:9–20	John 20
Appearances of Jesus at or Around the Tomb	none	Jesus meets the women, and they touch his feet; he repeats the message about Galilee	Jesus appears to Simon Peter	Jesus appears to Mary Magdalene	Jesus appears to Mary Magdalene; he speaks of ascending; Peter and another disciple run to tomb
Appearance of Jesus in the Country	none	none	road to Emmaus	two men walking in the country	none
Appearance of Jesus in Jerusalem	none	none	Jesus appears to the Eleven at meal on Easter night	Jesus appears to the Eleven at table	Jesus appears to disciples (except Thomas) on Easter night at a meal, and again a week later with Thomas present
Appearance of Jesus in Galilee	none	appeared to the Eleven on a mountain	none	none	appeared to seven disciples at the Sea of Tiberias

the empty tomb, but they fail to recognize Jesus as they meet and speak with him at length. It is only when they sit together and share a meal (with obvious Eucharistic overtones) that they recognize the risen Christ in their midst, but at that moment he disappears.

In John's Gospel, Mary Magdalene tells Simon and "the other disciple" about the tomb and the two disciples race back to the tomb. The "other disciple" comes to believe as soon as he sees the empty tomb, but the rest wait to see the risen Christ, particularly Thomas. Meanwhile, Mary Magdalene sees the risen

Christ and is sent to the other disciples to announce the good news. The story in John bears a number of similarities with the Synoptics, though always with a Johannine spin (e.g., the intimacy of Jesus and the Father is emphasized, the coming to belief of "the other disciple," and the doubt of Thomas).

The testimony of the New Testament reveals a wide range of accounts. These discrepancies are viewed as proof by those who would contend that the resurrection narratives are mythological, the products of vivid imagination or simple credulity. New Testament scholars suggest that discrepancies in the resurrection accounts point to the existence of two distinct traditions for proclaiming the resurrection. One tradition focused on the appearance of Jesus to the disciples and the other narrated the story of the empty tomb. This, along with other apologetic and theological interests, helps to account for the variations among the Gospels. Other scholars, however, assert that the discrepancies raise serious questions for the authenticity of resurrection stories. If the New Testament narratives are demonstrably unreliable, then one is free to speculate about what actually happened to give rise to the resurrection stories.

The Contemporary Debate

The Subjective Dimensions of the Resurrection

For Edward Schillebeeckx, a Dominican priest and theologian from the Netherlands, the story of the empty tomb is a late tradition from the Christian community in Jerusalem and not a historical recollection from the earliest disciples.[10] The earliest disciples had met on a regular basis to venerate the memory of Jesus at the place where they believed he was buried. In fact, Schillebeeckx contends that the discovery of Jesus' bones would not have posed a problem for the earliest Christians and their conviction that Jesus had been raised from the dead. Rather than focusing on the empty tomb, Schillebeeckx focuses on Paul and his conversion as the paradigm for understanding the resurrection (Acts 9, 22, and 26). The Easter experience is, thus, an experience of grace, an experience of conversion and forgiveness—the experience of Jesus' saving presence.

The New Testament testifies to the way Jesus' disciples abandoned him in his hour of suffering. It also testifies that they reassembled after Jesus' death. Schillebeeckx latches onto this event as the genesis of the resurrection stories. In the context of the reassembled disciples the presence of Jesus was felt and a collective experience of grace and forgiveness overwhelmed the assembled disciples so that they could indeed proclaim the resurrection. Schillebeeckx does not claim, however, that the resurrection experience was merely a psychological

---

10. For what follows see Edward Shillebeeckx, *Jesus: An Experiment in Christology*, trans. Hubert Hoskins (New York: Seabury Press, 1979), 320–97.

projection; rather, he asserts that God is at work here.[11] Yet, for Schillebeeckx, there is also a fundamental similarity between the early disciples' experience of resurrection and coming to faith and the way contemporary believers experience Christ's presence. The two experiences, however, are not identical: the first disciples bore special witness to their experience of the resurrection by drawing on their memories of Jesus' life and ministry, whereas contemporary Christians must rely on the disciples' witness.

The life and ministry of Jesus are decisive for any account of the resurrection. Schillebeeckx does not agree with those who say that one can only know the risen Christ proclaimed by the early church; rather, he argues that one's faith rests on the memory of Jesus, which provided the basis for identifying the risen Christ as Jesus of Nazareth. In telling of the risen Christ, therefore, the disciples tell something about the Jesus who lived among them. While the experience of the resurrection was central for the early Christians, Christian faith today is rooted in the life of Jesus. The resurrection provided the catalyst that enabled the early disciples to know and appreciate Jesus' life among them and its saving significance.

Roger Haight's account of the resurrection substantially agrees with Schillebeeckx's. For Haight, an American Jesuit theologian, Jesus was taken up into the life of God—exalted—at the moment of his death; there was no interim period between his death and resurrection.[12] So what happened to Jesus happened at the moment of his death and all narratives that report a series of events between the death of Jesus and his resurrection are legendary and artificial. Haight asserts that the Emmaus story in Luke offers the best and most historical account of the genesis of faith in the risen Christ. Through the remembrance of Jesus, particularly in the table-fellowship of those closest to him, the power of Jesus and the recognition of his vindication by God become apparent. Christian faith in the resurrection of Jesus arises out of a more basic faith in God mediated by Jesus, and a lingering commitment to his person as the one in whom God was encountered. According to Haight, following Jesus' death, the memory of his ministry, together with the work of the Spirit, was responsible for generating faith in Jesus' resurrection. When one says "Jesus is risen," one affirms what Haight calls "faith-hope," which expresses a religious commitment and trust in God on the part of both the individual and the community. It is pronounced partly on the historical grounds of Jesus' life and ministry but also on the grounds of the experience of the Spirit. Resurrection was, for Jesus, an intimate part of his life and not an add-on or an afterthought.

---

11. For a spirited and persuasive defense of the "objective" dimensions of Schillebeeckx's account of the resurrection, see Anthony J. Godzieba, "Schillebeeckx's Phenomenology of Experience and Resurrection Faith," in *Finding Salvation in Christ: Essays on Christology and Soteriology in Honor of William P. Loewe*, ed. C. Denny and C. McMahon (Eugene: Pickwick, 2011), 73–106.

12. Roger Haight, *Jesus Symbol of God* (New York: Orbis, 1999), 126. The material that follows is presented in chapter 5 of *Jesus Symbol of God*.

The Objective Dimensions of the Resurrection

Lutheran theologian Wolfhart Pannenberg issues important cautions regarding overly symbolic or thoroughly subjective interpretations of Jesus' resurrection.[13] Pannenberg stresses that the early Christians consistently affirm basic continuity between Jesus crucified and Jesus as he appeared to the disciples—it was Jesus who was transformed in the resurrection. While the appearance stories and the empty tomb stories appear to be different traditions for proclaiming the resurrection, the early disciples did suppose that the tomb was empty; for, it was the empty tomb that provided the necessary conditions for proclaiming the resurrection of Jesus.

In recent years a significant minority within the scholarly community, led by the Anglican bishop N. T. Wright, has taken Pannenberg's caveats a step further and has begun to challenge the subjective approach to Jesus' resurrection powerfully argued by scholars such as Schillebeeckx and Haight. Wright and others argue in favor of the basic historicity of the biblical narratives of the resurrection particularly because of the way it helps to explain why Christianity emerged and took the form that it did. For Wright in particular, the early Christians retained a belief in resurrection, but modified it substantially. They also retained belief in a coming messiah, but redefined that belief around their experience of Jesus. Why and how they redefined first-century Judaism points to the experience of the resurrection but not the experience as Schillebeeckx and Haight describe it.

Wright claims that certain fundamental assumptions corrupt the arguments of Schillebeeckx, Haight, and others who would argue that resurrection language was merely an opportunistic way of describing the disciples' belief that they were forgiven for their failings and given a mission to spread Jesus' message to the world. One such assumption is that the early Christians believed that God had exalted or vindicated Jesus in heaven, a belief that they expressed by using the language of *resurrection*. Another assumption is that the disciples came to believe in Jesus' divinity and then expressed that belief in resurrection language.

Wright argues that those who believe that resurrection language was simply a pious way of describing Jesus' exaltation have missed the point of resurrection language in the first century. First-century Jews, as was noted previously, had sophisticated language for honoring the martyrs and describing their resting place as they awaited the resurrection. If, as Wright argues, the earliest disciples thought Jesus had simply been lifted up to God (exalted) or had gone to a special place with God, resurrection language would have been out of place. But resurrection language makes sense if the earliest Christians indeed believed that

---

13. See Wolfhart Pannenberg, *Jesus-God and Man*, 2nd ed. trans. L Wilkins and D. Priebe (Philadelphia: Westminster, 1977), 88–108, esp. 96–101.

Person of Interest: N. T. Wright

N. T. Wright

© AP Photo / Max Nash

N. T. Wright is one of the most innovative scholars and churchmen the Anglican Church (Church of England) has seen in some time. Born in 1948, Wright earned his doctorate at Oxford University in 1981 and has worked diligently to offer a fresh understanding of the Apostle Paul. He argues against E. P. Sanders and the "New Perspective on Paul," which tries to harmonize or soften the lines that divide the apostle from first century Palestinian Judaism. Wright argues instead for a more "edgy" account of Paul, one that diffuses the anti-Judaism that has dominated the study of Paul over the centuries (by focusing on Romans 9–11) but one that also sees in Paul a radical theology of justification through faith (by also focusing on Galatians). Additionally, Wright has played an important role in contemporary historical Jesus research. He has demarcated the limits of the "third quest" for the historical Jesus and has offered an account that has engaged many English-speaking evangelical Christians in a debate that they had long found alienating. With a style that is combative but engaging, Wright's pastoral and evangelical sensibilities have won for him a wide audience in England and North America.

Jesus had been raised from the dead and the tomb was empty. After he ceased to appear, then exaltation language ("he is seated at the right hand of God"), which we find throughout the New Testament, would make perfect sense to explain the cessation of the appearances, but according to Wright, it cannot account for the assertion that Jesus had been raised from the dead.

Those who argue that conviction in the divinity of Jesus was the catalyst for the early Christian belief in the resurrection likewise run afoul of the evidence, according to Wright. Even if belief in the divinity of Christ was generated as early as the first moments after Jesus' death—and there is much evidence to the contrary—there is no logical connection between that affirmation and resurrection. How would the resurrection make sense? Wright affirms that it is belief in the resurrection that acts as a catalyst for affirming the divinity of Christ and for affirming the exaltation of Christ, not vice versa.

For Wright, the early Christians would not have regarded the empty tomb as theologically or religiously significant—tomb robbers were commonplace—and there was no expectation that Jesus would rise from the dead (Gospel passages in which Jesus predicts his resurrection are not stage-one material). As was noted previously, resurrection was a communal, corporate, and even cosmic event within early Judaism. Additionally, a vision of the risen Christ (whether real or imagined) would not have produced talk of resurrection among those who had the vision. Visionary experiences were manifold in first-century Judaism; yet no one used resurrection language to describe such experiences. For example, in Acts 12, when Peter, who was thought to be dead, suddenly appears, those present assume they were seeing was "his angel," not Peter risen from the dead (Acts 12:15).

In place of the arguments of Schillebeeckx and others, Wright believes the best explanation for the resurrection narratives—as well as the best explanation for how and why Christian belief and practice emerged as they did—was that the early followers of Jesus believed that God had raised him from the dead and that this same Jesus appeared to them. For the early Christians, Jesus really died, his tomb was empty, and he really did meet with the disciples, albeit in a transformed state.

Conclusion

Belief in a resurrection of the dead arose as an element of apocalyptic eschatology. The context for this development was the crisis precipitated by the oppressive policies of Antiochus IV, which also touched off the Maccabean Revolt. Apocalyptic eschatology attempted to address the problem of the righteous sufferer: Why are the righteous not rewarded for their faithfulness, and why are the wicked not punished for their wickedness? Why, instead, are the righteous suffering and the wicked prospering? Apocalyptic eschatology resolved the problem by asserting that God would, in time, intervene to set matters right. That future, divine intervention would include a general resurrection, following which all people would receive their just deserts.

Not all first-century Jews shared these beliefs. Some appear to have had no particular expectation of an afterlife, while others believed that the soul would survive death in disembodied form. Only those who accepted some form of apocalyptic eschatology expected a bodily resurrection. References to Jesus' resurrection in the New Testament must be understood within this context.

Theologically, some (e.g., Schilebeeckx, Haight) understood in a subjective sense the early Christian proclamation that Jesus was risen from the dead. In this view, the disciples spoke of Jesus being raised from the dead as a way of expressing their conviction that Jesus, as a divine figure whom God had exalted, was still present among them after his death. Those who hold to an objective model of the resurrection (e.g., Pannenberg, Wright) have questioned why the disciples would have employed resurrection language to describe their experience of Christ "appearing" to them after his death, when it is evident that first-century Judaism did not normally describe such phenomena as "resurrection." They argue, instead, that the best explanation is that the disciples believed that Jesus was in fact risen from the dead, and that this belief then explains their conviction that Jesus had been exalted to God's right hand—not the other way around.

Whatever the disciples meant by proclaiming that Christ was risen from the dead, it is clear that this was an event that changed things. Most obviously it changed the disciples. The same disciples who at the time of Jesus' arrest would rather flee naked into the night (Mark 14:51–52) would subsequently proclaim the name of Jesus and his resurrection to the point that it cost them their lives.

Questions for Understanding

1. Describe the Deuteronomic approach to life after death.
2. Explain the significance of the Maccabean crisis for the development of a theology of resurrection.
3. Describe the spectrum of positions on the afterlife in first-century Judaism.
4. The NT affirms that Jesus "was raised" and "was seen." Describe how these phrases use analogies to describe the resurrection and the appearances of Jesus.
5. Describe the position articulated by Schillebeeckx and Haight on the resurrection of Jesus. What are the merits of this approach? What are some of the problems?
6. How does N. T. Wright challenge the approach of Schillebeeckx and Haight? Do you find any merit in Wright's approach? Any problems? Explain.

Questions for Reflection and Action

1. In the middle part of last century, the great Israeli archaeologist Eleazar Sukenik uncovered an ossuary (a box used to burry the bones of a deceased person) bearing the inscription "Jesus son of Joseph." If this ossuary had been authentic (it was ruled a forgery by the experts), would this nullify Christian faith? Explain.

2. For a long time cremation was not permitted in Christian churches. It was seen as a denial of the Christian hope for resurrection (most churches now permit cremation). If Christians proclaim a hope for future resurrection, is allowing cremation consistent with that hope? Explain.

3. Apocalyptic eschatology was heavily political in its outlook. Many Christians today, particularly in the Western world, have abandoned the apocalyptic worldview that played such an important role in the New Testament. What do you think are the political implications of apocalyptic theology in today's world?

For Further Reading

O'Collins, Gerald, SJ, *Believing in the Resurrection: The Meaning and Promise of the Risen Jesus*. New York: Paulist, 2012.

Portier-Young, Anathea E. *Apocalypse against Empire: Theologies of Resistance in Early Judaism*. Grand Rapids, MI: Eerdmans, 2011.

Williams, Rowan. *Resurrection: Interpreting the Easter Gospel*. Berea, OH: Pilgrim, 2003.

CHAPTER 4

New Testament Christologies

Most Jews of the first century would have grown up hearing and praying the Shema (Deuteronomy 6:4), a prayer which boldly affirmed Israel's belief in one God: "Hear (*shema*) O Israel! The Lord is our God, the Lord alone." This affirmation was central to the life of first-century Jews, including Jesus! Jewish men used leather straps to bind small boxes containing this prayer (*tefillin* in Hebrew, *phylacteries* in Greek; see Exodus 13:9, 16; Deuteronomy 11:18; Matthew 23:5) on their forehead and left arm as they prayed. Even today, hanging on the doorposts of many Jewish houses are small cylindrical containers with the text of the Shema inside.

Given these rituals that reinforced the Jewish commitment to the oneness of God, it would have been absurd for Jesus to show up in a first-century synagogue and say, "Hello, I'm God." Yet, the earliest Christians believed that Jesus, through his life and ministry and the power of his resurrection, accomplished what God had promised to do for Israel. That is, in the resurrection they believed that they experienced God's presence with them, renewing their covenant relationship, empowering them in the face of oppression, and saving them from evil and destruction.

Jewish thought had long speculated about how God's power might be experienced in the world. In the older parts of the Old Testament, angels are the primary vehicles for this interaction (e.g., Genesis 16:7–14; Exodus 3:2–4), but in prophetic and early wisdom literature, God's Word and Wisdom become more pronounced as the means of this interaction (Proverbs 3:19; 8:22; Isaiah 55:10–11). In the first century, such speculation drew upon Greek ideas to amplify and even hypostasize (personify) notions of God's Word and Wisdom. Early Christians found in these speculations and expectations a framework to articulate the relationship between Jesus and God that was in keeping with Jewish belief.

The development of Christology in the New Testament, i.e., the attempt to articulate the religious significance of Jesus, involves the interplay of several factors: insight born of the resurrection experience, the memory of Jesus' life and ministry, developments within apocalyptic Judaism, and tensions with the limits of Jewish monotheism. The results of this interplay yield profound, yet somewhat uneven Christologies. One should not, therefore, expect a full and clear exposition of doctrinal orthodoxy from the New Testament; such clarity of expression was the product of subsequent generations. This does not mean that the New Testament offers a Christology that is less than orthodox—how could that be, as all of Christian theology rests upon Scripture? Rather, the New Testament shows the beginning of a process by which people of faith attempted to grasp the full significance of Jesus. It is a process that has continued to the present day.

The Background for New Testament Christology: "The One Who Is to Come"

As noted in chapters 2 and 3, several factors colored the theology of Judaism of the late Second Temple period (170 BCE to 70 CE). First, the end of the monarchy in Jerusalem had deprived the Judean people of self-governance and consequently affected greatly their covenantal identity. After all, God was the true king of Israel, and God had anointed David and his descendants to rule as divine representatives. Without these adopted "sons" of God (see 1 Samuel 10:6–11; Psalm 2:2,7; 18:35), Israel was lost (Hosea 3:1–5).[1] Kingship, in their theology, was closely connected to the covenantal relationship between God and Israel. The absence of a king created much uncertainty and anxiety in the Second Temple period, which only grew worse when the nation fell under persecution from foreign powers (the Seleucids and the Romans) and an illegitimate line took control of the High Priesthood. Eventually that anxiety birthed a bold hope that God would soon deliver them by sending an agent (or more than one) who would set things right, the Messiah(s).

Our word *messiah* comes from a Hebrew word (*mashiach*) meaning "anointed one" (the equivalent in Greek is *christos*). It is applied frequently to kings in the Old Testament, whether unnamed (1 Samuel 2:10; Psalm 2:2; 20:7) or named, including *Saul* (e1 Samuel 24:7), David (2 Samuel 22:51; 23:1), *Solomon* (2 Chronicles 6:42), *Zedekiah* (Lamentations 4:20), and even *Cyrus of Persia* (Isaiah 45:1). Additionally, priests could be called "messiah" (Leviticus 4:3, 5, 16; 6:15), as could prophets or patriarchs (1 Chronicles 16:22; Psalm 105:15). All of these figures, but especially the Davidic king, became the focal points

---

1. See e.g., Albert Rainertz, *A History of Israelite Religion in the Old Testament Period, Vol. I: From the Beginnings to the End of the Monarchy*, OTL (Louisville, KY: Westminster John Knox, 1994) 1:116–117.

Does the New Testament Call Jesus "God"?

Christians sometimes anachronistically read later doctrines back into the New Testament. For instance, many Christians, used to the assertions of the Nicene Creed (325 CE) that Jesus is "God from God, light from light, true God from true God," expect to see the term *God* applied to Jesus throughout the New Testament. In fact, there are only a handful of passages in the New Testament that appear to apply this term to Jesus, and a number of them are ambiguous, as illustrated in the chart that follows.

Passage	Greek Text	English Translation[2]
Romans 9:5	*kai ex hōn ho christos to kata sarka ho ōn epi pantōn theos eulogētos eis tous aiōnas*	"and through them according to the flesh is Christ, God who is above all, blessed forever" (author's translation); cf. the NABRE: "and from them, according to the flesh, is the Messiah. God who is over all be blessed forever." (Readers should note that the Greek manuscripts do not contain punctuation marks.)
Titus 2:13	*epiphaneian tēs doxēs tou megalou theou kai sōtēros hēmōn Iēsou Christou*	"the appearance of the glory of our great God and savior, Jesus Christ" (author's translation); cf. the NABRE: "the appearance of the glory of the great God and of our savior Jesus Christ" (The question is whether the words *God* and *savior* are joined or separated by the conjunction (*kia*/and); elsewhere in the Pastoral Epistles this precise expression joins the same two words: "our God and savior" [e.g. 1 Timothy 1:1; 2:3; Titus 1:3].)

Continued

2. The New American Bible Revised Edition (NABRE) was chosen for this exercise because it well conveys the potential ambiguity in several of these passages.

Does the New Testament Call Jesus "God"? *Continued*

Passage	Greek Text	English Translation
Hebrews 1:8	*pros de ton huion· ho thronos sou ho theos*	"but of the Son [he says]: 'Your throne, O God . . .'" (NABRE)
2 Peter 1:1	*en dikaiosunē tou theou hēmōn kai sōtēros Iēsou Christou*	"through the righteousness of our God and savior Jesus Christ" (NABRE)

In addition to the passages mentioned in the chart, several texts from the Gospel of John and the First Letter of John contain sections in which Jesus appears to be identified as God.

Johannine Passages

Passage	Greek Text	English Translation
John 1:1	*kai theos ēn ho logos*	"and the Word was God" (NABRE)
John 1:18	*monogenēs theos*	"the only Son, God" (NABRE)
John 20:28	*ho kyrios mou kai ho theos mou*	"My Lord and my God" (NABRE)
1 John 5:20	*en tō huiō autou Iēsou Christō, houtos estin ho alēthinos theos*	"in his Son Jesus Christ. This is the true God" (author's translation); cf. the NABRE: "in his Son Jesus Christ. He is the true God" (In context, the last phrase could refer either to Jesus Christ or God the Father.)

Given this scarcity of examples, it is clear that Christian claims regarding Jesus' divine status need to be based upon arguments other than a simple citation of New Testament passages in which Jesus is called "God." It is also fair to ask why the New Testament writers so seldom use this term regarding Jesus. In part, their reluctance may stem from a fear of describing the relationship of Jesus to the Father in a way that simply equates the two. Eventually the church would hit upon the language of *persons* as a way of addressing the tension between Jesus' oneness with, and distinction from, the Father.

of messianic expectations late in the Second Temple period. Without a king, Israel's covenantal status was compromised. As the Second Temple period drew on and apocalyptic eschatology came to the fore, the hope for a Messiah in Jerusalem took on a particular tone.

Jewish apocalyptic eschatology envisioned a radical in-breaking of God into human history at its consummation; an agent, "one who is to come" (variously interpreted) would bring about this in-breaking rule or reign of God. While expectation of a coming apocalyptic judge, "one like a son of man" (Daniel 7:9–14) was important, the key text in the emergence of messianism seems to have been in Daniel:[3]

> Seventy weeks are decreed for your people and your holy city:

> to finish the transgression, to put an end to sin, and to atone for iniquity, to bring in everlasting righteousness, to seal both vision and prophet, and to anoint a most holy place. Know therefore and understand: from the time that the word went out to restore and rebuild Jerusalem until the time of an anointed prince, there shall be seven weeks; and for sixty-two weeks it shall be built again with streets and moat, but in a troubled time. (Daniel 9:24–25)

Although the passage is bound with the events around the time of Antiochus IV Epiphanies and the Maccabean Revolt in the second century BCE, the forecast of an "anointed [one] and leader" (*mashiach nagid*, i.e., a "kingly Messiah") clearly looks to the future. This passage stands as the first example of an expectation of an unidentified future Messiah, a figure that will invite the reinterpretation of other Old Testament passages related to kingship and spur the development of messianic expectations in extrabiblical literature.

✳ For example, in the book of Numbers the pagan prophet Baalam utters the following words about the Israelites:

> I see him, but not now;
>> I behold him, but not near—
> A star shall come out of Jacob,
>> and a scepter shall rise out of Israel,
> it shall crush the borderlands of Moab,
>> and the territory of all the Shethites. (Numbers 24:17)

In the Second Temple Period, the rising "star" and the "scepter" of the Davidic monarchy in this oracle was sometimes reinterpreted as part of a messianic

---

3. See Joseph A. Fitzmyer, SJ, *The One Who Is to Come* (Grand Rapids, MI: Eerdmans, 2007), ch. 5.

prophecy, a return of the Davidic monarchy. Such a reinterpretation, for instance, stands behind the story of magi in Matthew 2:1–10. In its original context, the Numbers passage clearly refers to the rise of the Davidic household, but late reinterpretations of the passage point to a Davidic messiah coming in an unspecified future. Additionally, Nathan's prophecy regarding David's descendants—"I will establish the throne of his kingdom forever" (2 Samuel 7:14)—was invested with new significance, as were many of the royal Psalms (e.g., 21; 45; 72; 101; 110). Similarly, prophetic eschatology in Deutro-Isaiah (Isaiah 53) and Zechariah (Zechariah 9–11; 12:10–14) were gradually reinterpreted to refer to "one who is to come."

Apocalyptic eschatology and its reinterpretation of royal or Davidic biblical texts flowered in the extrabiblical literature of the late Second Temple period, particularly in the so-called *Similitudes of Enoch* (*1 Enoch* 37–71), several scrolls from Qumran (CD, 4Q; 1QS), and the *Psalms of Solomon*. These and similar works gave voice to an array of messianic ideas, forecasting a mighty ruler who would destroy the unrighteous and restore the kingdom of David. The often violent nature of this anticipated messianic rule is evident in *Psalms of Solomon*:

> Behold, O Lord, and raise up unto them their king, the son of David,
>> At the time in which Thou seest, O God,
>>> that he may reign over Israel Thy servant
>> And gird him with strength, that he may shatter unrighteous
>>> rulers,
>> And that he may purge Jerusalem from nations that trample (her)
>>> down to destruction.
>> Wisely, righteously he shall thrust out sinners from (the)
>>> inheritance,
> He shall destroy the pride of the sinner as a potter's vessel.
>> With a rod of iron he shall break in pieces all their substance,
>> He shall destroy the godless nations with the word of his mouth;
>> At his rebuke nations shall flee before him,
> And he shall reprove sinners for the thoughts of their heart.
>> And he shall gather together a holy people, whom he shall lead in
>>> righteousness,
>> And he shall judge the tribes of the people that have been sanctified
>>> by the Lord his God. (*Psalms of Solomon* 17:21–26)[4]

---

4. From "The Psalms of Solomon," trans. G. Buchanan Gray, in R. H. Charles, ed., *The Apocrypha and Pseudepigrapha of the Old Testament in English* (Oxford: Clarendon Press, 1913) 2:631–652.

Like so many extrabiblical works of the time, this passage expands biblical material, in this case Isaiah 11:4–5, to create an image of the messiah as the destroyer of the wicked and renewer of the covenant. Writings from Qumran emphasize at least two messiahs, one kingly, and the other a priestly messiah who would purify the Temple and the priesthood. One passage from Qumran (1QS 9:11) mentions not only the messiahs of Israel (i.e., a Davidic messiah) and Aaron (i.e., a priestly messiah; see Zechariah 4:14) but also the Prophet (i.e., Elijah) expected in the last days. After all, the priestly traditions had come, in some ways, to supplant the royal or Davidic traditions, and the dual missions of Zerubbabel (descendent of David) and Joshua (the high Priest) rebuilding the Temple following the Babylonian Exile may help to explain the rise of such a dual messianic expectation.

The messianic hopes and expectations of the first century BCE were far from uniform or precise. It was within this environment that Jesus articulated his own identity and significance, and it was within this environment that his followers continued to construct or amplify that identity, sometimes with competing imagery side by side. As one approaches the diverse waters of New Testament Christologies, one must be prepared to view them in the light of the variety of messianic expectations of the period.

The Growth of New Testament Christology: Titles, Roles, and Patterns

The Christology of the New Testament uses a variety of titles or roles that had been circulating within first-century Judaism to make sense of Jesus. In the present discussion of Christology in the New Testament, titles are like proper names; they are characters in the story of Israel and were used by early Christians to confess their faith in Jesus. Two obvious examples include "Lord" (e.g., Philippians 2:11), when it designates the divine name (YHWH), and "Messiah/Christ" (e.g., Matthew 16:16). A role, on the other hand, is more functional and descriptive. For example, the Letter to the Hebrews identifies Jesus as "a great high priest" (4:14). To call Jesus "a great high priest" is to describe the manner in which he functions, or a role he performs, and it was never used as a profession of faith in early Christian prayer or worship. To be sure, titles connect strongly to roles, but the opposite is not true: roles generally do not function as titles.

Additionally, New Testament Christology situates these titles and roles into narrative, sequential, or chronological patterns, thereby privileging certain moments that are understood to point to the identity and meaning of Jesus. For example, the title "Lord" was often associated with the exaltation of Jesus and not commonly associated with the life and ministry of Jesus (e.g., Philippians 2:11).

The relationship among these titles, roles, and patterns are not always stable—titles and roles overlap, Christological patterns can employ a variety of titles, etc. In what follows, titles, roles, and patterns will help structure a basic account of New Testament Christology. All of this is somewhat artificial and certainly not part of the thinking of the early Christians as they wrestled with language about Jesus, but it may prove helpful for gaining an understanding of the Christological language used in the New Testament.

As chapter 2 demonstrated, Jesus appears somewhat uncomfortable with self-description in the Gospel tradition. If one can talk about a "Christology of Jesus" as the starting point for a discussion of New Testament Christology in general, then one must begin with Jesus' self-designation as Son of Man.

The Son of Man is a notoriously complex topic in New Testament Christology and historical Jesus research.[5] It is a self-designation, or self-description, often used by Jesus but not used by others to refer to Jesus (for a possible exception, see Acts 7:56). The enigmatic phrase "Son of Man" can be understood in at least three senses: (1) the indefinite sense (i.e., "a human" or "mortal," common throughout the book of Ezekiel), (2) the generic sense (i.e., "a person in my position," thus "me"), and (3) the eschatological sense (a figure with a prominent role in the end times, according to the literature of Jesus' time).

Jesus appears to have used the phrase in the eschatological sense, connecting it to his role as "suffering servant of God." The suffering Servant was an enigmatic figure that, through suffering, would manifest God's glory (Isaiah 49:3). The figure of the Son of Man is found in Scripture in Daniel 7:13, but also in noncanonical books of Jesus' time such as *1 Enoch*. The Son of Man was interpreted by some Jews of the first century as a key figure in the story of Israel, a figure who vindicates God's fidelity toward Israel and his judgment against the wicked. However, the Son of Man, like Isaiah's suffering servant, is probably best understood corporately, i.e., as a figure representative of the righteous in Israel, rather than as an individual. In fact, the application of this role to an individual is a unique feature of Jesus' preaching and the preaching of the early church.

In both early Judaism and early Christian writings, the Son of Man is a figure that points to the future. When Jesus self-identifies with the Son of Man, he often associates this identification with some future event, sometimes pointing to his own suffering (as in Mark) but most often to his coming vindication: "you will see the Son of Man seated at the right hand of the Power' and 'coming with the clouds of heaven" (Mark 14:62). This quote also signals the importance of Psalm 110:1 for New Testament Christology ("The Lord says to my lord: 'Sit at my right hand, until I make your enemies your footstool'"). Through the

---

5. For a good summary of the major points in the discussion of the "Son of Man," see John R. Donahue, "Recent Studies on the Origin of 'Son of Man' in the Gospels," *Catholic Biblical Quarterly* 48 (1986): 484–98; John Collins, "The Son of Man in First-Century Judaism," *New Testament Studies* 38 (1992): 448–66.

Some Titles, Roles, and Patterns in New Testament Christology

Titles and Roles

Term	Title	Role	Description
Christ / Messiah	x	x	Jesus vindicates Israel over the forces of evil and oppression; he fulfills the promises God made to Israel through David and to the prophets.
High Priest		x	Jesus is able to offer the definitive sacrifice of himself; this sacrifice removes the sin of the faithful so that there is no further need of sacrifice.
Lord	x		Jesus has affected a union between God and Israel or the church; as Jesus destroys the power of sin, he receives the honor due to God.
Son of God	x	x	Jesus receives from God the task of bringing about the redemption of Israel from its period of oppression and servitude.
Son of Man		x	Jesus, through his suffering, will vindicate God and act as cosmic judge, condemning the wicked and blessing the righteous.
Son of David	x	x	Like "messiah" this title signifies the continuity of Jesus with the promises made by God through the prophets; Jesus is viewed as a figure of national hope for restoration and a sign of divine protection against oppression.
Suffering Servant		x	Through his suffering, Jesus atones for the people's sin and, thus, brings to a close the era of Israel's separation from God; the nation can find peace and union with God.
Word-Wisdom		x	Yahweh's Word creates, destroys, judges, and preserves the universe, yet God's Word also dwells with Israel in the Torah, and now, through the teaching and person of Jesus.

Continued

Some Titles, Roles, and Patterns *Continued*

Christological Patterns

Pattern	Titles and Roles Associated with This Pattern	Examples	Description
Parousia Christology	Lord, Christ, Son of Man	Acts 3:19–21; 1 Corinthians 16:22	At a point in the near future, Jesus will come in glory and power to judge the living and the dead and definitively inaugurate God's rule on Earth.
Resurrection-Exaltation Christology	Lord, Christ, Son of God	Philippians 2:1–11; Acts 13:33	Through the resurrection and the exaltation of Jesus the suffering and humiliation he had undergone is transformed.
Ministry Christology	Christ, Son of God, Son of Man, Suffering Servant; Lord	Mark 1:11; 10:45	Moments in the life and ministry of Jesus provide glimpses of Jesus' true identity as he serves the marginalized, encounters resistance and hatred, until he finally suffers to bring about the victory for God and God's people over sin and death.
Preexistent Christology	Lord, Word, Wisdom	1 Corinthians 10:4; Colossians 1:15–20; John 1:1–14	From the very origins of the universe and throughout the history of Israel, God's Wisdom, or God's Word, dwelt in the world and guided Israel; in Jesus, the Word of God has become incarnate to instruct and guide Israel to union with God.

resurrection, Jesus had been exalted to God's right hand, the place of intimacy, happiness, and power. In the future, he will come on the clouds as the vindicated Son of Man, execute judgment against the faithless and the unjust, and vindicate the righteous faithful. This orientation toward the future is an important pattern in New Testament Christology and often closely associated with the struggle to identify Jesus as the messiah.

The title "messiah" provides us with an appropriate point of transition from a "Christology of Jesus" to a Christology of the early church. It is apparent that Jesus had an ambivalent attitude toward the title *messiah*; he may have been put off by its connection to violent nationalism in the minds of many first-century Jews, as noted previously. While there was no uniform set of expectations concerning a messiah figure in first-century Judaism, the role of the messiah generally included achievements such as the inauguration of a new age, punishment of the wicked, resurrection of the dead, defeat of Gentile oppressors, purification of the Temple, and reestablishment of the Davidic monarchy. Given these connotations, the applicability of the title of messiah to Jesus seems curious—Jesus' role was not that of one who would bring defeat to Israel's political enemies, in accord with the violent nationalism that was popular in first-century Palestine. Yet Jesus did identify himself with messianic expectations through a variety of symbolic actions and provocative pronouncements. In light of such statements, the earliest Christians identified Jesus as messiah, even though Jesus had not performed many of the actions (performed the role) that many expected of the messiah. Rather, the earliest Christians anticipated Jesus' *future* vindication as messiah, at which time he would perform the basic functions associated with that role. This future event was called the Parousia.

The term *parousia* (Greek for "presence" or "arrival") was often used to describe the visit of an emperor. One can imagine the joy and horror such a visitation might evoke—those who were "good servants" of the empire might expect rewards and accolades, while those who were poor administrators would fear the repercussions of such a visit. The word became an effective image for the early Christians' apocalyptic expectations—Jesus would become Lord of all at the Parousia and execute judgment against evildoers. The expectation of the Parousia, or second coming, of Christ effectively bridged the early Christian experience of Jesus as decisive for Israel's future and the Jewish expectation of final judgment and resurrection. The Parousia would finally and definitively inaugurate the kingdom that Jesus had proclaimed as breaking into the world. It would bring about the defeat of evil, the resurrection of the dead, and vindicate Jesus' role as messiah. This future vindication stands in contrast with the ministry of Jesus, in which he is depicted as a lowly servant. The Christological pattern that shifts between these two stages, one lowly stage and one exalted stage, is often called "two-step Christology."

Two-step Christology seems to have characterized the early part of stage two, i.e., in the few decades immediately after the death and resurrection of

Jesus. Raymond Brown used the expression "Christological moment" to refer to scenes taken from the life and ministry of Jesus that became the vehicle for the expression of a post-resurrection Christology.[6] Jesus' lordship, recognized by his disciples in the resurrection, is transferred to various points in the life of Jesus. These points or moments tend to emerge earlier in the narrative of Jesus in the progressive development of the New Testament. For example, the earliest Gospel, Mark, uses the scene of Jesus' baptism as an inaugural Christological moment in the life of Jesus. However, in Matthew and Luke, the infancy narratives are the key early Christological moments. However, it is perilous to see this developmental pattern as perfectly linear.

The "Son of God" is often used to signify important Christological moments (e.g., Mark 15:39). Most modern Christians, however, immediately read this title in light of the Christian doctrine of the Trinity. However, one should be cautious about reading back into the biblical texts a doctrine that is not defined until the fourth century CE. Neither, however, should one pretend that such a doctrine emerged out of a vacuum. These doctrinal developments have their roots in the witness of scripture and the beliefs of the early church. Doctrinal development takes place as a movement from experience, to question, to formal doctrinal statements.

The "son of God" is a role rather than a title in the Old Testament. On occasion, it designates angels, as in the case of Job 1:6 in which even "the Adversary" (*satan* in Hebrew) is described as a "son of God." The people of Israel collectively or individually are designated as son(s) of God (Exodus 4:22; Hosea 11:1; Isaiah 1:2; 30:1). Because the king could be called "God's son" (2 Samuel 7:14; Psalm 2:7; 89:26), some have thought that this was a title to be used by the coming messiah, but even the Qumran literature does not necessarily support this view. The dominant view in the Old Testament is that a "son of God" was someone who had received a God-given task. As such, the title "Son of God" is applied to Jesus to signify his unique God-given task—redemption. The uniqueness of Jesus' task is emphasized in the Fourth Gospel, and in many early Christian writings, when Jesus is called "the only begotten Son" (*monogenēs*). However, it would be a mistake to consider the uniqueness of Jesus' relationship with the Father in terms of mission or function. Rather, in the New Testament, the title of Jesus as Son reflects the special intimacy that Jesus has with the Father and which, in his redemptive mission, he makes available to those who have faith: believers cry out to God, and they too call God *Abba* (Galatians 4:4–6). The title "Son of God," when applied to Jesus in the New Testament, while not Trinitarian in the later, Nicene sense, expresses the fundamental intimacy between Jesus and his Father that provides the foundations for an eventual statement about the Trinity in the early church.

---

6. Raymond Brown, "Aspects of New Testament Thought," in *The New Jerome Biblical Commentary*, ed. R. Brown, J, Fitzmyer, and R. Murphy (Englewood Cliffs, NJ: Prentice Hall, 1990), 1357.

The title, roles, and patterns that comprise New Testament Christology, however, are only partially understood when abstracted from the literature of the New Testament. In what follows, elements of New Testament Christology are given their proper form within their respective literary contexts.

Christology in Paul

One of the ironies of New Testament history is that the primary witness to the earliest theological reflections on Jesus comes to us from a man who never knew Jesus personally during his lifetime. Paul of Tarsus was, by all accounts, a persecutor of the church, but he had a revelatory experience of the risen Christ that he insisted was qualitatively the same as the experience of those who had been close to Jesus during his lifetime (1 Corinthians 15:1–11). His letters, while not Christological essays, stand as important witnesses to the theological developments described earlier.

Paul's letters are highly occasional—they do not offer a systematic presentation of his thought but address questions ad hoc. Nevertheless, one can piece together a pretty good idea of Paul's thoughts concerning Christ.

For Paul, the religious significance of Christ is grasped in conjunction with the story of Israel. Yet the gospel is also universal: it is meant first for the Jews and then for the Gentiles. God's love and fidelity are at the heart of the plan of salvation. This plan of salvation is historical, i.e., it unfolds through the course of history. God's plan is not exclusively focused on humanity but encompasses the entire cosmos so that all creation is to be reconciled to God in Christ.

Paul freely uses Christological titles to indicate the place of Christ in God's plan of salvation. Paul often uses the title "Son" to designate the preexistence of Jesus, i.e., that prior to his birth, Jesus existed with God in heaven. As was mentioned previously, in the Old Testament a "son of God" was someone who had received a God-given task. For Paul, God has given his Son the task of redeeming the world, and has been sent to Earth to carry out that task.

The title "Christ" was used in conjunction with Israel's hope of future restoration and deliverance. Paul uses the title to designate Jesus as the fulfillment of those hopes. In fact, Paul is so enamored with this title that it practically becomes a second name for Jesus: "Jesus Christ," or "Christ Jesus." It signifies understanding anew God's plan for the restoration of Israel and the redemption of the Gentiles.

The title "Lord" was, for Paul, a way of referring to the glorified risen Christ's dominion over creation—a dominion won through his obedience and death. When Paul calls Jesus "Lord," he is expressing the belief that Christ was due the same worship and honor as God—while always remaining distinct as the Son. One can easily see the tension here: Jesus appears to be equal to God in

Person of Interest: Paul

Apostle Paul

Paul has always been controversial. During his lifetime he was in conflict with other "apostles" and various groups within the Christian church (Galatians 1–2). Paul did not know Jesus; rather, he was a latecomer to the Christian movement.

Although born to Jewish parents in the Greek city of Tarsus in what is now southern Turkey, Paul, like the other citizens of his hometown, enjoyed the special status of "citizens of Rome" (Acts 22:25 ff.; 23:27). He grew up with one foot in the world of Greek thought and the other in Judaism; this is reflected in his two names—one Jewish (Saul) and the other Latin (Paul). Paul became an ardent supporter of the Pharisaic movement and even a persecutor of Christians (Acts 7:58; 22:20). At that time he underwent a dramatic call experience (Acts 9:1–19): Paul was said to be on "the road to Damascus" when he saw the risen Christ. In the years following his call, he seems to have spent time in "Arabia," in Damascus, at his home in Tarsus, and even a brief time in Jerusalem.

Paul moved into the spotlight when he was sent to Antioch with Barnabas. The church at Antioch, which was home to a community of both Jewish and Gentile Christians, commissioned Paul and Barnabas to spread the gospel among the Gentiles. Such inclusivity met with opposition from some Jewish Christians from Jerusalem; but in the end, the mission of inclusion won the day. The so-called Council of Jerusalem in 49 CE (Galatians 2:1–10; Acts15:6–12) decided that circumcision was not required for Gentile Christians to become full members of the Christian community. After further missions, Paul was martyred in Rome.

© The Bridgeman Art Library

some sense. While Paul and the early church have not really violated the monotheism of the Shema, one can imagine what non-Christian Jews of the time thought as they heard such bold statements about the preexistence of Jesus as God's Son and his exaltation at God's right hand.

Two sections from Paul's letters are of considerable interest for addressing the question of Christ's preexistence. The first of these speaks of Christ.

[W]ho, though he was in the form of God,
  did not regard equality with God
  as something to be exploited,
but emptied himself,
  taking the form of a slave,
  being born into human likeness.
And found in human form,
  he humbled himself
  and became obedient to the point of death—
  even death on a cross.
Therefore God also highly exalted him
  and gave him the name
  that is above every name,
so that at the name of Jesus
  every knee should bend,
  in heaven and on earth and under the earth,
and every tongue confess
  that Jesus Christ is Lord,
  to the glory of God the Father. (Philippians 2:6–11)

In this hymn, Christ is proclaimed Lord upon his exaltation, taking his seat at the right hand of God (cf. Psalm 110). Christ's exaltation comes about because of his self-emptying (*kenōsis*; see sidebar) to be born as a human and submit obediently to a humiliating death.

The basic pattern of the Philippians hymn is obvious enough—descent and ascent, emptying and exaltation—but some major Christological issues are signaled in the passage as well. The opening sentence envisions the preexistence of Christ: before Jesus was born, he existed "in the form of God." However, what does that mean? What does it mean to say, "He did not consider equality with God something to be grasped at"? This passage has long perplexed scholars. Some have seen here an early Christian belief in the full divinity of Christ. If Christ is "in the form of God," he is God. However, this phrase is not as simple and straightforward as it appears. Adam and Eve were created in the image and likeness of God, yet early (and contemporary) Christians did not understand them as equal with God. Other scholars contend that Christ is the preexistent heavenly man who empties himself out of humility but is rewarded with the divine title (Lord) because of his obedience to God. In effect, he wins by his obedience the divine prerogatives that Adam and Eve sought to gain by their disobedience (cf., Genesis 3:5). The Philippians hymn is a fascinating, early statement of Christology, but it raises more issues than it solves.

Kenōsis and Buddhism

Christianity and Buddhism have sustained a substantial dialogue for many decades. In particular, the Buddhist monk Thich Nhat Hahn and the late Christian monk Thomas Merton, OCSO, have both produced works that testify to common convictions about the nature of human existence and proper moral and spiritual responses to a world dominated by violence.

In recent years other scholars have engaged in substantial dialogue (e.g., John Cobb and Masao Abe) on another important area of common exploration that has emerged in conjunction with the Buddhist doctrine of *sunyata*, or the inherent emptiness of existence. The doctrine of *sunyata* was advanced by the Buddhist scholar Najarguna in response to certain developments within early Buddhism. He envisioned it as a faithful recovery of the Buddha's own teaching on the three marks or qualities of reality (*laksanas*). All reality is (1) *anitya* (i.e., all things in existence are transitory or passing), (2) *duhkha* (i.e., because all things are transitory, no-thing really satisfies; thus, reality is unsatisfactory), and (3) *anatman* (just like all aspects of existence, the self is *anitya*; it follows that there is no self, no *atman*). Such an account of reality, on the face of it, contradicts the Christian understanding of creation and the affirmation of creation in the Incarnation. In his popular book, *Crossing the Threshold of Hope* (San Francisco: Harper Collins, 1994), the late Pope John Paul II voiced concerns about the apparent contradictions between Christian and Buddhist understandings of the created world. Many Buddhist and Christian critics thought that he did not give Buddhist doctrine its due.

Some Buddhists and Christians have seized on the hymn in Philippians 2 as an important point of convergence between the two traditions. In that hymn, Paul asks the Philippians to adopt the mind of Christ who "emptied himself," and because of that self-emptying, was exalted. The Greek word for *self-emptying* in this passage is *kenōsis*. Some Christian theologians have begun to explore possible similarities between Paul's moral exhortation to the Philippians and the Buddhist doctrine of the inherent emptiness of existence and its corollary doctrine of non-attachment to the transitory world. The goal of the Buddhist "path" is realized, some would argue, not by trying to attain a comprehensive view of reality, which has been the concern of Christian theologians, but by using what Buddhists call "right understanding" to abandon all "view-making," or reality-making habits of the mind. The point is to let reality be and to become unattached, to resist the desire to control and dominate. This metaphysics is anti-metaphysical but still profoundly moral.

Another key Pauline text is 1 Corinthians 8:6: "There is one God, the Father, from whom are all things and for whom we exist, and one Lord, Jesus Christ, through whom are all things and through whom we exist." This passage asserts, in effect, that Christ was present at the creation of the universe and that all creation is sustained in existence through him. To this might be compared a passage from the letter to the Colossians:

> He is the image of the invisible God, the firstborn of all creation. For in him all things in heaven and on earth were created, things visible and invisible, whether thrones or dominions or rulers or powers—all things have been created through him and for him. He himself is before all things, and in him all things hold together. He is the head of the body, the church; he is the beginning, the firstborn from the dead, so that he might come to have first place in everything. For in him all the fullness of God was pleased to dwell, and through him God was pleased to reconcile to himself all things, whether on earth or in heaven, by making peace through the blood of his cross. (Colossians 1:15–20)

Most Pauline scholars believe that Colossians is "deutero-Pauline," meaning that it does not come from Paul himself, but from some follower of Paul writing in his name in the years after his death. Consequently it offers only indirect evidence of Paul's thought. With that caveat, however, it is obvious that the author has drawn heavily upon known Pauline themes. As in the Philippians hymn, Christ is said to be in the "image of God"—again leaving open the meaning of that phrase. In addition, it is obvious that the Colossian passage, like that of 1 Corinthians, asserts that Christ was present at the creation of the universe and that all creation is sustained in existence through him. This thematic connection of Christ with creation will prove fruitful for further elaboration on the precise relationship between the Son and God as the first century comes to a close.

Christology in Paul bears witness to the ferment and complexity in the early Church. On the one hand, Paul seems to present a Christology that is focused on the future and Christ's *parousia*, but this pattern is challenged by his inclusion of material like the Philippians hymn, which presents a Christological pattern that envisions Christ as preexistent. In fact, Paul's Christology resonates strongly with that of John, the latest Gospel (see section below entitled "The Gospel of Mark"). The Pauline data, therefore, put the lie to any account of New Testament Christology that posits a linear path of development either through titles or patterns.

Christology in the Synoptic Gospels

The study of New Testament Christology, particularly in the Synoptic Gospels, has moved away from an emphasis on roles, titles, and patterns to explore the distinctive Christological portraits offered in the New Testament. The previous discussion of roles, titles, and patterns still provides important background for understanding the Christology of the evangelists, but each of the evangelists acts as an artist, creating a distinctive portrait of Christ. Each of these portraits is designed to speak to a particular audience and to make the message of Christ's saving power apparent.

The Gospel of Mark

Mark identifies Jesus as the Messiah, the Son of God, and the Son of Man—titles with which the reader is somewhat familiar. However, Mark thoroughly redefines these titles in light of Jesus' suffering and death. His death casts a shadow over the entire Gospel and causes the disciples to misunderstand and fail in their attempts to follow Jesus.

For Mark, the proclamation of the kingdom of God provides the framework for a complex interplay between Christology and discipleship. "The kingdom of God" is an expression of hope for God to "break through" and rule the world definitively. Jesus' own life is a proleptic, or anticipatory, realization of the kingdom. The climax of Jesus' life is his suffering and death. This climax provides the interpretive key for his teaching and healing. Jesus' identity as Messiah is only realized at his death.

The disciples are generally depicted in the first part of the Gospel (through 8:27) as examples to be emulated; the second half of the Gospel depicts them in a much less favorable light. In the end, the real disciple must imitate Jesus, whose identity and mission are revealed in his suffering and death (Mark 15:39). To fail to do so is to reject Jesus. Perhaps one of the Gospel's most remarkable scenes is found in Mark 14:51–53, in which a young man observes the arrest of Jesus from a distance. All of Jesus' friends have left him and fled. When the authorities spot this young man, they try to arrest him also, but he is so desperate to escape suffering with Jesus that he runs out of his clothes and flees naked into the night. Mark highlights the failure of the disciples, particularly their refusal to accept the role of sufferer either for Jesus or themselves.

Mark's disturbing portrait of Jesus as God's Suffering Servant, and his insistence that disciples are called to follow Jesus in this regard, probably emerged from the Christian community at Rome shortly after the emperor Nero began a localized but brutal persecution.[7] Mark's emphasis on suffering and the failure of the disciples reflects the historical context of Jesus ministry, but Mark's Christology of suffering is also the product of his Christian community's concern to respond to the call of Jesus within its own historical context.

The Gospel of Matthew

Matthew's Gospel also reflects a Christian community torn by strife, but the strife is not with the Roman Empire but with its Jewish neighbors. One must be careful not to fall into the anachronism of talking about Judaism and Christianity in this context, as the boundaries of the two communities continued to

---

7. Some scholars have tried to argue for a Palestinian or Syrian setting for Mark, but a majority of scholars still identify Rome as the place of composition (for a complete discussion see Francis Moloney, *The Gospel of Mark: A Commentary* [Peabody, MA: Hendrickson, 2002]).

overlap until the second century CE. Matthew probably understood himself and his community as a viable expression of Judaism, competing with other expressions of Judaism in the first century—another form of what some would call "middle Judaism."[8] Others, however, contend that the inclusion of Gentiles in the Christian movement and its emphasis on the messiahship of Jesus moved the Christian community of Matthew further and further outside of emerging "normative Judaism" toward the end of the first century and into the second and third centuries. What is clear is that there has been a rift between Matthew's community and some important elements within Judaism, and this rift has important implications for reading the Gospel and understanding its Christology.

The Christology of Matthew is elegantly presented in summary fashion in the first two chapters of his Gospel. These chapters, often called the "infancy narrative," tell the story of Jesus' birth. In some ways the story acts like a theological overture to the rest of the Gospel. Like a musical piece at the start of a play or opera, the overture sets the mood and offers the audience some important musical signals for interpreting the story.

In Matthew, the evangelist begins with a list of generations. This is a common biblical device, used particularly in Genesis to link seemingly disparate stories (e.g., Genesis 5:1–32 where the stories of Adam and Noah are connected in this way). Matthew traces the lineage of Jesus from Abraham to David, through the kings of Judah, down to Jesus. The genealogy concludes with a note on its perfect symmetry: fourteen generations from Abraham to David, fourteen from David to the Babylonian Exile, and fourteen to the birth of Jesus. It is no coincidence that the numerical value of David's name was fourteen.[9] Jesus, therefore, is born at the perfect time. Yet the then king of the Jews, Herod the Great, did not know this, and when he learned of Jesus' birth, he arranged to have the child killed. Matthew deftly weaves his narrative so that Herod is foiled by the three astrologers (*magoi*) who, without the aide of the scriptures and having only the stars to guide them (cf. Numbers 24:7), are able to locate the messianic child and worship him with symbolic gifts. These Gentiles hail the Jewish messiah, while the rulers of Jerusalem only see Jesus as a threat and seek to destroy him.

Matthew's infancy narrative presents Jesus as the fulfillment of Israel's messianic hopes, but also as the figure who lays bare the fact that many who had waited for the messiah were unprepared to welcome him and unable to respond to his call to conversion and repentance. Matthew depicts Jesus as the royal, eschatological, and covenantal agent of God in human history, and this portrait unfolds throughout the course of the Gospel.

---

8. Anthony J. Saldarini, *Matthew's Jewish-Christian Community*, Chicago Studies in the History of Judaism (Chicago: University of Chicago, 1994).

9. In Hebrew, Latin, Greek, and most ancient languages, letters did double duty as numbers. Thus the sum of the numerical values of the letters/numbers in a person's name could be used symbolically to refer to that person.

The Parting of the Ways: Christianity and Judaism

Christians commonly read the New Testament with the assumption that Christianity and Judaism were two different religions even in the time of Jesus. Yet history demonstrates that no such distinction existed at that time or for some time thereafter—the parting of the ways between Christianity and Judaism was a long and complex process.

Some scholars would argue that the split began in the time of Paul when Gentiles started to enter into the Christian community without having to observe the Mosaic (Jewish) Law. Others point out that no definitive break between Christian and Jewish communities occurred until at least the end of the second century CE. All agree that during Jesus' lifetime, and immediately thereafter, "Christianity" was not a distinct religion. It was surely a distinct movement at this time and certainly controversial but so were many expressions of Judaism. The Pharisaic movement was not welcomed by everyone, and the Essenes were viewed as a marginal group and perhaps as dangerous by the aristocracy in Jerusalem—but this did not make them any less Jewish.

Jesus operated within bounds of Jewish thought and practice. The Gospel accounts of his controversies with established teachers within Judaism, though highly embellished (and in some cases invented) by the early Christians, were typical in Jewish circles—arguing a point of Torah is a sign of respect for Torah and allegiance to the covenant. Jesus challenged Jewish violence and sectarianism, and this certainly would have annoyed many people in first-century Palestine, but it was hardly a denial of Judaism. Additionally, Paul's insistence on grace and faith rather than Torah observance (i.e., "works of the Law") is a reformulation of the basic covenantal formula—after all, Torah was a gift (i.e., a grace) from God as well.

The differentiation between Judaism and early Christianity was accelerated by the destruction of the Temple in Jerusalem in 70 CE. Thereafter Judaism began a long process of transformation into a more homogenous or normative religious tradition. The diversity that had defined it earlier in the first century began to give way to the feeling that greater uniformity was needed in response to the pressure of political and cultural circumstances. This process continued well into the second and third centuries CE, eventually resulting in "normative" Judaism.

The Gospel of Luke

Luke's historical and social context, unlike Matthew's, was not defined by strife, but by circumstances that required the Gospel to adopt an apologetic tone. Luke's audience appears to have been comprised mainly of Gentiles. This audience seems to be concerned with two questions. First, what does a Jewish

Gospel Christologies: Portraits for Particular Audiences

Evangelist	Approximate Date	Circumstances of the Evangelist	Christological Portrait
Mark	around 70 CE	**Rome** The unpopular emperor Nero was accused of setting fire to part of the city of Rome. Nero shifted the blame to the Christians, who were disliked and mistrusted and made easy scapegoats. The Gospel of Mark was written to strengthen and encourage the church in the years following this persecution. Some scholars, however, would place the circumstances of Mark in southern Syria during the tumult and suffering surrounding the Jewish revolt in the late 60s and early 70s CE.	The climax of Jesus' life is his suffering and death. This climax provides the interpretive key for his teaching and healing. Jesus' identity as messiah is only realized at his death (Mark 15:39). The disciples are depicted in the first part of the Gospel (through 8:27) as examples to be emulated. In the second half of the Gospel, they are depicted as failing to grasp Jesus' true identity because they refuse to accept, as Jesus does, the way of suffering and death. In the end, the real disciple must imitate Jesus.
Matthew	around 85 CE	**Syria-Palestine** The Gospel seems to reflect the state of turmoil within Jewish Christianity that would be characteristic of the period in which the rabbis gathered in Jamnia and began to reform Judaism after the	Matthew depicts Jesus as "Son of God," Davidic messiah, and supreme teacher, or a "new Moses." Matthew is concerned about demonstrating continuity between Jesus and the story of Israel by using several devices including the

Continued

Gospel Christologies *Continued*

Evangelist	Approximate Date	Circumstances of the Evangelist	Christological Portrait
Matthew (*cont.*)	around 85 CE	destruction of the Temple. From this reformation of Judaism eventually emerged a form of normative Judaism that increasingly excluded other expressions of Judaism (e.g., Sadducees, Essenes, etc.). One of the groups excluded was the Christian community of Matthew. The dispute centered around the question of who was the authoritative interpreter of the Mosaic Law: Jesus or the rabbis?	list of generations at the beginning of the Gospel. Jesus' ministry begins with the Sermon on the Mount, in which Jesus lays out a more demanding interpretation of Torah.
Luke	around 80 CE	Greece/Asia Minor Luke's Gospel is not shaped by crisis as are Mark's and Matthew's; rather, Luke's concern is to make Jesus—the Jewish messiah—intelligible in a non-Jewish context.	Jesus is depicted as the universal savior and the fulfillment of all of Israel's aspirations. As such, Jesus is the friend to the outcast and the marginalized (especially women).
John	around 95 CE	Asia Minor (Ephesus?) The history behind the Fourth Gospel is notoriously complex, but it appears that the community was torn by internal and external strife concerning the person of Jesus.	John's Gospel emphasizes the preexistence of the divine Word and develops a Christology of Jesus as the fulfillment of Torah and Temple.

messiah have to do with the salvation of Gentiles? In other words, how can a religious figure from a tradition so apparently suspicious of foreigners be the way of salvation for these outsiders? Second, the destruction of Jerusalem coupled as it was with the rejection of the Christian message by most Jews seemed to suggest that God has abandoned the covenant. However, how can this God be trusted if the covenant can be abandoned? Isn't God faithful to the promises made to Israel?

Luke's answers to these questions run something like this: Jesus is the friend of the outsider, the neglected, and the weak. The marginalized become the focus of Jesus' proclamation to an extent not found in the other Gospels, and this focus proves to be the key for understanding the Gentile mission. Second, Luke emphasizes the continuity of the covenant Jesus announces and the covenant between God and the people of Israel. This continuity with the Old Testament is essential for Luke's overall argument: God is faithful to his promises.

The infancy narrative in Luke is remarkable, especially when compared to Matthew's version. First, when one compares his genealogy with Matthew's one notices at least two important differences: Luke traces Jesus' ancestry back to Adam, all humanity's common ancestor, and to David, but through a line that does not include any of the kings of Judah (Luke 3:28–31; cf. Matthew 1:6–11). Luke thus portrays Jesus as a commoner, like everyone else, universally identified. This theme of universalism is accentuated by Luke's propensity to have socially marginalized figures like a young virgin and shepherds figure prominently in the birth story. These figures attend to the advent of Jesus as the first to hear and respond to the gospel, for he is their savior and has come to despoil the rich and the mighty (Luke 1:51–53; 6:20–26).

Luke's portrait of Jesus, however, is not simply that of social contrarian; rather, he portrays Jesus as one led by the Spirit, whose actions are informed by a deep prayerfulness (e.g., 11:1) and intimacy with God. It is out of this intimacy with God that Jesus reaches out to those on the margins—particularly women. Perhaps the most poignant example of this is the familiar story of the woman who interrupts a meal at the house of Simon the Pharisee by anointing and kissing Jesus (a similar story is found in Matthew and Mark). Only in Luke's Gospel is the woman described as a "sinner" (what sin she had committed is not known), and Simon, the host, grows increasingly uncomfortable and annoyed with the extravagance of her gesture. Jesus' response to the woman emphasizes the offer of forgiveness—her love is great because her sin is great. The story is, thus, transformed by Luke so that forgiveness and compassion for the most vulnerable, a chief characteristic of Luke's portrayal of Christ, receive special emphasis. Luke's special source collection (L) also emphasizes this theme, particularly his parables. The familiar story of the Good Samaritan depicts Jesus as offering a Samaritan, a member of a community despised by "orthodox" Jews of Jerusalem and Galilee, as an example of what it means to love one's neighbor.

Both of these stories illustrate Luke's fundamental interpretation of Jesus: he is God's universal offer of salvation. Such a portrait cannot be captured by a single title but requires the complex narrative offered by Luke.

Together, the synoptic evangelists created powerful narrative portraits of Jesus—portraits that do not focus on titles or definitions but tell a story. It is through the story of Jesus' life, told in light of the resurrection, that the gospel proclamation of the early church comes to life. Yet none of these Christological portraits address the nagging question raised in the Christological material in the Pauline letters: what is the precise relationship between God and Jesus?

Wisdom and Logos: The Confluence of Jewish and Greek Ideas

The titles, patterns, and Christological portraits discussed in the previous sections culminate, in a sense, with the flourishing of wisdom Christology toward the end of the first century and the close of the New Testament period. The wisdom tradition helped the early church more adequately understand the intimacy between Jesus and God and was decisive for subsequent doctrinal formulations. Like the prophetic tradition and the priestly tradition, the wisdom tradition was one of the many forms or expressions of Judaism in the centuries up through the time of Jesus. As its name suggests, the wisdom tradition placed a heavy emphasis on the wisdom of God and God's communication with the created world and provided a means for understanding the convergence of the divine and the human in Israel's story.[10]

The wisdom tradition encompasses both a particular theological content and a literary style. Its origins are in the life of the clan or tribe, the courts of royalty (this explains the association of wisdom with one of Israel's great kings, Solomon), and in the Temple services: the Psalms offer many examples of wisdom literature. In Jewish wisdom literature, different kinds of wisdom appear: judicial, natural, theological, and experiential. Wisdom is not conscious of tradition but concerned with the "here and now." Significantly, wisdom is not restricted to Israel and includes all nations; this last feature will prove useful to early Christians as they attempt to articulate the significance of Jesus beyond the confines of Judaism. However, most important for early Christology is the tendency of the tradition to personify divine wisdom, particularly by associating the wisdom of God and the word of God. Both expressions—wisdom and word—signify the active presence of God in the word. This presence creates, communicates, sustains, and guides Israel.

---

10. Roland Murphy, one of the foremost experts in the wisdom literature, outlined some of the main features of the wisdom tradition. See Roland E. Murphy, "Wisdom Literature," in *NJBC*, ed. R. Brown, J. Fitzmyer, and R. Murphy (Engelwood Cliffs, NJ: Prentice Hall, 1990), 447–50.

God's word was the means by which God created: "By the word of the Lord the heavens were made, and all their host by the breath of his mouth" (Psalm 33:6; see also Genesis 1:1–2:4). God's word is also powerful and effective, healing the dead in their graves (Psalm 107:20) and changing the course of nature (Psalm 147:15, 18). Perhaps the best expression of the dynamic power of God's word is found in Isaiah:

> For as the rain and snow come down from
>   heaven,
>   and do not return there until they have
>   watered the earth,
> making it bring forth and sprout,
>   giving seed to the sower and bread to the
>   eater,
> so shall my word be that goes out from my
>   mouth;
>   it shall not return to me empty,
> but it shall accomplish that which I propose,
>   and succeed in the thing for which I sent it (Isaiah 55:10–11).

The author of the Wisdom of Solomon describes the presence of God through his word in the actions of the "angel of death" at the time of the Passover-Exodus:

> For while gentle silence enveloped all things,
>   and night in its swift course was now half gone,
> your all-powerful word leaped from heaven,
>   from the royal throne,
> into the midst of the land that was doomed,
>   a stern warrior
> holding a sharp sword of your authentic
>   command,
> stood and filled all things with death
> and touched heaven while standing on the
>   earth. (Wisdom of Solomon 18:14–16)

Notice that the word of God is given the role of the warrior—defeating the enemies of God and connecting heaven and earth as the plan of God is enacted.

The notion of heaven and earth being connected through the word of God is further developed in the thought of the great Jewish philosopher, Philo of Alexandria. Philo, a contemporary of Jesus, used Greek philosophy to interpret the Hebrew Scriptures. Drawing upon Greek philosophy, Philo emphasized the utter perfection of God and, therefore, God's remoteness and separation from the created world. If God were to be directly connected to the world, then God's perfection and immutability would be compromised; God would appear far too similar to the mythological images of the pagan gods of Greece. For the Greeks, reason had long been thought of as a divine principle, a spark of divinity, in the created world: this was often called the *logos spermatikos*, or "the seminal word." For the Greeks, the Logos stood between God and the created order as a conduit or a point of connection. The following passage from Philo reflects his indebtedness to Greek philosophical speculation about the Logos:

> And the Father who created the universe has given to his archangelic and most ancient Word a pre-eminent gift, to stand on the confines of both, and separated that which had been created from the Creator. And this same Word is continually a suppliant to the immortal God on behalf of the mortal race, which is exposed to affliction and misery; and is also the ambassador, sent by the Ruler of all, to the subject race. And the Word rejoices in the gift, and, exulting in it, announces it and boasts of it, saying, "And I stood in the midst, between the Lord and You." (Philo, *Who is the Heir of Divine Things?* 42. 205–206)

The Logos is divine; it is the thought of God coming to expression. As such it connects the world of ideas—the real world, for Greek philosophers like Plato—with the material world of the senses. The Logos thus connects God to the world, but it also acts as a barrier between the contingent material world and the infinity of God. It is from this milieu that the early Christians developed a Christology of the divine Word, or Logos Christology.

Wisdom and Logos in John's Christology

Perhaps the premier example of Logos Christology in the New Testament is the Prologue to the Fourth Gospel:

> In the beginning was the Word, and the Word was with God, and the Word was God. He was in the beginning with God. All things came to be through him, and without him not one thing came into being. (John 1:1–3)

From these brief verses one can begin to identify several benefits of Logos Christology. First, Logos Christology makes possible a much clearer identification of Jesus with God. Second, the life and ministry of Jesus, as well as his death and resurrection, are not innovations in the history of Israel. Rather, the life, death, and resurrection of Jesus were viewed as an extension of God acting on behalf of humanity from the first moment of creation. Through the Logos, God

Person of Interest: Origen

© Private Collection / Ken Welsh / The Bridgeman Art Library

Origen

Origen (185–254 CE) is one of the greatest Christian writers before the fourth century, yet some of his doctrines came under suspicion in later centuries and were condemned. Origen, thus, does not enjoy the title saint, though he is regularly listed among the most influential church fathers. His writings were highly influential in the early church and continue to be read by Christians who pray the Liturgy of the Hours (the daily prayers that are the "official" daily prayers of the church and include Psalms, Scripture passages, and devotional readings from great Christian writers).

Origen was a prolific writer and the leader of the great Christian catechetical school in Alexandria. He devoted himself to a strict, disciplined life that included, unfortunately, self-mutilation: he took Jesus' admonition in Matthew 19:12 literally! He suffered from church politics in Alexandria and was later tortured by the Roman imperial authorities during the persecution led by the emperor Decius.

Origen's most important contributions lie in his ability to synthesize Greek philosophy with the Christian scriptures. Many would assert that the result was not always positive. His most celebrated work is *On First Principles* (*Peri Archōn*) in which, like Philo, he offers an allegorical understanding of scripture. For Origen, the literal sense of the text is only one of its meanings, and often its least important meaning; the literal sense is meant to spur the reader on to discern its allegorical meaning, its spiritual reality. Additionally, Origen wrote an influential commentary on John in which he subordinated the divinity of the Son to that of the Father on the basis of John 1:1. He also popularized the idea that all things, even Satan, would be restored to God in the end of time (the Greek word for this "universal restoration" is *apokatastasis*). These theological innovations set up many problems for the generations of theologians who followed Origen, and some of his positions were condemned at church councils held in the fifth and sixth centuries.

has created the universe, spoken to Israel, and fought on their behalf against the forces of evil and destruction.

If one examines closely the Greek text of John 1:1, the apparent clarity of the verse is clouded, however. The Greek reads as follows (with a slavishly literal translation in parentheses):

1a *en archē ēn ho logos* (In the beginning was the Word)
1b *kai ho logos ēn pros ton theon* (and the Word was with the God)
1c *kai theos ēn ho logos* (and God was the Word)

Our concern here is with the second and third clauses. The Greek term for *Word*, as noted previously, is *logos*, and the word for *God* is *theos*, while *ho* and *ton* are different forms of the definite article in Greek (i.e., *the*). Note that the Word was with "the God" in 1b, but 1c states that the Word was "God," and not "the God." Most commentators agree that the Prologue makes a distinction between "the God" (with article) that the Word is with and the "God" (without article) the Word is with. This is occasionally rendered in English translations as, "The Word was with God and the Word was divine." Others argue that such a translation goes too far, for Greek has a perfectly good adjective for *divine*, but John chose not to use it.[11] Although Christians today affirm that the Word is fully divine and read John 1:1 as reflecting this, it was not so clear to many ancients. The apparent distinction offered in this passage will be cited by luminaries such as Origen and will lend fuel to the fires of Christological speculation in the years after the writing of the New Testament.

The Logos Christology is not found only in the Prologue. Indeed the entire Fourth Gospel identifies Jesus as the Word incarnate while also employing other devices to round out what is often called a high Christology. This high Christology is further reflected in the so-called I AM statements found in the Gospel (John 8:24, 28, 58). These passages are more striking in the original Greek because they include the first-person pronoun; like Spanish and many other modern languages, the use of the first-person personal pronoun is rare in Greek and grammatically unnecessary. These I AM statements evoke the image of Yahweh revealing himself to Moses as I AM (Exodus 3:14), especially in those cases in which no predicate, no "what" completed the I AM (John 8:58; 13:19). With these emphatic statements Jesus is, in a sense, identifying himself with the God of Moses and giving special weight to all he says and does—even to the extent of prefixing teachings with an emphatic double *amen*, an Aramaic word which means "it is so" (John 1:51). The double amen is used twenty-five times in John to emphasize the power and authority of Jesus' teaching. The Fourth Gospel also

---

11. The New English Bible translates the passage as "the Word was what God was," though other commentators have argued that "the Word was divine" is appropriate. Scholars such as Raymond Brown have argued that while there is an important distinction between 1b and 1c, translations like the NABRE and the NRSV (i.e., "the Word was God") are accurate so long as one does not thereby read into the passage Trinitarian theology, which did not develop as such until the fourth century.

emphasizes Jesus as the new Torah (John 1:16) and as the new Temple (John 1:14) so that the Christology of John echoes the diversity and the narrative richness of the other Gospels even as Logos Christology pushes New Testament Christology in a new direction.

Conclusion

The New Testament uses a variety of images and symbols to explore the experience of God in Jesus. These efforts culminate in the development of Logos Christology, which emphasizes the creative and redemptive power of God's self-communication.

These efforts did not settle the precise question of Jesus' relationship to God, however. The New Testament offers the Christian faithful a set of stories and symbols that communicate the proclamation of God's salvation in Christ, stories that are just that—narrative creations that early Christians regarded as decisive for Christian life and worship. Following the close of the first century CE, as the canon of the New Testament began to achieve a fixed form and exercised an increasingly normative role for the Christian community, the limitations of its Christological formulations became apparent—as will be discussed in the next chapter.

Questions for Understanding

1. What is the Shema, and how does it complicate the Christology of the earliest Christians?
2. Describe the basic set of expectations surrounding the "one who is to come," or the messiah in late Second Temple Judaism.
3. What is the difference between a Christological title, a Christological role, and a Christological pattern?
4. What is the origin of the phrase "Son of Man," and what does it mean?
5. Why might it have been difficult to convince first-century Jews (or anyone for that matter) that Jesus of Nazareth was the messiah?
6. List some of the titles and roles associated with Paul's Christology.
7. Does the hymn in Philippians 2 state that Jesus is God? Explain.
8. How do the infancy narratives in Matthew and Luke function as "Christological moments"?
9. What is the Logos, and why is it important for understanding the development of New Testament Christology?
10. Does John's Prologue proclaim that Jesus is God? Explain.

Questions for Reflection and Action

1. Christians read the Hebrew Bible (the Old Testament) as their own scripture and see in it many pointed references to Christian doctrine. Given what you have read in this chapter, is such a practice legitimate? Are there limits to such a practice?

2. The Christology of the New Testament is rather ambiguous. Are there benefits to such ambiguity? Are there problems? Explain.

3. If the New Testament offers a primarily narrative account of Jesus' identity, are Christians committed to narrative (i.e., stories) in a unique way? In other words, if the religious truth about Jesus is delivered primarily as a narrative rather than as a proposition, does this fact mean anything for how these truths should be understood?

For Further Reading

Dunn, James D. G. *Christology in the Making: A New Testament Inquiry into the Origins of the Doctrine of the Incarnation.* 2nd ed. Grand Rapids, MI: Eerdmans, 1996.

Hurtado, Larry W. *Lord Jesus Christ: Devotion to Jesus in Earliest Christianity.* Grand Rapids, MI: Eerdmans, 2003.

Matera, Frank J. *New Testament Christology.* Louisville, KY: Westminster John Knox, 1999.

CHAPTER 5

The Development of Classical Christology

The New Testament testifies to the difficulty encountered by the earliest Christians when they tried to reconcile their experience of the risen Christ, the traditions of Jesus of Nazareth, and their understanding of God from the Old Testament. However, as chapter 4 demonstrated, the earliest Christians were also open to innovation—to restructuring their understanding of God and their patterns of worship. In fact, it was through Christian worship that important Christological insights were gained. In the first century, Christian communities inaugurated a process of redefining the major symbols and the entire story of first-century Judaism, yet these redefinitions, these innovations, were not without controversy.

Any description of the early Christological controversies tends to stumble on the fact that the vocabulary and the cultural setting of these controversies appear hopelessly opaque. The controversies make more sense when seen from the perspective of the issues they addressed. Two basic Christological questions will guide this chapter. The first has to do with the precise relationship between the Logos, incarnate in Jesus, and God.[1] The second Christological question hinges upon the human Jesus. While some groups such as the Gnostics denied that Jesus was human, or even material, the vast majority of Christians affirmed the humanity of Jesus. However, just how human was he? What is the relationship between the human Jesus and the Logos or the Son?

These two Christological questions, taken together, provide the impetus for exploring what Christians have experienced in the life, death, and resurrection of Jesus Christ. The novelty of this experience demanded new ways of speaking about Jesus and new ways of speaking about God. In sum, Christological orthodoxy is born from theological innovation, but these innovations, in turn, set up new boundaries, new limits, to guide Christian thought, worship, and practice. The classical Christological doctrines emerged to affirm both the humanity and divinity of Christ.

---

1. The Logos was discussed in chapter 4.

The Way to Nicaea (100–325)

The close of the New Testament saw an important move toward Logos Christology with its focus on the Jewish and Greek ideas of the divine Word (Logos) and its relationship to God and the world. The combination of early Jewish and Greek thought helped to set up the controversies and the doctrinal developments that took place in the two-and-a-half centuries following the close of the New Testament and culminated in the theological battles at Nicaea and afterward.

Students of Christology have often been tempted to see Greek thought as an intrusion into early Christian theology. However, scholarship in the twentieth and twenty-first centuries has demonstrated that, even in the world of Jesus (i.e., first-century Palestinian Judaism), one cannot always easily separate Jewish, Christian, and Greek thought. Greek ideas influenced and were affected by all of the cultures and religions in the Mediterranean basin. Additionally, the development of Christological orthodoxy involves more than just the confluence of culture, or even politics; it involves the capacity to affirm judgments beyond the narrative and symbolic discourse characteristic of more strictly literal or highly subjective and even quirky approaches to biblical interpretation.

Developments before the Fourth Century

By the end of the first century CE, Christian communities had become increasingly Gentile in composition (mostly Greek) and had begun to orient themselves and their mission to the urban centers of the Roman Empire. Around 160, Justin Martyr undertook to argue on behalf of the Christian faith, but the task was not easy.[2] He needed to explain how a man who was crucified by the Romans as a Jewish nationalist and revolutionary could be religiously meaningful for the diverse and cultured peoples of the Roman Empire. Jesus may have been the Jewish messiah, but the messiah was obviously no friend of Rome. What value could Jesus have for Romans or Greeks?

Justin employed Logos Christology in his First Apology (*apologia* means "defense" in Greek) against those who thought a Jewish messiah had no relevance beyond Palestine.[3] Specifically, he drew upon the idea of the *logos spermatikos* (seminal word): the divine Word was present in the world through a rationality that permeated everything. The ordering of the sun, moon, and stars, the order of nature, and especially the rationality of the human mind signified the connectedness of the created order with the realm of the divine. Justin reasoned that all

---

2. Justin was eventually killed for his faith during a Roman persecution of Christians; he is therefore known as Justin Martyr.

3. Justin also attempted to address Jewish objections to Christian claims in his *Dialogue with Trypho*.

philosophies and religions before Christ were well intended but limited human attempts to respond to the "seminal word." However, these philosophies and religions were really pointing to and preparing for the definitive moment when the divine Word would arrive in the world, in the person of Jesus. For Justin, Jesus was the fulfillment not just of Israel's hopes but also of the hopes of the entire world. Logos Christology thus provided an important point of intersection between the world of Greek thought and early Christian theology.

Meanwhile, other theologians began to tackle pressing questions regarding the relationship between God and the Word, or the Son. For many second- and third-century theologians, the problem of how the one God could share his divine power or *monarchia* with the Son helped to focus this issue. For one group of theologians, often called Adoptionists (or Dynamic Monarchians), the Son is given a share in the divine power or authority because of his virtue. That is, the human Jesus practiced virtue to such a heroic extent that God bestowed on him a share in his *monarchia*. Proponents of this position did not see the Son as inherently divine but understood that the Son shared in the authority of God through God's gracious will. While this understanding seemed consistent with belief in the oneness of God[4] it failed to adequately distinguish the Son from other charismatic leaders from Israel's past (e.g., Jeremiah). In addition to the Adoptionists, there was a group called the Modalists (or Modal Monarchians) for whom the Son was a mere "mode" or operation of God. That is, the Modalists asserted that words *Father* and *Son* do not signify anything about God's nature or being; rather, these words simply describe the manner in which one experiences God; the Father is the Son, and the Son is the Father. Again, the Modalists were able to safeguard the oneness of God but failed to grasp the distinctions between Father and Son so central in the Gospels.

In order to avoid these two problematic positions, the great African theologian Tertullian (c. 160–220) argued that the Father, who is God from all eternity, is the origin of the divine power or *monarchia* because he is *spiritus* (spirit)— the stuff, the material, of divinity (a fine grade of matter like ether). When the Father decided to create the universe he "extruded" the Son, so the Son also was *spiritus*. The Son was distinct from the Father, but this distinction did not divide or diminish the divine *monarchia* any more than the emperor divides his authority when he commands an agent to do his bidding.

Tertullian successfully refuted the Adoptionists and the Modalists, but made two important mistakes. First, Tertullian radically subordinated the Son to the Father: in his model, the Son is less divine than the Father. Second, Tertullian articulated the relationship between the Father and the Son in materialistic terms: they are both divine because they are made of the same stuff.[5]

---

4. Cf. the importance of the Shema, discussed in chapter 4.

5. See Tertullian, *Against Praxeas*, 7.

Tertullian's materialistic subordination of the Son was rectified, to some extent, by Origen (c. 185–c. 255), the controversial third-century Alexandrian theologian and biblical exegete. As the successor to Clement of Alexandria, the leader of the catechetical school of Alexandria, Origen was a Platonist and, therefore, suspicious of materialistic thought.[6] In the context of Tertullian's materialistic understanding of the relationship between the Father and Son, Origen's Platonic idealism provided an important insight.

According to Origen, God fully transcended the created order and was beyond any material form. The properties of God were unknowable, but the Son, or the divine Word, was the expression of God, not "extruded" as a material substance, but immaterially and eternally. However, while Origen corrected Tertullian's materialism and emphasized the eternity of the Son's participation in the Father, he nonetheless subordinated the Son to the Father. For Origen, the Son was still a step down from God because the Son is divine through "participation" while the Father is divine in himself. Origen made this explicit when he differentiated the Father from the Son using "the God" (*ho theos*) for the former and "God" (*theos*) for the latter.[7] This subordination of the Son and the theological tension it created would prove important in the fourth century, as the Christian church moved from the status of a persecuted community to that of an institution sponsored by imperial power.

The Council of Nicaea (325)

Legend has it that in 312, on the eve of a great military campaign, the young emperor Constantine had a vision of the *chi rho* (X and P—the first letters of the Greek word *christos*) and heard a voice saying, "in this sign you shall conquer."[8] Constantine went on to defeat his rival and subsequently became a defender and sponsor of the Christian church and its politics. The young emperor believed that as the sponsor of the church he had an obligation to preserve good order in the church as well as in the empire. When a controversy broke out in the city of Alexandria between its bishop, Alexander, and a priest, Arius, Constantine intervened.[9]

---

6. Recall that for Platonists, ultimate reality is to be found beyond the material, which is only a shadow of the real world of forms or ideas.

7. See Origen, *Commentary on John* 2.2.

8. Lactantius, *On the Deaths of the Persecutors*, 44. Eusebius, *Life of Constantine*, 1.28, offers the Greek version: *touto nika*).

9. N.B., the bishops of Rome, Alexandria, and Antioch (later this list would include Jerusalem and Constantinople) were greatly revered in the early church. They had enormous power and influence over other churches in their areas. Starting in the sixth century these bishops will be called patriarchs (eventually to include the bishops of Constantinople and Jerusalem) but during the period in question, the leaders of these churches were titled simply bishops.

Arius (c. 260–336) is often regarded as the greatest heretic of the early church. Contemporary scholars rightly note that most of our information about Arius and his position comes to us from his opponents—Arius's own works were destroyed after he was condemned—and should, therefore, be taken with a considerable dose of salt. Nevertheless, the basic contours of Arius's thought are fairly clear and undisputed. Based on surviving quotations in the lost work known as the *Thalia*, Arius demonstrated continuity with the philosophical and theological tone of Alexandrian theology—especially as exemplified in the works of Philo and Origen. Like his predecessors, Arius wanted to preserve an essentially Greek understanding of God as removed from the material world. He, therefore, constructed an account of the world in which the divine Word was an intermediary being standing between the one God and creation. Such an understanding of the Word had the effect of distinguishing the divinity of the

Caesar and the Church

The conversion of Constantine and his patronage of the Christian church was a mixed blessing. The Edict of Toleration he issued jointly with his co-emperor Licinius in 313 gave Christianity legal standing and ended the horrible persecution that had broken out periodically in the empire. With the emperor's favor came the emperor's influence. Because religion was a public and civil matter in the empire, Christians began to appeal to the emperor to adjudicate their disputes. For example, in a controversy in North Africa the emperor lent imperial weight to the condemnation of a group known as the Donatists.[10] In the Arian controversy, first one, then another of the emperor's bishop-advisers influenced his position, with the result that Athanasius and other supporters of Nicaea fell in and out of favor. In the East, a model that many call "Caesaro-papism" emerged as the dominant ideal for church-state relations. Caesaro-papism was the idea that the emperor was the supreme ruler of the church and had the responsibility to protect and safeguard it. In the West, however, with no strong imperial figure, the Bishop of Rome began to emerge as dominant, and he sought to subordinate secular officials to the power of the church, with varying degrees of success. The ongoing tension between civil and religious authorities erupted into conflict during the Protestant Reformation. With the rise of nationalism, pressure was increasingly brought to bear on the Roman Catholic Church to cede power to national leaders and subject the church to civil authority; but such attempts were usually rebuffed and in many places the Catholic Church lost its political standing and governmental support.

---

10. Donatists asserted that churchmen who had recanted their faith during persecution could not subsequently repent and be restored to office. The Donatists refused to accept the authority of such church leaders.

Father from that of the Son by means of a radical subordinationism that defini-tively separated the Father and Son. Two important Arian slogans indicate this: "There was a time when he [i.e., the Son] was not," and, "Before he [the Son] was begotten he was not." For Arius, God alone is unchanging and unbegotten (i.e., without beginning or origin); the Son was created out of nothing by the will of the Father. Additionally, Arius asserted that only God knows himself and all things perfectly; the Son only knows God and himself imperfectly, and can only reveal God imperfectly.

The Arian position gained considerable popularity because of Arius's appeal to scripture and his use of passages from notable theologians like Origen. How-ever, Arius's bishop, Alexander, called upon Arius to recant his position. Arius refused to submit to his bishop, and when the controversy dragged on, the emperor stepped in.

Constantine's initial intervention took the form of a letter to both Arius and Alexander in which he instructed the two parties to be reconciled to one another: "For as long as you continue to contend about these small and very insignificant questions, I believe it indeed to be not merely unbecoming, but positively evil, that so large a portion of God's people which belong to your jurisdiction should be thus divided."[11] The letter demonstrates that the moti-vation behind the emperor's intervention had more to do with his concern for order than theology. The theological issues at stake, however, were not lost in the drama; in fact, the debate provoked by Arius's position helped to crystallize the importance of the Incarnation for understanding Christian worship and the Christian experience of salvation.

When the emperor's attempts to impose a solution failed, a council of bish-ops assembled to judge the case. The council was convened in the late spring of 325 in the small village of Nicaea at the emperor's summer palace. Thus, the council became known as the Council of Nicaea, or Nicaea I. The bishops were quick to condemn Arius and his theology, but that was not enough for the emperor, who sought some statement of faith, a creed, which could be regarded as the standard for the church.

Although creedal statements were commonly used for catechumens (i.e., persons preparing for baptism), they were not applied to bishops, so the emper-or's request that the bishops formulate and bind themselves to a creed was unusual. However, the bishops yielded and used as their template a largely scrip-tural creed as the basic statement of faith. Because its language was primarily scriptural, that creed was open to a variety of interpretations—including Arian interpretations. As seen in chapter 4, scriptural language is complex and highly symbolic, and because of this, the fathers at Nicaea could not construct a binding statement based on biblical images alone. Therefore, the council added several

---

11. Constantine's Letter to Alexander and Arius, quoted in Leo Davis, SJ, *The First Seven Ecumenical Councils 325–787: Their History and Theology* (Collegeville, MN: Liturgical, 1983), 55.

phrases to the creed to preclude the supporters of Arius and other sympathizers from interpreting it in terms of their own Christology.

The decisive Greek phrase was *homoousion tō patri*, which is translated as "[the Son is] one in being with the Father" in the creed many modern Christians still use in the liturgy (often called The Nicene Creed or The Niceno Constantinopolitan Creed). The word *homoousios* was highly controversial at the time. It had been condemned by a local church council (i.e., a gathering of local bishops to address regional issues) held in the third century when the term was associated with the teachings of the Gnostics. Yet before the Council of Nicea Constantine's theological advisor, Ossius, the bishop of ancient Cordova, had adopted the term as a translation of the Latin word *consubstantialis*, which had become accepted in the Latin-speaking western half of the Empire: Italy, Gaul, Spain, and North Africa. He urged the emperor to adopt the term, and its acceptance at the council was, thereby, assured, even though there were strong objections to making a non-scriptural word normative for Christian faith. While the condemnation of Arius was the result of general consensus, the adoption of *homoousios* was more controversial and provided the occasion for many bishops subsequently to have reservations about Nicaea.

In the heated battles that followed the Council of Nicaea, the foremost proponent of Nicaea's statement of faith against those who sought compromise was a man named Athanasius. Although Athanasius (c. 295–373) was only a deacon at Nicaea, he eventually succeeded Alexander as bishop of Alexandria. He became the staunchest defender of Nicene orthodoxy in the theological and political battles that took place in the decades following the council and was the person most responsible for the eventual victory of Nicaea in the East. His work *On the Incarnation*, though written before the Arian controversy, defends the faith as it would be formulated at Nicaea and offers reasons for Arius's condemnation. In this work, Athanasius sums up the purpose of the Incarnation by stating, "God became human in

Athanasius

order that humans might become God."[12] This startling statement of divinization (*theōsis*) is at the heart of Nicaea's condemnation of Arius and helps to put
into bold relief the issues at stake.

Christians claim that in Christ they have experienced salvation—that is,
a transformative union with God, a participation in God's existence. Christians experience this salvation through faith in Christ, through baptism into
Christ's death and resurrection, through partaking of the Eucharist, and
through adhering to the teaching of Christ. Christ, therefore, gives the believer
salvation and mediates the presence of God; through Christ believers participate in God's own existence. Now if the Son was merely a creature and not
truly divine, how could one participate in God's existence or how could one
have salvation? This line of reasoning carried the day for the pro-Nicaea party
in the following decades when political considerations threatened to reverse
the council's decision. Athanasius tenaciously fought for this theology and was
successful to the point that he and the symbol, or creed, of Nicaea became the
standards of orthodoxy for centuries.

The importance of Nicaea for the development of the Christian tradition
can hardly be overestimated. The late Canadian Jesuit Bernard Lonergan particularly has helped to clarify this point. According to Lonergan's reading of
second- and third-century theology, the church was struggling to express a judgment about the precise relationship between the Father and the Son.[13] Tertullian attempted to set forth an adequate understanding of this relationship but
did so by envisioning that relationship materially: the Father and Son are made
of the same stuff. Origen corrected Tertullian by going beyond his materialistic explanation, but Origen's Platonic idealism confines his attempt to a world
of gradations. For Origen there is only one origin of the divine—the Father—
and the Son is divine only by participation. Neither Tertullian nor Origen could
adequately express what Christians had experienced in Christ. The triumph of
Nicaea was its ability to express the relationship between the Father and Son in
a way that goes beyond "picture thinking" and idealist explanation.

In the work of Lonergan, the Christological controversies in the early
church become the means for exploring human understanding and the power
of language to shape that understanding. Affirmations of what is true, what is
real, force one to transcend "picture thinking" and materialism to affirm what
is so. The truth of any claim transcends its capacity to be presented in terms of
materiality. The development of the Christological tradition offers a lesson in
human cognition and the relationship between different types of discourse or
what Lonergan calls "realms of meaning."

---

12. *On the Incarnation* 54. 11.

13. Bernard Lonergan, *The Way to Nicea: The Dialectical Development of Trinitarian Theology*
(Philadelphia: Westminster, 1976).

Political and Theological Conflict as Engines for Doctrinal Development: Constantinople I (381)

The battles over Nicaea spanned several decades, but eventually gave way to a second Christological question. Surprisingly, the controversy over how to understand the relationship between the divine Son and the human Jesus emerged from one of the most ardent supporters of Nicene orthodoxy, Apollinaris (also sometimes spelled Apollinarius), the bishop of Laodicea in Syria.

Apollinaris (310–390) was a vigorous opponent of Arius and a consummate Alexandrian theologian. Apollinaris's Alexandrian roots are apparent in his theology, for Alexandrian theologians, particularly following the defeat of Arius, increasingly emphasized the full divinity of the Son and the unity of the divine Son with the human Jesus. In fact, Alexandrian Christology tended to start with the affirmation of the divine Son as *homoousios* with the Father and only then asked the question as to how the divine Son connects with the flesh of humanity. While this was perfectly orthodox, the Alexandrian approach to Christology could be developed in a way that was less than orthodox—as was the case with Apollinaris.

Apollinaris's Christology related the divine Son to the human Jesus at the expense of the humanity of Christ. He understood the human person to be a composite reality made of two "parts": (1) the body, or the flesh (*sarx* in Greek) and (2) the rational soul, or the mind. If the divine Son was to be united to the human Jesus, where could the Son "fit in"? For Apollinaris, the conscious subject of Jesus (the ego or the *I* of Jesus) is the divine Son, period. Although this seemed to answer the question of the relationship between the Son and Jesus, it compromised the humanity of Christ—it was reduced to mere flesh.

Essentially Apollinaris is removing the mind and the will from Jesus so that the divine Son can take its place. If such is the case, then what is human about Jesus is only the physical. If you remove the rational soul, or the mind, from the human Jesus, then the Son would be united to the flesh of the man Jesus but not to his rational soul, because he had none.

The First Council of Constantinople (Constantinople I, 381) met to consider the teaching of Apollinaris, among other things. The council emphasized the significance of Jesus' complete humanity for understanding Christian salvation. Gregory Nazianzen, bishop of Constantinople, put it most pointedly when he affirmed, "What was not assumed [i.e., taken on by Christ] was not redeemed; whatever is united to God is saved."[14] This is actually a corollary of Athanasius's famous maxim mentioned previously: "God became human in order that humans might become God." The union between God and

---

14. *Letter 101 to Cledonius.*

humanity involves reciprocity—God solves the problem of sin in Christ by uniting all that God is with *everything that humans are*. If one were to leave out some aspect of humanity from this union, then that aspect would not participate in God's own life, and would be unredeemed. If Christ does not redeem the human will, then he does not redeem from sin at all, for sin does not originate in the flesh but in the operations of the mind—the will. The Gospels draw attention to the crucial role of the mind in salvation when they report that Jesus summoned people to repentance, for the term used there (*metanoia*) literally means "change of mind."

Alexandria and Antioch

By the end of the fourth century, around the time of Constantinople I (381 CE), a theological and political rivalry had developed between the schools of thought of Alexandria and Antioch. Each of these "schools" had distinctive theological outlooks, and each tried to gain the upper hand in the imperial capital of Constantinople. This rivalry figures into the Christological controversies of the early Christian church.

Early Christological Controversies

School	Alexandria	Antioch
Christology	This school adopted a Logos-sarx approach to Christology. This approach emphasizes the unity of the subject, Christ. This unity is achieved, to put it simply, by having the divine Word (Logos) take over the higher functions of the human person, Jesus, while the lower function is controlled by the flesh (*sarx* in Greek).	This school adopted a Logos-anthropos approach to Christology. This approach emphasized the distinction between the human Jesus and the divine Word (Logos). The two realities are conjoined yet maintain their respective properties. Jesus maintains his integrity as a human (*anthrōpos* in Greek).
	Potential Problem: The full humanity of Christ can get lost.	*Potential Problem*: The approach can leave the human Jesus separate from the divine Son.

Continued

Alexandria and Antioch *Continued*

School	Alexandria	Antioch
Scripture	The Alexandrian approach to scripture was allegorical. Every passage had a literal sense (what the words on the page said) and a spiritual sense. The literal sense was open to anyone who could read or understand the language, but the spiritual sense of scripture—the deeper and more profound sense of scripture—was available only through the eyes of faith.	The Antiochene approach to scripture was historical and literary. Every passage had a history behind it, and every passage was subject to literary convention. The Antiochene approach was, therefore, much closer to contemporary academic approaches to scripture.
Some Chief Representatives	Athanasius, Apollinaris, Cyril of Alexandria, Dioscorus, Eutyches	Theodore of Mopsuestia, John of Antioch, John Chrysostom, Nestorius

The condemnation of Apollinaris at the first Council of Constantinople set Alexandrian theology on its heels. Alexandrian clerics were in competition with their rivals to the north, in the Syrian city of Antioch, where another approach to Christology had developed. The Antiochene approach was to start with the human Jesus and then ask how he is united to the divine Son. This Christological approach is commonly called Logos-anthropos Christology (the Greek word *anthropos* means "human being"). The condemnation of Apollinaris vindicated the Antiochene emphasis on the full humanity of Jesus, but it left unanswered how one was to speak of the union of humanity and divinity of Christ. This resulted in a heated controversy in the early fifth century in the imperial city of Constantinople.

Political and Theological Conflict as Engines for Doctrinal Development: Ephesus (431)

Constantinople was built by Constantine as his new capital—a city that would unite the culture of the eastern part of the Roman Empire with the western part. Though it was built on the remains of a small fishing village named Byzantium, it had no real history that would privilege one people over another or one theology over the other. However, the unifying force of such a capital could never be fully realized. In fact, in the third canon, or law, of Constantinople I, it was declared that the church of Constantinople should rank above all others churches in the east and second only to Rome.[15] As such, the city, and the church of Constantinople, became a cause of division: bishops of both Antioch and Alexandria resented the prestige granted to the young city and tried to control its bishop and, perhaps, the emperor.

In the early fifth century, Nestorius († c. 451), an Antiochene, was made bishop of Constantinople, setting the scene for a major battle among these power centers. A large number of Alexandrian monks lived in the imperial city at the time, and it was their custom to honor Mary, the mother of Jesus, with the title *Theotokos*, which means "God bearer," or "mother of God." For Nestorius and his supporters, this was a theological misstatement. Mary was the "mother of Christ" (*Christotokos*) by virtue of the fact that she bore the God-man Jesus, but to call her *Theotokos* was inaccurate, because the divine is eternal while Mary is obviously not. Nestorius provocatively made his case in a series of sermons around Christmas in 428. These sermons angered the Alexandrians and alienated many of the other residents of Constantinople. Having picked a fight, Nestorius suddenly realized that he had no allies close enough to protect him when the storm broke.

Cyril (c. 376–444), the bishop of Alexandria, heard of these developments. He was sincerely concerned over the theological attack on the title *Theotokos* and the Christology it rested upon, but he also recognized an opportunity to seize the upper hand in the imperial city for Alexandria. Cyril urged the emperor to convene a council in 431 at the city of Ephesus on the Aegean coast of Asia Minor. Cyril brought with him a large contingent of bishops and monks from Egypt, who supported him. Nestorius, meanwhile, waited for his supporters, including John of Antioch, to travel from as far away as Persia before making his appearance. Before Nestorius's supporters arrived, Cyril convened the council and condemned Nestorius in absentia. Some suspect that the tardiness of Nestorius and his contingent was deliberate, because they knew that they did not have enough votes to prevail in the council. When they arrived in the city four days later, they held their own meeting and condemned Cyril. Both sides appealed to the emperor: Cyril was vindicated and Nestorius was condemned and removed as bishop. His supporters were furious.

---

15. The canon actually states, "The bishop of Constantinople shall have primacy of honor after (*meta*) the bishop of Rome because Constantinople is the new Rome." Many Orthodox Christians would argue that the word *after* (*meta*) in the canon does not make Constantinople inferior to Rome but should be read in a temporal sense, i.e., Constantinople is chronologically "after" Rome.

The theological reasons for Nestorius's condemnation are important for understanding subsequent Christological discussions. Nestorius, along with virtually all Christians at the time, insisted that the Son's *physis*, or nature, was divine and had its own *hypostasis*, or concrete existence. This was the orthodox teaching against the Modalists. This teaching was laid out first at Nicea and then in the debates about the Holy Spirit at Constantinople I. Both councils defended the unity of God first by declaring that the Father and Son were "one in being" (Nicaea) and by declaring that there were three coequal *hypostases* in God (Constantinople I). Nestorius, as a good Antiochene theologian, also insisted that Jesus was a human with a human nature (*physis*). This human nature had its own concrete existence, or "person" (*prosōpon*). The latter term carried the meaning of the observable manifestation; it was occasionally used interchangeably with *hypostasis*. For Nestorius, the Incarnation involved the "conjoining" (*synapheia*) of these two natures so that each retained its own properties. Thus, Nestorius posited a *prosōpon* of the union, a single object of perception, which he calls "Christ."

While Nestorius tried to articulate a Christology that defended the full humanity and the full divinity of Christ against what he saw as another version of Apollinarianism, he fell into a position that failed to adequately express the full union of the divine Son with the human Jesus. Nestorius believed that the conjunction between the divine Son and the man Jesus was voluntary, that is, the conjunction came about because of God's gracious will, which united with the man Jesus. In the subsequent letters defending his position, Nestorius argued that he really is concerned to articulate a substantial (i.e., real) coming together of the divine and human in Christ, but the formal maneuvers he used to articulate his position left his attempts suspect in the eyes of his contemporaries.[16]

To Cyril, Nestorius's explanation sounded like a form of Adoptionsim and, therefore, a denial of the Incarnation.[17] Cyril insisted upon the union of the two natures in Christ, so that one could predicate of Jesus things that were proper to divinity and things proper to human nature, as had been customary for centuries; this is called the *communicatio idiomatum* or the communication of attributes. However, as Cyril vigorously attacked the unpopular Nestorius, he adopted some controversial formulations himself. One formula stated that "out of two natures (i.e., the divine and human natures) one incarnate nature of the Logos."

---

16. Note that the controversy sounds like it revolves around Mary but, in fact, centers on Christ. Theologians have observed that Marian doctrines as a rule are primarily about Christ.

17. Cyril accused Nestorius of having embraced the adoptionist Christology of Paul of Samosata, who was remembered as a notorious heretic.

Cyril thought that this phrase was completely orthodox, as he believed it came from one of Athanasius's writings, but it had actually come from Apollinaris! Athanasius was such a popular figure after his death that he became synonymous with orthodox Christian faith. When Apollinaris was condemned, many of his supporters sought to preserve his works, and because his ideas were, in some ways, inspired by the theology of Athanasius, these supporters protected Apollinaris's writings by attributing them to Athanasius. These writings, generally known as "pseudo-Athanasius," were taken unknowingly by Cyril as genuine works of Athanasius and, therefore, completely orthodox. This "one incarnate nature" formula, so robustly presented by Cyril, would become the basis for the next round in the Christological and political battles between Antioch and Alexandria.

Schism and Compromise: Between Ephesus and Chalcedon (433–448)

Following the Council of Ephesus in 431 and its condemnation of Nestorius, there was a major split, or schism, in the church. The Antiochene bishops, many of whom were not entirely in support of Nestorius's theology, nonetheless, felt Cyril and his supporters had treated them unfairly. Cyril, on the other hand, felt that truth had triumphed; he was not terribly concerned over the ecclesiastical cold shoulder he received from the Antiochene bishops. The schism, however, attracted the attention of Emperor Theodosius II, who desired unity and a measure of uniformity in order to protect the common good—Germanic invasions were ravaging the western empire at the same time. Theodosius insisted that Cyril and John of Antioch work out their differences. In 433, John and Cyril, under imperial pressure, hammered out a formula of faith, called the Formula of Reunion, to end the schism. The main section of the formula reads as follows:

> We confess then our Lord Jesus Christ, the only begotten Son of God, perfect God and perfect man, consisting of a rational soul and body, begotten of the Father before the ages as to his Godhead, and in the last days the Same, for us and for our salvation, of Mary the Virgin as to his manhood; the Same *homoousios* with the Father as to his Godhead, and *homoousios* with us as to his manhood. For there has been a union of two natures; wherefore we confess one Christ, one Son, one Lord. In accordance with this thought of the unconfused union, we confess the holy Virgin to be *Theotokos*, because the divine Logos was incarnate and made man, and from the very conception united to himself the temple that was taken of her.[18]

18. See Robert V. Sellers, *The Council of Chalcedon: A Historical and Doctrinal Survey* (London: SPCK, 1953), 17–18.

The formula contains passages characteristic of both Alexandrian and Antiochene Christology. Notice the Alexandrian emphasis on identification of the divine Son as the subject of Jesus ("the Same"), the "union" (*henōsis*) of the divine and human rather than Nestorius's "conjunction" (*synapheia*) of the two natures, and the identification of Mary as *Theotokos*. The formula also contains several Antiochene elements: Christ is *homoousios* with both God and humanity and the full affirmation of the human nature in Christ such that it is not diminished in any way. The Formula of Reunion testifies that while Alexandria and Antioch had very different approaches to Christology, their positions were not irreconcilable, provided each side demonstrated flexibility. The politics of the day and the pettiness of many figures in these disputes made compromise impossible apart from pressure from the civil authorities.

More Politics and More Doctrine: The Council of Chalcedon (451)

Shortly after the reunion between Alexandria and Antioch, both Cyril and John passed away and the truce between them began to show signs of instability. Their successors carried on the theological and political battles.

In 434, Proclus became bishop of Constantinople. A great supporter of Alexandrian theology, he was moderate enough to show respect to his great predecessor in the see of Constantinople, the Antiochene John Chysostom, by bringing his body back from exile and burying it with high honors in the Basilica of the Apostles in the newest part of city. Proclus had written a letter to the church of Armenia (called *The Tome of Proclus*) setting out for them the orthodox doctrine of the Incarnation. It stated, "There is only one Son, for the natures are not divided into two hypostases, rather the awesome economy of salvation has united the two natures into one *hypostasis*."[19] Here one finds an example of a crucial distinction made neither by Nestorius nor Cyril—the distinction between "nature" and "person" (*hyspostasis*).

After Flavian became the bishop of Constantinople in 446, the Alexandrian desire for a fight reached a climax. During the Synod of Constantinople (448), a meeting of all the bishops in the region, Bishop Eusebius of Dorylaeum brought an indictment against the monk Eutyches, who was a powerful figure and very close to the imperial family. Eusebius charged that Eutyches had repudiated the Formula of Reunion signed by John and Cyril in 433. Eutyches had been insisting that "out of two natures" there was only "one incarnate nature of the Logos"—a position called Monophysitism. This phrase, used years earlier

---

19. Migne, *Patrologia Grecae*, 65. 651, quoted in Davis, 164.

by Cyril, became a battle cry for those Alexandrians who felt that too much had been given away to the Antiochenes in the Formula of Reunion; Eutyches decided to make a stand.

The bishop of Constantinople, Flavian, put Eutyches on trial for heresy. Such a trial is a combination of what modern readers would think of as both a criminal and a civil procedure. The defendant stood to lose a lot: property, job, freedom (a conviction often meant exile), and perhaps even one's life. Meanwhile, keeping abreast of these developments was the new bishop of Alexandria, Dioscorus, for whom the condemnation of Eutyches represented an opportunity to undo the Formula of Reunion and gain a definitive victory for Alexandria.

The indictment and conviction of Eutyches centered on his denial of the Formula of Reunion, which represented a serious problem for Flavian's attempts to stabilize Constantinople. Years earlier, at Ephesus in 431, the bishops became hesitant about adding to or changing the basic statement of Christian faith that had been articulated at Nicaea. The bishops, therefore, declared that no one was to add to that statement of faith and that Nicaea was the only standard of orthodoxy. Eusebius and Flavian, however, had used the Formula of Reunion as the standard of orthodoxy when they condemned Eutyches; this was in violation of the rule set forth at Ephesus. The enemies of Flavian and Eusebius now had a powerful weapon to use against them.

Dioscorus, the bishop of Alexandria, was able to persuade Emperor Theodosius II to convene a council at Ephesus again. The council was held in 449 with Dioscorus presiding and Flavian as the defendant. Leo, the bishop of Rome (pope) at the time, supported Flavian in an important letter (Leo's Tome) and sent two legates, or representatives, to the council, but it soon became evident that the deliberations at Ephesus were even less fair and transparent than Cyril's council had been. Through intimidation and threat, Dioscorus engineered the exoneration of Eutyches and the condemnation and eventual death of Flavian; Flavian died on his way into exile at the hands of his captors. The papal legates at the council were forced to flee the scene and stow away on a ship to report to Leo the disastrous events that had taken place. In a letter to Empress Pulcheria, Leo characterized the meeting at Ephesus as a "Robber Council."

The death of Theodosius II, however, began to reverse the fortunes of Dioscorus, and at the behest of Leo, the new emperor, Marcian, called for another council, this time at Chalcedon. In 451, the council met and reversed the findings of the Robber Council. Eutyches' position was condemned and Dioscorus was deposed and even taunted in the council chamber as the "murderer of Flavian." The bishops then set forth a formula (not a creed) to articulate the orthodox belief of the Christian church regarding the divine and human natures in Christ. The formula combined the best aspects of Cyril's theology (from his second letter to Nestorius), Flavian's statement of faith against Eutyches, and Leo's tome. The Formula (or Definition) of Chalcedon provides a synthesis of Christological insights in the fourth and fifth centuries:

> Therefore, following the holy Fathers [i.e., the bishops at Nicaea], we all teach with one accord all to acknowledge one and the same Son, our Lord Jesus Christ at once complete in Godhead and complete in humanness truly God and truly human consisting of a rational soul and body; of one substance of the Father as regards to his Godhead, and at the same time of one substance with us as regards His human-ness; like us in all things except sin; as regards His Godhead, begotten of the Father before all the ages but yet as regards his humanity begot-ten for us and for our salvation of Mary the Virgin the God bearer; one and the same Christ, Son, Lord, Only-begotten recognized in two natures, without confusion without change without division without separation; the distinction in the natures being in no way annulled by the union, but rather the characteristics of each nature being pre-served and coming together to form one person [*prosōpon*] and one subsistence [*hypostasin*] not parted or separated into two persons but one and the same Son and Only-begotten God the Word, Lord Jesus Christ even as the prophets from earliest times spoke of Him and our Lord Jesus Christ Himself taught us, and the creed of the Fathers has handed down to us.[20]

The essential clarification made at Chalcedon was the distinction between nature (*physis*) and person (*prosōpon* or *hypostasis*), a distinction Cyril himself and many others had failed to make, but which Proclus had begun to articu-late. Like Nicaea's *homoousios*, the Formula of Chalcedon does not provide the reader with a picture of the union of natures in Christ; rather, the formula provides theological-grammatical rules for talking about this union: "without confusion without change without division without separation; the distinction in the natures being in no way annulled by the union." Chalcedon, therefore, answered the second Christological question (what is the relationship between the human Jesus and the divine Son?), much like Nicaea had answered the first Christological question (what is the relationship between God and the Son?). In addition, like Nicaea, Chalcedon self-consciously set out its formula as a definitive guide for "acknowledging" Christ, that is, the right way to think and talk about Christ.

---

20. In Davis, *The First Seven Ecumenical Councils*, 186.

The First Four Ecumenical Councils: A Time Line

This table summarizes the dynamics of the councils in the context of Alexandrian and Antiochene theological battles.

Alexandria ⟷ Antioch

Nicaea I (325)

Nicaea's affirmation of the full divinity of the Son became a central piece in Alexandrian theology. Defense of Nicaea became the concern of those who succeeded Athanasius as bishop of Alexandria.

Constantinople I (381)

The condemnation of Apollinarianism and the assertion that Christ was fully human, including a rational soul, was an important victory for Antiochene Christology.

Ephesus (431)

Nestorius's caution about too closely identifying the divine nature with the human Jesus was tantamount to denying the Incarnation in the ears of Alexandrian theologians. The condemnation of Nestorius was a great victory for Alexandria, and in the subsequent battles, the Alexandrians were ever watchful for the reemergence of Nestorianism.

Chalcedon (451)

Chalcedon's affirmation of the full humanity of Jesus, without confusion or mixture with the divine, was precisely what the participants felt Nestorius had tried, rather clumsily, to express. The Alexandrians had a difficult time accepting Chalcedon, and many of them did not. Subsequent attempts to put an Alexandrian "spin" on Chalcedon (i.e., Leontius) made little difference to the Alexandrians.

The Aftermath of Chalcedon (451–553)

It may appear as though Chalcedon brought the story of classical Christology to its conclusion with a consensus uniting the church. Nothing could be further from the truth. Dioscorus and many of his supporters remained defiant and used the politics of the empire to separate themselves from the other churches, despite the efforts of several emperors and bishops to counter such moves. To this day, the vast majority of Egypt's ten million Coptic Christians do not subscribe to Chalcedon. Additionally, the Christians of Armenia, and the thirty million Christians of Ethiopia are Cyrillian-Monophysite and do not accept Chalcedon.[21] For them, the impasse was stated clearly by the great champion of Cyrillian-Monophysitism, Philoxenus of Mabbugh (440–523). Philoxenus insisted that every nature (*physis*) has a person (*prosōpon*); if there are two natures in Christ, then there are two Christ's. This sounds inescapably Nestorian to those who do not affirm a distinction between *person* and *nature*. Philoxenus repeatedly affirms, however, that the Son became a perfect human, and this perfection necessarily included a human soul and human intelligence. It seems obvious, therefore, that even though Philoxenus might be identified as a Monophysite, his position is perfectly orthodox when properly understood and contextualized.

While the Latin-speaking West was largely content with Chalcedon, the battles in the Eastern Church continued. In the sixth century, several theologians emerged to support and defend Chalcedon against many attackers, both civil and ecclesiastical. Leontius of Byzantium tried to win over the Cyrillian-Monophysites by explaining the orthodoxy of Chalcedon in a way that allowed opponents to hear something other than Nestorianism in the "two natures" language of Chalcedon. Leontius stated that the human nature of Christ is neither an acted *hypostasis* nor without *hypostasis*; rather, the human nature of Christ was *enhypostasia*.[22] What Leontius means is that the human nature of Christ does not have its own separate concrete existence (*hypostasis*); rather, it has its concrete existence "in" the *hypostasis* of the divine Word. This relationship between the *hypostases* of the divine and human nature has often been described as "the

---

21. While the acceptance of Chalcedon has proven problematic for these churches, there are still many Christian churches that reject the Council of Ephesus and support Nestorius. These churches, mostly in modern-day Syria, Iraq, and Iran, sent missionaries as far as western China in the fifth and sixth centuries. The reading of the Christological councils here is done from a Roman Catholic perspective, though I hope Coptic, Assyrian (so-called Nestorian), and other Christians do not take offense. Many aspects of these early theological debates reflected conceptual and linguistic issues as well as political and cultural ones at the time.

22. For an excellent discussion of the issues involved and the implications of misreading Leontius's Christology, see LeRon Shults, "A Dubious Christological Formula: From Leontius of Byzantium to Karl Barth," *Theological Studies* 57 (1996): 431–46.

hypostatic union." Leontius's formulation does not say that the human nature of Christ is diminished in any way; it retains all of its properties, including a rational soul. However, the human nature of Christ does not exist alongside the divine; rather, these two are united. The human nature of Christ is "in" the *hypostasis* of the divine nature.

Leontius's Christology was vindicated at Constantinople II in 553. Yet, the circumstances in which it was articulated—at a time when the state was looking for ways to heal the schism that had divided the church between Monophysitism and Chalcedon—conspired to distort its contribution over time. For Constantinople II posthumously condemned the great Antiochene theologians of the fourth and fifth centuries, including Theodore of Mopsuestia. Many contemporary scholars feel that these condemnations, along with approval of Leontius's theology, had the effect of diminishing Christ's humanity in Christological reflection. Such a move, though not formally intended, has caused many contemporary theologians to rethink the teaching of Chalcedon and "recover" the full humanity of Jesus; in so doing, they are also revisiting the theology of Theodore of Mopsuestia and even Nestorius. Such developments have raised the important and controversial question of the value and applicability of classical Christology for contemporary theology.

Person of Interest: Theodore of Mopsuestia

Theodore of Mopsuestia (350–428) was one of the greatest and most articulate of the Antiochene theologians. As the bishop of Mopsuestia, he was great friends with another Antiochene theologian, St. John Chrysostom, the bishop of Constantinople. While his account of the Incarnation was used by Nestorians to support their doctrines, he had developed his doctrine to combat the threat posed by the teaching of Apollinaris. Nestorius and his supporters began using Theodore's Christology after he died. This Christology supplied Nestorius with some of his ammunition: a hard distinction between the eternal Word and its shrine, the human Jesus and the notion of a single *prosōpon* resulting from the conjunction (not union) of the two natures. Many bishops at the time viewed the posthumous condemnations of Theodore and other Antiochene theologians at Constantinople II (553) as excessive and inappropriate. Contemporary scholars tend to take a much more sympathetic view of his Christology. Additionally, Theodore was a great interpreter of scripture who advanced a less allegorical and more historical approach. Many contemporary biblical scholars continue to find his biblical commentaries highly instructive.

ecascaseaisecaisececaisececaisececaisececaisececaisececaisececaisececaisececaisececaisececaiseececaisececaisececaisececaisececaiseececaisececaisececaisececaisececaisececaisececaisececaisececaiseececaisececaisececaisececaisececaisececaisececaisececaisececaiseececaisececaisececaisececaisececaisececaisececaisececaisececaiseececaisececaisececaisececaisececaisececaisececaisececaisececaiseececaisececaisececaisececaisececaisececaisececaisececaisececaiseececaisececaisececaisececaisececaisececaisececaisececaisececaiseececaisececaisececaisececaisececaisececaisececaisececaisececaiseececaisececaisececaisececaisececaisececaisececaisececaisececaiseececaisececaisececaisececaisececaisececaisececaisececaisececaiseececaisececaisececaisececaisececaisececaisececaisececaisececaise

Conclusion

Many question the relevance of the Christological controversies. However, these controversies remain important for several reasons: First, they illustrate the importance of theological clarity and right judgment. For believers, some ways of thinking about Jesus Christ are better than other ways. In fact, some lines of thought have the effect of negating Christ's ability to function as savior. The disputed points in the Christological controversies may appear to be mere speculation, but speculation, or theory, is important for the health and vitality of religious faith and its expression, both on a corporate and an individual level. Second, the story of the Christological controversies demonstrates that theological orthodoxy—discerning the most truthful ways of thinking about Jesus Christ, or at least ruling out the really poor or inadequate ways—is not a matter of merely repeating received formulae. Rather, orthodoxy is the product of innovative and creative thinking. As this thinking always reflects the particular cultural and historical circumstances in which that thinking takes place, orthodoxy must always remain an open rather than closed system. It always calls for some measure of innovation. Finally, the story of the Christological controversies provides the necessary foundation for understanding and assessing contemporary Christological debates.

Questions for Understanding

1. How did the Modalists understand the relationship between God (the Father) and the Son? Why might this position be problematic?
2. Describe Origen's views on the relationship between God (the Father) and the Son. How is his position different from Tertullian's?
3. Explain Arius's position on the relationship between the Logos and God. What scripture passages helped Arius to make his case?
4. Who was Apollinaris, and what did he say about Jesus? Why was his Christology condemned at Constantinople I?
5. What role did politics play in the Council of Nicaea and its aftermath?
6. Why did Nestorius object to honoring Mary with the title of *Theotokos*?
7. Why did the Alexandrians object to the statement of faith made at the Council of Chalcedon?
8. Some have described Nicaea and Chalcedon as "bookends" to classical Christological questions. In what way can these two councils be understood to encapsulate or enclose the debate?

Questions for Reflection and Action

1. Jesus is depicted in a variety of ways and this variety often says as much about humans as it does about Jesus. For example, in a Vietnamese church, one may encounter an image of Christ with Asian features and dressed in traditional Confucian style. In Ethiopian iconography, Jesus and his disciples are depicted as Africans. These images reflect the conviction that in Jesus everything that it means to be human, including ethnicities, has been taken up into God and redeemed through the Incarnation. This conviction is reflected in Gregory Nazianzen's famous statement, "What was not assumed is not redeemed." With this in mind, respond to the following questions: Are these ethnocentric depictions of Jesus appropriate? Are there any limits in such iconography? Given Gregory's maxim, could Jesus be depicted as a woman in liturgical art? Explain.

2. This chapter treated a lot of important philosophical terminology (e.g., *homoousios, prosōpon*). These terms do not play any important role in New Testament Christology, but they play decisive roles in normative statements of Christian faith (in creeds, in catechisms). Is it appropriate to move beyond the New Testament in this way in order to standardize Christology? Furthermore, should Christians try to move beyond these terms and categories, or are these terms essential for understanding what Christians believes about Jesus? Explain.

3. Politics and rivalry seem to play important roles in the unfolding of Christological doctrine. This is also a factor in modern times (cf. the history of Vatican II or recent meeting of the World Council of Churches). Are politics and rivalries antithetical to real religious dialogue, or are these realities simply an inescapable aspect of dialogue? Explain.

For Further Reading

Anatolios, Kahled. *Retrieving Nicaea: The Development and Meaning of Trinitarian Thought*. Grand Rapids, MI: Baker 2011.

Davis, Leo D. *The First Seven Ecumenical Councils (325–787): Their History and Theology*. Collegeville, MN: Liturgical, 1990.

Grillmeier, SJ, Aloys. *Christ in Christian Tradition, Vol. 1: From the Apostolic Age to Chalcedon (451)*. Atlanta: John Knox, 1975.

CHAPTER 6

The Work of Christ

Imagine the infant Jesus, wrapped in swaddling clothes and lying in Mary's arms in Bethlehem. Suddenly, a menacing silhouette appears in the doorway. One of Herod's soldiers has been sent to Bethlehem on orders from the king to destroy all children less than two years of age (Matthew 2:16–18). He seizes the child as his mother clutches the baby desperately in a futile attempt to stop the insanity, but the soldier prevails and takes the child out to the town center where he unceremoniously slaughters the baby along with the other children. Mary weeps and mourns as she commits the body to an appropriate burial place. In this imaginary scenario, would the death of the child Jesus still have religious significance, or would it simply be a horrific crime?

This exercise of the imagination is intended to suggest the problems that result when one attempts to articulate Jesus' saving work *solely* in terms of his death. The present chapter deals with this issue of "soteriology"—i.e., how Christ saves (from the Greek, *sōtēr*, meaning "savior"). Even the word *save* raises questions: saved from what and for what purpose? Quite often, one's understanding of sin will structure one's account of how Jesus saves. For example, if one conceives of sin as tantamount to disturbing the gods, as in the Babylonia creation story *Enuma Elish*, then one might expect that salvation would consist of placating the god whose anger has been aroused. If, on the other hand, one understands sin as a crime against the sovereign ruler of the kingdom, then perhaps salvation would entail finding some way of averting the punishment that such a crime incurs. This chapter will explore some of the most popular images of sin and the corresponding approaches to soteriology that have flourished in the Christian tradition.

Biblical Images of Salvation

The Prophets and Salvation History

The primary model for understanding God as savior emerges from the prophetic tradition in the Old Testament. The evangelist Luke developed this "prophetic" model of salvation further in the New Testament.[1] When most of the Old Testament prophets were active, there was no consistent vision of afterlife. To be "saved," meant being preserved from death and destruction in the "now." God was savior to the extent that God acted in history to secure justice. For the eighth-century BCE prophets, God's saving action in history involved the use of humans, entire nations, and historical events to correct injustices and mete out punishments. The process by which justice was restored and Israel was saved from destruction unfolded over the course of centuries.

In the book of the prophet Isaiah, for example, salvation is something that is worked out over the long haul of history. In the first part of Isaiah (1–39), which contains the oracles and poetry most closely associated with the eighth-century Jerusalem prophet, humans suffer for the sins of the nation. The inability or unwillingness of various kings and the people in general to trust in God and abide by the covenant makes this suffering appropriate. Second and Third Isaiah (40–55 and 56–66, respectively), were written by other, anonymous prophets in the final decades of the exile in Babylon and during the return to Jerusalem at the end of the sixth century BCE. These two late additions to the oracles of Isaiah of Jerusalem, the eighth-century prophet, bring the prophetic warning around full circle and offer an expansive account of God's *chesed*—his loving mercy. The canonical book, therefore, testifies that over the long course of history, God's purpose, God's faithfulness, unfolds and brings about the salvation of Israel and all of creation (see, e.g., Isaiah 66:10–24).

The Priestly or Cultic Approach to Salvation

The priestly traditions of Second Temple Judaism, which understood soteriology in a cultic sense, strongly influenced the soteriological language in the New Testament. The sacrificial culture of Israelite religion has ancient roots, dating to the thirteenth century BCE or even earlier, but the final form of the cultic material in the Torah was authored or edited by priestly traditions around the time of the Babylonian Exile or possibly later, receiving their final form around 400 BCE.[2]

Some of the vocabulary and idioms of sacrifice suggest more primitive and anthropomorphic notions of payment and manipulation. Of particular interest are expressions such as "pleasing odor," (e.g., Genesis 8:24), and various

---

1. Some of the material in this section comes from the first section of Richard Clifford and Khaled Anatolios, "Christian Salvation: Biblical and Theological Perspectives," *Theological Studies* 66 (2005): 739–69.

2. Jacob Milgrom has been at the forefront of scholarship on Old Testament sacrifice. See his massive study: *Leviticus*, 3 vols., AB (New Haven, CT: Yale University Press, 1998, 2000, 2001). For an appreciative critique of Milgrom's focus on cleansing, see Roy E. Gane, *Cult and Character: Purification Offerings, Day of Atonement and Theodicy* (Winona Lake: Eisenbrauns, 2005).

expressions suggesting that sacrifices are "food for God" (e.g., Leviticus 21:6, 8). The notion of "propitiation" or placating God's wrath occurs frequently in the Old Testament accounts of sacrifice (e.g., Numbers 8:19 or Exodus 32:30). This primitive imagery continues to lurk behind much of the more developed material that reflects a more spiritualized approach to the Temple rites reflected in the rituals associated with *Yom Kippur*.

The *kapporet* plays an important role in these rituals (Leviticus 16). It is often translated as *mercy-seat* or *propitiatory* and refers to the Ark of the Covenant's gold cover over which YHWH was enthroned. This is God's "throne," hence the notion of "mercy-seat." The Ark was a major symbol in the history of Israel. At a literal level, it was a box, made out of gopher wood, clad in gold, and containing the two tablets of the Law given to Moses on Mt. Sinai (1 Kings 8:9), along with Moses' staff by which God showed his power (Hebrews 9:4) and a jar of manna (i.e., the bread that fed the Israelites when they wandered in the wilderness after departing Egypt). The Ark had a lid, or cover, on which stood the figures of two cherubim with wings folded over the Ark. The Ark was the symbol of God's presence with Israel, but God was not identified with the Ark; rather, God sat "enthroned above the cherubim" (see, e.g., 1 Samuel 4:4; 2 Samuel 6:2; Psalm 80:2). This throne (the *kapporet*) was the focal point of the rituals on the Day of Atonement.

On the day on which the high priest made a sacrifice to take away the sin of the people of Israel, the high priest had to offer a bull and a goat as sacrifices before he entered the inner sanctuary where the Ark was kept. This was the only day out of the year that anyone entered this holiest place. The high priest was to apply the blood of the sacrificed animals on the *kapporet*. He would then go outside to another goat—the scapegoat—and pronounce the sins of the people and touched the goat, thereby transferring the sins of the people to the goat. The goat was then driven out of the community. The blood offering eradicated impurities, but deliberate sins could not be eradicated, only carried to the wilderness from where, it was hoped, they would never return.

The *Yom Kippur* ritual revolves around two important concepts, or elements.[3] First, there is a sacred substance: blood. Blood contains the life force, which has power that properly belongs to God and not humans. This dangerous and dynamic force can destroy as well as cleanse. In this context, blood has the force to cleanse the sanctuary of impurities. Second, sin is transferred and expelled from the community, so that through a combination of ritual actions Israel may be both purged of sin and cleansed. Both these themes will reemerge as New Testament authors explore the religious significance of Christ's death.

---

3. See Stephen Finlan, *Problems with Atonement* (Collegeville: Liturgical, 2005), 11–38.

Sacrifice in Ancient Israel

Human Sacrifice

Although not condoned in scripture, the practice of human sacrifice is not far removed from the experience of ancient Israel. In *cherem*, or "holy war," humans and animals were dedicated to God through their destruction (e.g., Joshua 6:17). Jephthah, one of the judges, made a vow to kill whoever was the first to greet him upon his return from a victorious battle (Judges 11:29–40). His daughter rushed out to greet him upon his arrival and Japheth made good on his promise to God. In the *Aqedah,* or "binding," of Isaac, God commands Abraham to sacrifice his son and, at the last minute, stops him and prohibits human sacrifice in Israel. The prophets refer to the practice of child sacrifice for a deity named Molech (2 Kings 23:10; Jeremiah 32:35), though the practice was condemned in scripture (e.g., Leviticus 18:21).

Animal Sacrifice

Various animals were regularly sacrificed in Israel. These sacrifices fell into different categories based on the purpose of the ritual involved and how the animal was disposed.

Holocaust or Burnt Offerings

The Holocaust was an offering exclusively designated for Yahweh and meant to acknowledge God's holiness. After the animal's throat was cut and the blood was drained from the body and offered to God, the sacrifice was skinned, quartered, and burned. The fire and the smoke rose toward heaven and delivered the sacrificial victim to God. Such a sacrifice was offered on very solemn occasions.

Peace Offerings

In the peace offering, the most prized portion of the animal (fat, kidneys, and liver) is offered to God while the remainder is split between the priest and the beneficiary of the sacrifice.

Expiatory Sacrifices

Scripture distinguishes two types of expiatory offerings: "sin offerings" and "guilt offerings." The precise distinction, however, is unclear. While the words used to designate each of these sacrifices differ, the rituals outlined in Torah and the reasons for each ritual often overlap. With these offerings, the priest ate the portions of the animal not offered to God (fat, kidneys, liver).

Grain Sacrifice

The *minha* was the standard offering of grain and oil. Sometimes it was offered raw, and at other times, it was offered as a baked product. The priest would burn a portion of the offering to God and eat the rest. Additionally, two rows of six cakes each (the "showbread") were placed on a table every Sabbath. At the end of each week, the priest would eat the old cakes.

The Saving Work of Jesus in the New Testament

By the first century CE, the theology of Jerusalem's sacrificial system had been substantially spiritualized; the rituals were being interpreted metaphorically or analogously in order to give expression to a drive toward personal interaction with God. Although sacrifices were still taking place in the Temple, and all Jews—including the followers of Jesus—regarded these sacrifices as religiously meaningful, the meaning of these rituals had developed considerably.

A good example appears in Paul's letter to the Romans, particularly Romans 3:25, where Paul expresses the redemptive value of Christ's death through the Greek word *hilastērion*, a translation of the Hebrew word *kapporet*. Because the *kapporet* was central to the biblical instructions for the removal of impurity and sin and because it had long been removed from the Temple after the Babylonian destruction of Jerusalem in 586 BCE, it necessarily became invested with great symbolic and metaphorical power for Paul and other Jews of his time. For Paul, sacrificial terms like *hilastērion* could be used to express an understanding of Jesus' death as the effective means for gaining reconciliation with God.

In the Letter to the Hebrews, an early non-Pauline Christian sermon, Christ's death is the culmination and end of the Temple's sacrificial system. Hebrews shares the Hellenistic propensity for dualism: matter and form, old and new, imperfect and perfect. Its understanding of the Temple and priesthood in Jerusalem reflects this dualism. For the author of Hebrews, the Temple merely foreshadowed and prepared for the death of Christ, so it makes perfect sense to explain the meaning of Christ's death via the Temple. In Hebrews 4–10, an elaborate analogy argues that the literal Temple service is ineffectual and banal; Christ is the true high priest, who offers himself as the perfect sacrifice. In contrast with the oft-repeated and ineffectual Temple sacrifices, Christ offers himself once for all in the definitive and ultimate effective sacrifice.

Another image used by Paul and other early Christian writers centers on the term *ransom*, a transaction that sets humans free. A ransom was the price paid to free or "redeem" a slave from bondage; metaphorically, Christ redeems humans from sin. Primitive accounts of Israelite sacrifice, however, also involved giving a ransom to God so that the offender's life would be spared. Several Old Testament texts suggest this aspect of sacrifice and evoke very disturbing notions of God (see, e.g., Exodus 30:12–16; Numbers 31:50).[4]

The notions of ransom or expiation was also used within the martyr tradition of the Maccabean period (160s BCE). The deaths of righteous Jews at the hands of their persecutors were understood as a "ransom" for the nation:

> These, then, who have been consecrated for the sake of God, are honored, not only with this honor, but also by the fact that because of them

---

4. The Hebrew word *kopher* means "payment" and is closely connected to *kipper*, or *atonement*.

our enemies did not rule over our nation, the tyrant was punished, and the homeland purified—they having become, as it were, a ransom[5] for the sin of our nation. (*4 Maccabees* 17:21–22; RSV)

The author of Maccabees interprets the death of these righteous martyrs as the means by which the nation is released from its enslavement to foreign oppression. Their deaths are vicarious, i.e., their deaths were for others, specifically, "for the nation." Similarly, Jesus' death is said to be "for us" (e.g., Romans 5:8).

Similar to the discussion of New Testament Christology, New Testament reflection on the meaning of Christ's death made use of the symbols and narratives at the heart of Jewish life. Such language—*sacrifice, ransom*, and *redemption*—is profoundly metaphoric. Unfortunately, there has never been the soteriological equivalent to the Council of Nicaea that could bring clarity to the maze of biblical images. Theologians and preachers throughout the centuries have had to proceed without such a guideline for their soteriological discourse.

Soteriology through the Middle Ages

Soteriology in the Patristic Era (100–700)

In the patristic era, biblical imagery became the catalyst for imaginative approaches to soteriology. Augustine of Hippo (354–430) and Gregory the Great (540–604) understand the death of Jesus as a necessary act whereby God was appeased by the human sacrifice of Christ, who paid the debt incurred by sin.[6]

Origen, the great third-century theologian from Alexandria, was clearly troubled by the cultic approach to soteriology, even as he remained wedded to the biblical language of sacrifice. He connected the sacrificial language of the New Testament to the sacrificial deaths of martyrs (Revelation 6:9) and to the horrifying passage from Judges 11 in which Japheth sacrifices his own daughter:

The story suggests that the being must be a very cruel one to whom such sacrifices are offered for the salvation of men; and we require some breadth of mind and some ability to solve the difficulties raised against Providence, to be able to account for such things and to see that they are mysteries and exceed our human nature. (Origen, *Commentary on the Gospel According to John*, 6. 36)

---

5. The original Greek is *hilastērion* (*expiation*) and not *apolytrōsis* (*ransom*).

6. See, e.g., Augustine, *Contra Faustum* 14. 4 and Gregory's *Moralia in Iob* 9.54.

Origen also moves beyond the sacrificial account of Jesus' death and employs the ransom concept to develop a distinctive narrative for interpreting the saving power of Christ's death. This move would be repeated among theologians for several centuries thereafter.

The symbolic language of the ransom theory is narrative and not theoretical. The sin of Adam enslaved humans to sin; Christ was, therefore, offered as a ransom, a payment to the devil. Gregory of Nyssa (335–395) likens the Incarnation and Christ's death to a fisherman using a fishhook.[7] The devil had held humanity as slaves since Adam had sold himself to the devil. The sinless Jesus was then offered as payment for the release of the devil's claim to humanity. The bait (Jesus' humanity) masked the hook (the divinity of Christ), so that when the devil seized Jesus in death, the divine nature of Christ was revealed, and like a fish who swallows the hook along with the bait, the devil was caught in a trap from which he could not escape and was forced to give up his claim on humanity and his claim of Christ. Contemporaries criticized Gregory of Nyssa for his approach, especially Gregory Nazianzen (329–389), who felt it was a mistake to assert that the devil had rights over humanity.[8]

Other theologians of the period also included the notion that, with the devil conquered, Christ was able to summon the souls of the dead that he had won and lead them out of death and into heaven. This last image is rooted in passages such as 1 Peter 3:18; 4:6, in which Christ is described as penetrating the abode of the dead in order to preach the gospel, making all creation accountable to God's mercy.[9]

Several early Greek theologians managed to transcend such an exclusive focus on Christ's death in their soteriologies. Two of the most prominent in this regard are Irenaeus and Athanasius. Irenaeus (c. 130–200) was a bishop in what is the modern French city of Lyons, but he wrote in Greek and was originally from Smyrna in Asia Minor. In the second century, he forged a systematic approach to soteriology that drew upon both the model of Isaiah and Luke and on Paul's Adam Christology: "Yet death exercised dominion from Adam to Moses, even over those whose sins were not like the transgressions of Adam, who is a type of the one who was to come" (Romans 5:14). For Irenaeus, God saves humanity through history by uniting himself with the history of the world. Salvation unfolds in a drama of human and divine action as the divine plan progresses through several interrelated stages. The Incarnation is the key event for Irenaeus, for Christ sums up, or recapitulates, the story of God and humanity. Christ reverses the disobedience of Adam (Romans 5:12–21). Christ, the

---

7. Chapters 22–24 of *Catechetical Orations*.

8. See his *Orations* 45. 22.

9. Cyril of Jerusalem, *Catechetical Lectures* 14. 18–19.

Incarnation of God, affects a union between God and humanity that destroys sin and brings about a transformation of humans so that they become divine. In effect, Irenaeus synthesizes the wide variety of images found in the New Testament to offer a systematic narrative account of Christ's saving work, one that brings together cultic imagery, a battle motif, and the didactic or moral dimensions of Christ's saving work.

Like Irenaeus, Athanasius, the champion of Nicaea, refused to focus on any one moment in the life of Christ as decisive for salvation. Rather, the entire life of Christ brings salvation.[10] The cross plays a special role, and Athanasius uses sacrificial as well as redemptive language to describe its effectiveness. However, coupled with such imagery is Athanasius's emphasis on divinization (*theōsis* or *theōpoiēsis*). Chapter 5 alluded to Athanasius's famous maxim: "God became human so that humans might become God." The Incarnation not only removes sin but also provides a model of the moral life. Christ restores the divine image, the original gift of creation that was lost through sin. The power of his resurrection empowers believers to treat death without fear and even with disdain, unlocking the possibility of living fearlessly as well.

> For as when a tyrant has been defeated by a real king, and bound hand and foot, then all that pass by laugh him to scorn, buffeting and reviling him, no longer fearing his fury and barbarity, because of the king who has conquered him; so also, death having been conquered and exposed by the Savior on the Cross, and bound hand and foot, all they who are in Christ, as they pass by, trample on him, and witnessing to Christ scoff at death, jesting at him, and saying what has been written against him of old: "O death , where is your victory? O grave, where is your sting?" (Athanasius, *On the Incarnation of the Word*, 27)

Divinization describes the saving work of Christ in terms of "participation," whereby all that is human is taken up into God so that God is not lowered, but humans are elevated and participate in God's own life: "[God] gave himself to us through his Spirit. By the participation of the Spirit, we become communicants in the divine nature. . . . For this reason, those in whom the Spirit dwells are divinized."[11]

The patristic era concentrated on narrative and symbolic soteriologies. Such approaches vividly portray the saving power of Christ's death. However, vivid narration often raises as many problems as it solves. The patristic accounts fall

---

10. George Bebawi, "St. Athanasios: The Dynamics of Salvation," *Sobornost* 8 (1986): 24–41; Christopher Smith, "The Life of Christ Structure of Athanasius' *De Incarnatione Verbi*," *Patristic and Byzantine Review* 10 (1991): 7–24.

11. *Letter 54* quoted in *CCC*, 1988.

short of answering difficult questions such as, "How does Jesus take away the sin of the world?" It is through theoretical language that a faith community is able to form and pronounce judgments—doctrines—in a clear and systematic way. More theoretical accounts of Christ's saving work began to appear in the Middle Ages.

Medieval Soteriology (1000–1500)

Anselm of Canterbury (1033–1109), a Benedictine monk and archbishop, famously defined theology as "faith seeking understanding" and used a sharp sense of reason to explore the truths he affirmed in faith. Perhaps his most famous, and most misunderstood, contribution to theology is *Cur Deus Homo?* ("Why Did God Become Human?"). In this work, Anselm sets out to discover "the necessary reasons" why humanity had to be redeemed through the Incarnation, death, and resurrection of Jesus. Like all theology, the answer Anselm constructs reflects his own context.

In Anselm's day, when one who was under the power and protection of a lord failed to be loyal or if he somehow offended the lord's honor, he was required to make "satisfaction." That is, he had to perform some act whereby the honor, the right relationship between servant and master, could be restored. Sometimes the offense was of such a kind or degree that the only act of satisfaction was death.

Anselm explicitly excludes the notion that God resembles a medieval lord, but at the same time, one cannot ignore the political and social context behind Anselm's language about atonement. For Anselm, God is "One than whom nothing greater can be conceived." God is the creator of existence, and humans owe God complete obedience of intellect, will, and complete love. However, humans have sinned and violated God's honor by denying that their existence comes from God and that they owe God everything. By so doing, they have disrupted the order of the universe.

God's honor is not the petty pride of some self-important nobleman. Rather, God's honor is really God's godliness, God's very divinity. Sin, in a sense, compromises, challenges, or threatens God's divinity because it separates creature from Creator. For Anselm, God is utterly justified in allowing creation to cease, to give humankind the destiny it has chosen: oblivion. This would be fitting for God's justice. However, God's love will not permit it. The resulting tension between God's justice and God's love seems irreconcilable.

Anselm finds the solution to the problem of sin in the Incarnation and the resolution of the apparent tension between God's love and God's justice. Humans, because they already owe God everything, cannot offer anything to God that would make "satisfaction" for their offense and restore the order of the universe. Even if they gave everything to God in an effort to make satisfaction, they would only be giving God what is already and always required. What is necessary is a sinless human who would not be required to die; the death of this person would be an offering to God because this person would not deserve death. A mere human, however, could not really make satisfaction for the sins of humanity as that sin is an infinite offense against God. However, if the perfect human offering described here were also divine, and thus infinite, the death of that person would have infinite value. Because Jesus was perfectly human and perfectly divine, he was able to make satisfaction for humans as a human, by offering God his death. This satisfaction has infinite value for others. That is, it is vicarious insofar as others participate in it indirectly, and it is a "supererogatory" act; it benefits others rather than Christ. It restores balance and order in the universe, and it restores God's honor.

Anselm's emphasis on the death of Christ as vicarious satisfaction was supplemented in later years by the work of the great scholastic theologian Thomas Aquinas (1225–1274). For Aquinas, the theologian is not concerned with the "necessary reasons" for Christ's death as was Anselm. Rather, the theologian's task is to ascertain how the saving work of Christ was the "appropriate" way God freely chose to redeem the world from sin.[12] Thomas determined that it was appropriate for many of the same reasons Anselm deemed it necessary but with an important twist: for Aquinas, the death of Christ was not the primary offering to God. Rather, Christ's loving obedience (even to the point of death) was the offering that makes satisfaction for sin. Christ offered to God, not "what was required," but something God loved more than he hated the offense.[13] Humans are reconciled to God through God's love and the love and obedience of Christ.

Aquinas perceives that any adequate soteriology must not only account for human salvation from sin (a negative soteriology) but must also account for the idea that the Incarnation made the sin of Adam a *felix culpa*, a "happy fault" that was able to bring salvation in a way that contributed something more to the human condition.[14] In his *Summa Theologica*, an "introductory" textbook for theology students of his day, Aquinas offers a clear overview of the negative and positive dimensions of Christ's saving work as he responds to the question: "Whether it was necessary for the restoration of the human race that the Word of God should become incarnate?" (*Summa Theologica* III. Q. 1 a. 2.) Aquinas's response to this question unfolds as a series of points whereby he clarifies succinctly how the Incarnation helps human beings progress in goodness and withdraw from evil.

---

12. Thomas uses *convenientia* frequently in the following articles on Christology: *Summa Theologica*, III, Q.1; Q. 46; Q. 50.

13. *Summa Theologica*, III, Q. 49, a. 4.

14. See *Summa Theologica*, III, Q. 1. a. 3.

Furtherance of Good

- Faith is made more certain and humanity's journey in faith is made more sure when the Truth becomes human.
- Hope is strengthened in the Incarnation because it shows us how much God loves us.
- God's love is "greatly enkindled by this [Incarnation, death, and resurrection]."
- Humans are given an example of how to live as humans.
- Humans are given full participation in the life of God ["God became human so that humans might become God"].

Withdrawal from Evil

- Humans are taught not to prefer the devil to humanity [God dignifies humanity-corporeal nature through the Incarnation].
- Human dignity is affirmed and makes sin unbecoming.
- Human presumption [i.e., confidence in one's own merit] is done away with because the grace bestowed in Christ is utterly gratuitous [free].
- Human pride is challenged by the humility of God in Christ.
- The devil is overcome by the justice of the man Christ through the satisfaction made by Christ on the cross (cf. Anselm).

Peter Abelard (1079–1142), the controversial Parisian theologian, challenged Anselm's approach more directly by envisioning Christ as a model, an example of God's love for humanity. The crucified Christ summons humans to enkindle the love of God within themselves and put away sin. In his *Exposition of the Epistle to the Romans*, Abelard modifies the sacrificial language of Paul to create a very different image of God and the work of Christ.

> Now it seems to us that we have been justified by the blood of Christ and reconciled to God in this way: through this unique act of grace manifested to us—in that his Son has taken upon himself our nature and persevered therein in teaching us by word and example even unto death—he has more fully bound us to himself by love; with the result that our hearts should be enkindled by such a gift of divine grace, and true charity [love] should not now shrink from enduring anything for him. . . .
>
> Our redemption through Christ's suffering is that deeper affection in us which not only frees us from slavery to sin, but also wins for us the true liberty of sons of God (Romans 8:21), so that we do all things out of love rather than fear. (Peter Abelard, *Exposition of the Epistle to the Romans*, 2.3)[15]

---

15. Peter Abelard, *Exposition of the Epistle to the Romans*, 2. 3, quoted from *A Scholastic Miscellany: Anslem to Ockam*, trans. and ed., Eugene R. Fairweather (New York: Macmillan, 1970), 283–84.

Person of Interest: Peter Abelard

© Bettmann / CORBIS

Peter Abelard

Abelard (1079–1142) was a prodigy—and a problem for his superiors. A gifted student, he was able to poke holes into the arguments of his teachers, who were some of the most respected minds in France at the time. He began his teaching career in Paris at a young age and attracted enormous audiences. In the Middle Ages, students paid their professors directly, and popularity among students translated into wealth and security, sometimes to the detriment of other faculty. He eventually fell in love and had a torrid affair with Heloise, one of his pupils and the niece of a very important church official. When their secret marriage was discovered, Abelard had Heloise sent to a monastery in an effort to protect his reputation. In retaliation for the treatment of his niece, Heloise's uncle had Abelard castrated. Abelard left Paris in 1118 to enter a monastery. Heloise and Abelard kept up a correspondence over the years and these letters attest to their mutual devotion. Controversy continued to hound him later in life: his doctrine on the Trinity was condemned at a council in the French city of Soissons in 1121, and St. Bernard of Clairvaux, the great mystic, also led a heresy trial against him. Happily, he and Bernard were later reconciled, and Abelard spent his final years in the great Benedictine abbey of Cluny.

Abelard was not alone in his emphasis on a "moral" or "subjective" approach to soteriology. Among the great theologians of the Middle Ages was the English mystic Julian of Norwich (1342 to around 1414). She was a lay woman who took a vow as an anchoress—a recluse attached to a church. She received a series of revelations in 1373 and published her account of these revelations, along with elaborated reflections on these revelations, some twenty years later under the title of *Shewings*. In this work, Julian uses the term *oneing* to describe the union between the divine and the human through God's love. Julian's revelations are anchored in the conviction that God's very being is love, such that even sin cannot challenge the loving nature of God. Julian describes God's love as both intimate (*homely*) and respectful (*courteous*)—God desires to be generous and faithful to his creatures, but in a way that demands a similar response. Her soteriology rejects the image of God as judge and offers, instead, the possibility of imaging God as a loving mother who refuses to allow us to be lost.

In *Shewings*, Julian describes the human self as suffering between reluctance and freedom. Freedom rests with God, and the human heart's deepest desire is to do God's will, but humans refuse to believe that. They fear that by doing God's will, their desires will be lost. Freedom is, thus, compromised by choosing against what God wills. Yet God embraces humans in an eternal bond of love that enables the exercise of human freedom.

Julian describes the role of humans in the economy of salvation through the imitation of Christ—a free response to God's love. Through the contemplation of Christ's life, death, and resurrection, one begins to exhibit the loving obedience of Christ. Christ thus "wants us to be his helpers, giving all our intention to him, learning his laws, observing his teaching, desiring everything to be done which he does, truly trusting in him."[16] Through contemplation and imitation, the believer's oneing with God is furthered. Julian thus provides a fine example of medieval moral soteriology that emphasizes the importance of prayer and the process of personal transformation.

The tendency of Julian and Abelard to emphasize the subjective dimension of Christ's saving work, as well as the patristic idea of divinization (*theōsis*), has been obscured in the history of Western theology, particularly through an over-emphasis on the death of Christ and its role in Anselm's theology. His account of atonement as vicarious suffering and the restoration of divine order in the universe had great appeal in a world in which order, especially hierarchical order, was paramount. The pluralism and rich ambiguity of the patristic and medieval accounts of Christ's saving work eventually succumbed to the pressures of modern societies and the polemics of the Reformation and Counter-Reformation and the corresponding demise of soteriology in Christian theology through the nineteenth century. Today many theologians dismiss such subjectivist accounts of soteriology in favor of more objectivist accounts (i.e., Anselm's approach, or more likely the approach of the Reformers discussed later) because subjectivist approaches seem to make human salvation contingent on human response and neglect much of the cultic language found in scripture.[17]

---

16. *Julian of Norwich Showings*, Classics of Western Spirituality, trans. Edmund Colledge and James Walsh (New York: Paulist, 1978), 57:292.

17. See, e.g., Gustav Aulén, *Christus Victor: An Historical Study of the Three Main Types of the Idea of Atonement* (New York: Macmillan, 1969). Hans Boersma offers a robust appreciation for subjectivist approaches, especially what he finds in Irenaeus, but he ultimately falls back onto a traditional (his term) emphasis on God's violence in the atonement. See his *Violence, Hospitality, and the Cross: Reappropriating the Atonement Tradition* (Grand Rapids, MI: Baker, 2004).

René Girard's Theory of Sacrifice

French literary critic René Girard understands the origins of human violence in terms of "mimetic desire." Girard's theory states that humans actually learn to desire that which their peers, and especially their elders, teach them to desire. It logically follows that if we all desire the same things, and there is a limited number of desirable "things" that we all desire, the result is anxiety and violence.

Such anxiety and violence is regulated by a society through the scapegoat mechanism—a society will transfer the guilt and anxiety that permeates its relationships onto an individual who is then driven out and destroyed. The scapegoat restores balance within society and paradoxically becomes an object of worship, invested with supernatural or even divine power. From this enactment of the scapegoat mechanism, societies develop moral codes, rituals, and myths, all of which serve to both mask foundational violence and perpetuate the "benefits" of that violence. Girard argues that Jesus is the perfect scapegoat, the one who lays bare all of the violence inherent in religious systems and throughout human culture and ends thinly masked violence that saturates human social arrangements. Yet, Girard notes that Christians soon forgot the power of Jesus' death as anti-sacrifice and were co-opted by the power of sacrificial language (e.g., Hebrews, Anselm, penal substitution). Some of his interpreters have suggested (e.g., Raymund Schwager and Robert Daly), however, that Girard may have room for a positive account of sacrificial language, leaving some room for a more positive account of sacrifice in the Christian theological tradition.

The Reformation and the Doctrine of Penal Substitution (1500–1600)

The great reformer, Martin Luther (1483–1546), sought to retrieve a more biblically oriented and simpler form of Christian faith in response to the outrageous excesses of late medieval theology and church practices. Late medieval scholasticism had introduced a range of ideas that many thought had strayed from the basics of Christian faith as expressed in the New Testament. Luther and the other Reformers rejected traditional ecclesiastical authority; some Reformers called for a less centralized and more democratic form of church governance. At the theological level, Luther insisted upon the autonomy of the believer in the interpretation of scripture. Perhaps most central to Luther's theology was an insistence on the essentially gratuitous nature of redemption: salvation is a gift, pure and simple.

Luther asserted that humans are redeemed through the work of Christ and receive these benefits through God's gift of grace in faith: humans are "justified"—made right with God—through faith. Luther's Catholic opponents argued that while justification was a gift and totally unmerited in the strict sense, what was required from Christians was the response to grace that included not only faith but also works of penance and charity, or love (*caritas*).[18]

Because the response of love was itself a grace freely given by God, it is incorrect to speak of acts of love as a means of earning or "meriting" salvation. On the contrary, when God saves, God merely crowns or rewards God's own gifts. Any talk of "earning" one's salvation was absurd.

At the popular and even the pastoral level, however, there was a great deal of ignorance, minimal catechesis, and poor practice, such that many people apparently believed that one could, in fact, "earn" one's salvation through penance and other good works. In the sixteenth century, a practice emerged that helped to push Luther into public conflict with the church: the buying and selling of indulgences. The logic ran as follows: as part of one's penance, and not as a condition for the forgiveness of sin, Christians could choose to donate funds to the work of the church. Such actions helped to make satisfaction for sins—provided these actions were sanctioned by the church and united to Christ's act of satisfaction.

In the early sixteenth century, one of the major "charitable" works for which the Catholic Church sought funds was the rebuilding of St. Peter's Basilica in Rome. The clergy who were tasked with raising the necessary funds succumbed to very bad theology in order to meet their "fundraising" goals. If one contributed to the work, the church, through its power to bind and loose sin and through its treasury of merit, would accept this gift as penance. One could also transfer the "indulgence" purchased to a loved one, living or dead, so that that person's penance, either in this life or in the next, would be shortened. Luther, in response, insisted on a theology more explicitly focused on the grace of God's saving work. In the ensuing debate, Luther accepted only arguments based directly upon scripture; the positions of the church fathers and scholastic theologians, for the most part, were accorded only secondary value as they often wander far from scripture to focus upon philosophical speculation.

Luther's insistence upon the literal sense of the text was an important corrective to the speculative theology of the scholastic period. For Luther, the literal sense could be historical, proverbial, or parabolic, provided such a nuanced meaning is evidently intended in the text. Scholastic theology tended to regard the literal sense of the text as the least important and argued that the real or spiritual meaning of scripture could be unlocked only through allegory or other complex forms of interpretation, usually appealing also to authorities like church

---

18. For a wonderful and provocative account of the issues related to justification, sanctification, and love, see, Paul A. Rainbow, *The Way of Salvation: The Role of Christian Obedience in Justification* (Milton Keynes, UK: Paternoster, 2005) and the now classic historical account, Alister E. McGrath, *Iustitia Dei: A History of the Christian Doctrine of Justification*, 3rd ed. (Cambridge: Cambridge University Press, 2005).

The Work of Christ   **163**

fathers. Some modern theologians have misinterpreted Luther's soteriology as simply a return to biblical imagery, particularly its narrative dimensions.[19]

Luther's robust appropriation of the narrative dimensions of soteriology in the New Testament has led some scholars to characterize his approach to the work of Christ as "Christus Victor." In this model, the Incarnation of the Son brings about direct confrontation with evil in which Christ, through his life, death, and resurrection, defeats the power of evil and sin in battle. These images are present throughout the New Testament and the writings of Luther. Yet, as many have noted, Luther's approach to soteriology has much in common with Anselm and moves beyond a simple rehearsal of the biblical material.

Luther's soteriology also emphasized Jesus' role as a representative of all humanity. As such, Jesus is the individual who endures the suffering and death humans merit because of their sins. This constitutes a "happy exchange": Christ takes on the punishment that would otherwise fall upon humans, while they share in Christ's righteousness. While Luther's "penal substitution" model draws heavily upon biblical images, the net result is a novel understanding of soteriology:

> All the prophets of old said that Christ should be the greatest transgressor, murderer, adulterer, thief, blasphemer that ever was or ever could be on earth. When He took the sins of the whole world upon Himself, Christ was no longer an innocent person. He was a sinner burdened with the sins of a Paul who was a blasphemer; burdened with the sins of a Peter who denied Christ; burdened with the sins of a David who committed adultery and murder, and gave the heathen occasion to laugh at the Lord. In short, Christ was charged with the sins of all men, that He should pay for them with His own blood. The curse struck Him. The Law found Him among sinners. He was not only in the company of sinners. He had gone so far as to invest Himself with the flesh and blood of sinners. So the Law judged and hanged Him for a sinner. (*Commentary on the Epistle to the Galatians*)[20]

Sin incurs the penalty of death, but Christ takes on this penalty, substitutes himself in the place of humans, and bears their punishment. Because Christ suffered the penalty for sin, humans do not need to suffer the penalty, provided they are united to Christ in faith. Luther's soteriology, whether focused on the Chistus victor model, as some would argue or on the notion of penal substitution, both emphasize the utter gratuity of God's work in Christ for the salvation of the world. In other words, Luther's theology always and everywhere sought to emphasize the role of God intervening in human history to bring about

19. Cf. Gustav Aulén, *Christus Victor* (New York: Macmillan, 1961). Aulén's account of soteriology wrongly characterizes the soteriologies of both Anselm and Luther.

20. *Commentary on the Epistle to the Galatians*, trans. Theodore Graebner (Grand Rapids, MI: Zondervan, 1949).

Soteriologies: A Simplified Comparative Chart

Model	Major Figures	Understanding of Sin	Summary	Some Strengths and Shortcomings
Prophetic	(Isaiah) Luke	Sin is failing to exercise mercy toward the oppressed and marginalized, forgetting God's covenant. The effects of sin are oppression and violence.	God acts in history, through concrete events and people, to rescue the righteous and judge the wicked.	This model emphasizes the concrete realities of sin and death, but it can also ignore the moral significance of the individual in favor of a long-term communal approach to sin and salvation.
Sacrificial	Paul and the author of Hebrews	Sin compromises God's holiness, God's justice, and God's mercy to Israel.	The sacrifices of the Temple were designed to foreshadow the work of Christ, whose blood, like that of the bulls and the goats, unleashes the power of divine forgiveness and reconciliation.	This model integrates Israelite Temple theology with the story of Jesus, providing for continuity between the covenants, but by concentrating on Jesus' death, it fails to incorporate the salvific significance of his life and ministry.
Ransom (Patristic)	Origen, Augustine	Sin is offering allegiance to the devil rather than to God. Sin results in the subjugation of humanity to the devil.	The devil has dominion over humans. Christ, in the disguise of human flesh, gave himself over to death to take the place of humans in death. As the devil takes Jesus into death, the devil discovers that Jesus is without sin and cannot be touched by death. The devil, having overplayed his hand, must sacrifice his dominion over all humans.	The playful and vivid imagery of this model is evocative, but one might question whether such a theology of deception is consistent with the God of Israel.

Continued

Soteriologies: A Simplified Comparative Chart *Continued*

Model	Major Figures	Understanding of Sin	Summary	Some Strengths and Shortcomings
Divinization	Athanasius	Sin is turning away from God, our creator. The result of this turning away includes the loss of the divine image with which humans were created.	God became human in Christ. This union restores the divine image and raises humans to participate in God's own life—a life beyond the fear and ignorance in which sin thrives.	This approach incorporates the entire life of Christ in an account of redemption, but it also employs a range of images and metaphors that lack theoretical rigor and fails to explain how divinization occurs.
Vicarious Satisfaction	Anselm	Sin violates God by dishonoring him. Sin has the affect of disordering the universe God has created.	The death of a sinless human is an offering to God, but the infinite offense that humanity has committed requires an act of infinite value—so Jesus, as the God-man, makes satisfaction for our sins.	Anselm introduces a theoretical approach to soteriology, but both his search for the necessity of the Incarnation and his focus on the death of Jesus limit its value. Also, the social setting for his theory raises questions, as does the minimal role played by conversion.
Moral Exemplar	Abelard, Julian of Norwich	Sin is a failure to love God above all. It both results from and causes forgetfulness of God's love for humans.	The cross is a sign of God's love for us, and it calls us to remember that love and turn away from sin.	Abelard and Julian focus on the love of God, the teachings of Jesus, and the importance of conversion, but they do not adequately differentiate Jesus from other martyrs.
Penal Substitution	Luther, Calvin	Sin is a violation of divine law. The sanction for such violation is death.	Christ takes our place. Christ dies so human beings do not have to die.	This approach emphasizes the complete gratuity of God's salvation but also makes God the origin of Jesus' suffering. Also, it is not clear what role conversion has in this approach.

salvation as a gift that humans are only able to accept in faith as gift or reject. The complexities and nuances of Luther's soteriology are far more intricate than the preceding paragraphs have suggested, but the focus is always the same: salvation is pure grace-gift.

John Calvin (1509–1564), another prominent Reformer, presented a similar version of penal substitution and emphasized the utter gratuitousness of God's saving work in Christ. Calvin used the idea of criminal law to understand the saving significance of Christ's death. For Calvin, Christ "was made a substitute and a surety in the place of transgressors and even submitted as a criminal to sustain and suffer all the punishment which would have been inflicted on them."[21] This drama of salvation played out in accordance with God's sovereignty, God's control over history, and was solely for those elected and predestined for salvation.[22]

Many Christians today accept penal substitution as a full and clear account of the salvation that has been accomplished in Christ. However, more and more Protestant scholars have begun to find penal substitution wanting for at least three reasons. First, its understanding of sin is problematic. Sin seems to be a violation of God's law, and the relationship between sin and death is simply willed by God's justice; sin and death have no intrinsic relationship. Second, penal substitution offers an utterly objectified account of redemption: the problem of sin is taken care of, with no reference to the decisive significance of Jesus' call to conversion. In other words, "Jesus died so I don't have to." Third, in penal substitution God wills and inflicts the violent death Jesus experienced. God decrees that sin merits death, and God is the enforcer of this punishment. "The wrath of God" toward sin is visited upon Jesus so that the suffering of Jesus is at the hands of the Father. Some have complained that this model essentially depicts God as a child-abuser.

While penal substitution originated among the Protestant Reformers, Catholic Counter-Reformation piety developed a similar emphasis on the suffering of Christ. In the pastoral theology and practice of many Catholic churches, meditation on the suffering of Christ became central. In some versions of the Catholic devotional called "The Stations of the Cross," one is encouraged to believe that the pain Christ endured was caused by one's own sin—the more one sins, the more suffering Christ endures. Additionally, one can share the suffering of Christ. Believers can make up for what is lacking in Christ's afflictions (Colossians 1:24) when they unite their suffering to that of Christ. Such devotional language is powerful and not to be casually dismissed—it has tremendous value when understood properly. However, at the same time, such language envisions a world in which pain and suffering are punishments for sin, and they can be divided or borne away provided one is sufficiently disciplined.

---

21. *Institutes of the Christian Religion*, 2. 16. 10.

22. See *Institutes of the Christian Religion* 1. 5. 1–15.

Conclusion

Most Christians today, if asked to explain the salvific work of Christ, might say something like, "Christ died for our sins"; in effect, they would attempt to express some form of penal substitution theory, the only soteriology they know. Soteriology, however, is a far broader topic embracing a variety of models. Penal substitution is only one such model and a relative latecomer, at that. Increasingly, theologians focus on three elements in any soteriology. First, does the model provide an appropriate understanding of Jesus' own call to conversion? Second, does the model offer an account of the importance and limitations of the practice Jesus modeled? And third, does the model responsibly interpret Christ's death and resurrection? Contemporary theologians seek to address these concerns and to speak more intelligibly to the modern context, not by abandoning the tradition, but by attempting to formulate original soteriology that stands in continuity with that tradition. Contemporary developments in Christology and soteriology will be discussed in chapter 7.

Questions for Understanding

1. Describe the prophetic model of salvation. Are any features of this approach troubling? Are any features appealing?
2. Describe the liturgical or sacrificial model of salvation. Why do you think so many Christians still spontaneously identify Christ's saving work with sacrifice? What makes it so attractive?
3. Describe Anselm's theory of the atonement. Is it dependent upon medieval social structures? Explain.
4. How do Abelard and Julian of Norwich challenge Anselm's approach to soteriology?
5. Describe the doctrine of penal substitution. How does it differ from Anselm's approach?

Questions for Reflection and Action

1. Ask three people the following question (regardless of their religious identity): "In Christian understanding, how is Jesus supposed to save humans from sin?" Do the answers of Christians and non-Christians diverge or are they similar? How do you account for the differences or similarities? Do their responses reflect one of the theories or approaches to soteriology mentioned in this chapter?
2. Mel Gibson's film *The Passion of the Christ* (2004) stirred a great deal of controversy when it was released. Do some basic research on the

Web and identify some of the reasons for this controversy. Were these reasons theological?

3. What is your response to the primitive images of God that lurk behind the biblical language of sacrifice? Should sacrificial language have a place in contemporary society or religious practice?

For Further Reading

Baker, Mark. *Recovering the Scandal of the Cross: Atonement in New Testament and Contemporary Contexts*. Downers Grove, IL: InterVarsity, 2000.

Finlan, Stephen. *Problems with Atonement: The Origins of, and Controversy about, the Atonement Doctrine*. Collegeville, MN: Liturgical, 2005.

Young, Frances M. *The Use of Sacrificial Ideas in Greek Christian Writers from the New Testament to John Chrysostom*. Eugene, OR: Wipf & Stock, 2004.

CHAPTER 7

Christology and Social Transformation

More than forty years ago, a young Joseph Ratzinger (later Pope Benedict XVI), began his celebrated book *Introduction to Christianity* with Søren Kierkegaard's familiar parable about a clown who, after seeing a major fire in the village, tried to warn the villagers of the danger.[1] The villagers, knowing what clowns do for a living, simply thought it was part of his clown act. So they laughed and ignored the seriousness of his warning. In order to save the village, the clown needed to do more than just remove his makeup and don more "respectable" clothes. According to Ratzinger, Christianity requires more than a change of costume or updated language to win a hearing from "the villagers." The current situation requires recognition of the fundamental commonality between the nonbeliever and the believer.

Ratzinger and many other Christian theologians are convinced that the credibility of Christian faith, and the nature of Christian faith itself, demands that Christians recognize that they are not in possession of "all the answers" but are on a journey of faith often fraught with uncertainty. Christianity teaches that the journey is made possible by the assurance of faith, an assurance produced by God's outreach and self-communication. Perhaps modern culture, even post-Christian culture, offers resources that can help the Christian community to find its voice.

In a world in which injustice and suffering abound, how do Christians respond to the pervasive experience of evil? Many Christians have chosen to emphasize salvation in a way that makes it a personal project. Such an approach can lead to escapism; this world is simply a test that is passing away. Individualism and escapism do not address the suffering of the world or its causes, however, and they thus undermine Christianity's credibility and relevance in the modern world. If Christian faith proclaims that God has redeemed the world in

---

1. Joseph Ratzinger, *Introduction to Christianity*, trans. J. R. Foster (New York: Herder, 1969), 15–17.

Person of Interest: Søren Kierkegaard

Søren Kierkegaard

Søren Kierkegaard (1813–1855) is often credited as the founder of modern existentialism and one of the most important theologians of the nineteenth century. He was annoyed and dismayed at the kind of Christianity that had taken root in his native Denmark and throughout Europe in his day. Kierkegaard saw orthodox Christianity as a puppet of the state and believed it affirmed the world's petty morality. Christianity had become bourgeois and superficial. As an ardent individualist, Kierkegaard insisted that human reason, and reflection on God can only lead to frustration because God is beyond human reason, and any reflection on God can only yield paradoxes. Because humans are self-absorbed, they need to experience despair in order to make a "leap" of faith in order to emerge on the other side of the despair and the vertigo that constitutes human existence. His thought has been highly influential among Protestant Christians in Germany, Scandinavia, and the English-speaking world. Some of his most important works are *Fear and Trembling*, *The Concept of Anxiety*, and *Either Or*.

© Private Collection / The Bridgeman Art Library

Christ, such salvation must be demonstrable, not simply a "mystery" in the most evasive sense of the term or one that condones unresponsiveness to the Christian imperative to bear witness to that salvation. The discussion that follows will consider the contributions of several theologians who have made a case for the credibility of Christian claims about salvation.

Sin, Conversion, and Society

Chapter 6 addressed the history of soteriology, or the way earlier Christians have understood the saving work of Christ. The present chapter begins with some contemporary reappraisals of the soteriological tradition, particularly as offered in the work of Bernard Lonergan and René Girard.[2] Both theologians have worked to renew the soteriological tradition, particularly by articulating a more adequate understanding of sin and using it as a heuristic notion, or a pattern of inquiry, for constructing a more adequate soteriology.

Accounts of soteriology often fail to address sin as concrete, real-world evil: injustice, oppression, exploitation, and the degradation of individuals, societies, and even the environment. Sin is often characterized as a spiritual problem for the individual: sin is when one lies to avoid looking bad in public or when one grows angry when stuck in traffic. Theologians working in the tradition of both Lonergan and Girard recognize that Christians need a new account of sin, one that moves beyond the notion of "breaking God's law." While the notion of divine law is still valuable, taken by itself, as it often is, it fails to adequately account for sin understood as a this-world force that produces suffering and dehumanization.

Two Contemporary Accounts of Sin

William Loewe, a prominent interpreter of Lonergan, argues that the modern historically conscious world necessarily moves one away from what the French philosopher Paul Ricoeur calls first naïveté: the mythological view of the world. For Ricoeur, modern religious understanding begins with a first naïveté, which emphasizes the importance of myth and symbol. One recognizes these elements as essential in an account of a religious worldview—e.g., one reads the story of Adam and Eve as a straightforward account of the first two humans and their confrontation with a talking snake. However, when that faith is exposed to a series of critical questions that arise from one's experience of the modern world, that initial trust in myth and symbol is broken. At this point many faithful people become skeptical and irreligious. Ricoeur, however, holds out the possibility that faith can persevere and integrate critical questioning with the myth and symbol of the first naïveté.

What Ricoeur calls a second naïveté emerges on the other side of this process. Here one freely engages myth and symbol while recognizing their true power as well as their limitations. For Loewe, when one realizes that human history is mostly a product of human choosing and doing, one recognizes human responsibility for the tragic direction of history (though not all tragedy is the product of human action). Christians cannot blithely dismiss evil as the work of unseen demonic forces or explain disasters as God's punishment for sin. An

---

2. Of special interest here is William P. Loewe, "Toward a Responsible Contemporary Soteriology," in *Creativity and Method: Essays in Honor of Bernard Lonergan, SJ*, ed. Matthew Lamb (Milwaukee, WI: Marquette University Press, 1981), 213–27. Additionally, Girard's work has found elaboration among many theologians, including James Allison (e.g., *The Joy of Being Wrong: Original Sin through Easter Eyes* [New York: Crossroad, 1998] and Raymund Schwager, SJ, *Must There Be Scapegoats? Violence and Redemption in the Bible* [San Francisco: HarperCollins, 1987]).

adequate contemporary approach to sin must address the paradox of history: history is a product of human achievements, and yet it eludes human understanding and control, leaving humans helpless in the face of suffering and evil.

Any contemporary understanding of sin must move away from the symbolic narratives found in scripture and toward a formal account of sin that acknowledges the massive scale of alienation and dehumanization in the modern world. In our globalized society, economic systems reinforce the exploitation of resources (including people) for the sake of a small segment of the population. These systems are legitimated by a wide range of ideologies, including religious ideologies, resulting in a subtle but profound transformation of moral discourse. Questions of meaning and value are reduced to merely pragmatic questions of what "works."

Pragmatism is not bad, but pragmatism can prevent one from suffering or self-sacrificing for what is truly good. Current political and economic debates in the United States and around the world reflect this unwillingness to embrace suffering. Take for example the decision of the Internet search company Google, which, under pressure from the Chinese government, agreed to curtail the ability of its search engine to locate and provide access to sites advocating democracy, because the government deems them subversive.[3] Google's decision was pragmatic: if one wants to have access to the fastest-growing market in the world, one needs to play by the government's rules, even if that means cooperating in the suppression of basic human rights. Such pragmatism leads to a general resignation to and acceptance of current conditions. Acceptance, in turn, legitimates current conditions and structures a limited field of moral vision. It is attributable to what Lonergan calls "bias."

Lonergan describes three different forms of bias: individual, group, and general. Each of these biases impedes real progress in history and results in decline, destruction, and alienation. Individual bias takes the form of egoism, a pervasive form of selfishness. Egoism is not the spontaneous, instinctual acts of the human animal to self-preservation; rather, egoism sabotages intellectual operations in order to serve self-interest; one's thinking and valuing are skewed in favor of one's own selfish desires. Similarly, group bias is self-interest at the level of a particular group—a religious sect, nation, class, or racial group. Because the criteria for satisfaction have shifted from the individual to the group, it is easy for one to become deluded and mistake group bias for "good order." What is truly good, and what might require a particular group to suffer for the benefit of others, is ignored in favor of decisions that promote group interests. A nation's foreign policy is often phrased in a manner that is explicitly biased: "We will act to protect our interests." These interests coincide with concerns over trading and energy rather than justice or human rights.

---

3. For a fuller exploration of the controversy and Google's business practices, see Steven Levy, *In the Plex: How Google Thinks, Works, and Shapes Our Lives* (New York: Simon & Schuster, 2011).

Lonergan and the Notion of Bias

Individual Bias

Individual bias makes people focus upon themselves. They fail to ask, "What is true?" and "What is good?" Instead, they are stuck in the rut of asking, "What is true for me?" and "What is good for me?"

Group Bias

Group bias is individual bias that is enacted within a group. The questions of value (What is good?) and questions of fact (What is true?) are asked and answered from the perspective of the group. Nationalism is a common example of group bias.

General Bias

Common sense is not a bad thing, but when it is celebrated as a pervasive assumption about reality, or when it gives over to the tyranny of "what works" and "what I can see," it wreaks havoc in history. When humans simply defer to the general bias of common sense, they ignore the human vocation to transcend themselves, their group, and what can be sensed, and fail to pursue what is really real and really good.

Conversion

Lonergan describes the process by which bias is overcome as "conversion." It is a dramatic leap beyond the horizon of meaning and value that defines people and the world in which they locate themselves. Intellectual conversion entails recognizing that reality is not simply a matter of sense experience. Moral conversion means no longer thinking that what is good for oneself is really good; rather, what is really good may work against one's interests in the short run. In religious conversion, one comes to understand that one is loved by God beyond all reason and called to complete self-transcendence and union with God in love. These conversions can happen in any order, but they tend to have an impact upon each other.

The general bias of common sense is a deeper, more pervasive force capable of underwriting the other two forms of bias. By *common sense*, Lonergan means the universal or common concern for the concrete and the practical. It is essential for the day-to-day business of human living. The general bias of common sense extends "its legitimate concern for the concrete and the immediately practical into disregard of larger issues and indifference to long-term results."[4] Humanity

---

4. Bernard Lonergan, *Insight: A Study in Human Understanding*, Collected Works of Bernard Lonergan, vol. 3 (Toronto: University of Toronto Press, 1992), 250–51.

turns to common sense to deliver it from individual and group biases that are motivated by self-interest. Common sense, however, is unable to meet this challenge; it must be led, at a deeper level, by something more. General bias prevents one from addressing questions concerning long-range consequences of actions or values. Pervasive and insidious, general bias can contribute to "the longer cycle of decline" within a given culture.[5] It fuels the other biases, resulting in both social and personal decline and decay. Suffering and evil result when people fail to move beyond the moral horizon of common-sense, fail to surpass self-interest or the interest of their tribe, and fail to embrace authentic value—that which is truly good.

The position of French cultural theorist René Girard could be read as complementary to that of Lonergan. Girard offers an account of the origins of violence and culture that has been widely influential among Christian theologians.[6] For Girard, human interactions center upon desire and the way humans learn to desire or imitate desire. This mimetic desire leads to competition and violence. As humans learn to desire the same things, they compete for and even fight or kill one another for that which they desire. The violence generated becomes entrenched through a system called "the scapegoat mechanism."

In Girard's theory, the violence of human social relationships is transferred or displaced onto a third party—the scapegoat (cf. Leviticus 16:5–10). This third party then becomes the recipient of abuse and violence and is expelled from the community. As the focal point of the community's violence, the scapegoat transfers the violence inherent in human social relationships and, in a ritualized manner, absorbs that violence and carries it away. Through the ritual of the scapegoat, the community exorcises, celebrates, and even perpetuates the violence of its social order and culture. Over time, the destruction or expulsion of the scapegoat fades within the memory of the community, and the community both reveres the scapegoat as the source of the community's unity and reviles it as the source of its original discord. Moreover, the community misremembers its role in the violence inflicted on the scapegoat and its complicity in the scapegoat's victimization. Both ignorance and violence become entrenched as this cycle repeats itself throughout history, inscribing pathological fear, suspicion, and violence deeply within the human psyche and social systems. Paradoxically, through the spiritualization of Israel's sacrificial system and the ethical monotheism of the prophets, Girard sees Israel evolving beyond the scapegoat mechanism into a new cultural form.

Both the Lonerganian and Girardian accounts of the social and cultural dimensions of sin and violence invite a corresponding account of Jesus' saving work within contemporary Christian theology. Both of these approaches tend

---

5. On Lonergan's account of the "longer cycle of decline," see *Insight*, 251–67.

6. See René Girard, *Violence and the Sacred* (Baltimore, MD: Johns Hopkins University Press, 1977).

to emphasize the social and cultural dimensions of sin—not just the personal, individual, or spiritual dimension—and help to structure a corresponding soteriology, one that addresses the social and cultural dimensions of salvation.

Conversion, Sacrifice, and the Law of the Cross

Both the Lonerganian and the Girardian approaches to soteriology develop Aquinas's insight that Jesus does not simply save humans *from* sin, but also his saving work transforms human existence and possibility so that they are saved *for* something more. In both approaches the cross of Christ is interpreted as deeply connected to the life and ministry of Jesus, and both understand the evil inflicted upon Jesus and evil in general as transformed into a higher good through the cross.

Lonergan identifies "the law of the cross" as a principle of transformation. This principle, presented in the story of the life, death, and resurrection of Jesus, unfolds through three distinct moments. First, sin brings death. Sin kills. However, if the death and suffering caused by sin is accepted out of love, it can be transformed, and this is the second movement in the law of the cross. In other words, when one is injured by the thoughtlessness, the bias, or the sin of others, one can respond out of love. Though humans experience pain and suffering, the death of sin, they have the capacity to see sin as the product of negative value and can embrace the suffering that has been inflicted, not passively, but proactively.

The law of the cross formulates a principle of transformation or conversion that makes it possible for humans to become fully what God has created humans to be. Lonergan calls this state *authenticity*, and describes it variously as "being in love in an unrestricted fashion" or "unreserved openness to value." This "being in love" enables one to live the law of the cross, but the law of the cross also structures one's "being in love." Authenticity is not a personal achievement, gained through self-help books and seminars, but the result of God's self-gift in grace experienced and received in community. This self-gift is uniquely mediated to the world in the person of Jesus and perpetuated by the witness of the church, particularly through its stories, symbols, and uniquely in its liturgy.

James Alison, building upon the work of Girard, argues that the scapegoat, the victim, is uniquely equipped to bring about a conversion. Alison understands conversion as the grasp of a new intelligence that unmasks the violence and ignorance of the people who have victimized the scapegoat.[7] The scapegoat's identification with the outsider, the marginal, the intruder makes possible the disclosure of a new intelligence. The ultimate instance of this disclosure of a new intelligence was the resurrection of Jesus. In the resurrection, Jesus approaches those who abandoned him and victimized him precisely to forgive them. In the

---

7. See James Allison, *The Joy of Being Wrong*, 237–65.

forgiveness of the disciples, Alison sees two important dimensions of revelation. First, the truth about all human complicity in violence and ignorance comes to light here. The disciples need forgiveness and not just the soldiers, Pilate, or the Sanhedrin. Second, the truth about God is made known in revelation. God is revealed as source of love and acceptance, and that love and acceptance is fundamentally subversive in character. Human cultural and social structures, built as they are on ignorance and violence, fall under God's judgment. This subversive realization, this conversion, is made possible only in the identification with the victim, the scapegoat, Jesus. Moreover, an accurate understanding of sin can only be gained from the perspective of graced forgiveness: it is only through "Easter eyes" that humans can understand the true nature of sin.

The Importance of Christian Doctrine for Social Change

The horrific cry of those millions who senselessly suffered and died as the result of Nazi atrocities and Allied indifference has profoundly shaped twentieth-century theology and made it come to terms with Christian theology's own role in the concrete suffering of millions. There is probably no better example of the impact the Holocaust has had on Christian theology than the work of Jürgen Moltmann, who, like many theologians in the twentieth century, has worked to connect God with human history, particularly through his conviction concerning the nature of God, revelation of that nature, and the process of history.

Revelation is not to be understood as a supernatural incursion into the natural world; rather, revelation is a promise about the future, experienced and anticipated in the here and now. God becomes known, indeed becomes God, within history. In his book, *The Crucified God*, Moltmann begins with the bold truism that the concept of God is determinative for a given culture, society, and individual. If humans are cruel and vindictive, their "god" tends to be cruel and vindictive.

> Without a revolution in the concept of God . . . there can be no revolutionary faith. Without God's liberation from idolatrous images produced by anxiety and hubris, there will be no liberating theology. Man always unfolds his humanity in relation to the divinity of his God, and experiences himself in relation to what appears to him as the highest being.[8]

The modern God is a God of apathy, and the modern human is the apathetic person of success. "Faith in the apathetic God leads to the ethics of man's liberation from need and drive, and to dominion over body and nature."[9] The result

---

8. Jürgen Moltmann, "The Crucified God," *Theology Today* 31 (1974): 16–18, 16.
9. Ibid., 11.

of this apathy is carelessness about one's actions and the suffering and oppression that they create. This apathy is poignantly reflected in the scene from Elie Wiesel's *Night* in which three prisoners are hanged for attempting to escape from a Nazi internment camp. One of the condemned prisoners, a small boy, dies slowly as the other prisoners are forced to watch. As the prisoners file past, someone asks, "Where is God?"

Moltmann responds that, in the context of Wiesel's story, we can only talk about God's presence in the person of the youth hanging from the gallows. In other words, God is present as the suffering one. Such a notion deeply disturbs the Western concept of the *apatheia*, or impassibility, of God since it serves to reinforce the relationship between God's freedom and God's love. Traditionally, Christian theology accepted a concept of love that demands absolute freedom: "True love arises out of freedom from self-seeking and anxiety, and because it loves *sine ira et studio* [without passion or prejudice], one understood apathy as the presupposition for *agape* [love]."[10] Moltmann argues that the classical idea of God's *apatheia* cannot be fully reconciled with the Jewish and Christian experience of God. In the prophets and in the story of Jesus, both the Jewish and Christian traditions insist that God suffers with and does not stand apart from the oppressed. Post-Holocaust theologies like that of Moltmann serve to recall such powerful traditions.

The Christian experience builds on the message and promise of the prophets in continuity with the covenant of Israel, but Christians also find themselves in a new "God-situation" as a result of their experience of Christ. In the cross of Christ, Christians find their own inescapable suffering as it exists in God. So if humans form themselves and their societies based on their image of God, a revised image of God then creates a different kind of society, one not built on progress, success, and action, but on fellow-suffering, sympathy, and radical patience. In such a theology, God cannot be the God of the establishment, whether church, government, or dominant social class. God must be identified with what and who are marginal; the suffering of the marginal is to be recognized as the suffering of God and as something to be embraced. In the end, what emerges is something like Lonergan's "law of the cross."

> Where [human beings] suffer because they love, God suffers in them and they suffer in God. Where this God suffers the death of Jesus and thereby demonstrates the power of his love, there men also find the power to remain in love despite pain and death, becoming neither bitter nor superficial. They gain the power of affliction and can hold fast to the dead . . . and despite [this] remain in love. (Moltmann, "The Crucified God," *Theology Today*, 17)

---

10. Ibid.

Moltmann transforms Christian doctrine through an appeal to the historical specificity of the encounter with God. This appeal enshrines the virtue of hope rather than so-called progress. The hopeless world is condemned to progress that is determined by the canonization of general bias, condemned to rely upon its own devices, which are unequal to the good intentions of humans. Such a world ignores suffering and cannot embrace the God who suffers and yet promises liberation. For Jews and Christians, God is the one who suffers with humanity amid the promise that suffering is not the last word; rather, God calls humans to faithfulness, to live beyond the desire to control that lies at the heart of progress. Jesus is the sure sign to Christians of God's suffering with humanity and the hope that history will unfold God's lordship over time.

Revolutionary Christology

Much of contemporary theology has been heavily influenced by liberation theology. Liberation theology emerged in the mid-twentieth century in response to the suffering of the marginalized in Latin America. The Catholic Church had long been allied with Latin America's colonial powers and the ruling class; liberation theologians sought to transform the Church so that it identified instead with the poor rather than their oppressors. Gustavo Gutierrez, regarded as the father of liberation theology, was educated within the European system, as were many of his followers. In European universities, liberation theologians appropriated the philosophical and political thought that dominated the region, a form of Marxist humanism (see the sidebar, "Marxism, Liberation Theologies, and the Catholic Church"). That political philosophy, along with the theological revolution precipitated by the Second Vatican Council, with its emphasis on the laity and its call to action on behalf of justice, contributed to the emergence of liberation theology as a distinct religious and theological movement.

While contemporary feminist theology has roots that reach back into the nineteenth century and beyond, it is closely related to liberation theology. Both theologies share a common methodological approach that runs through several distinct moments or steps:[11]

1. The suffering of the marginalized provides theology with its primary data, and a lived commitment to addressing this suffering is the starting point for theology.

2. The starting point for theological reflection is not philosophy but the social sciences, which help to explain in concrete terms how and why

---

11. See Francis Schüssler-Fiorenza, "Systematic Theology: Tasks and Methods," in *Systematic Theology: Roman Catholic Perspectives*, eds. Francis Schüssler Fiorenza and John Galvin, 2nd ed. (Minneapolis: Fortress, 2011), 47–59.

the marginalized are oppressed while also providing for ways to address that oppression.

3. The Christian tradition is to be read with a "hermeneutics (principle of interpretation) of suspicion." A hermeneutics of suspicion helps to uncover the way the Christian tradition itself has contributed to the oppression and marginalization of people.

4. A "hermeneutics of retrieval" recovers some elements of the tradition that have been omitted, lost, or suppressed in the history of the tradition; voices that have been silenced must be given recognition and new symbols need to be created and offered as the tradition is resymbolized to promote the liberation of the oppressed.

5. Praxis, or critically informed action on behalf of the marginalized, is the unique criterion for theology. The worth or value of any theology is determined by how well it promotes a way of living that remedies injustice and oppression. Praxis thus leads back to point 1: commitment to the oppressed. Additionally, this theology must maintain continuity to the proclamation of the gospel. The use of the term *praxis* affirms that liberation theologies seek a liberation that is religious, social, political, economic, and personal.

Marxism, Liberation Theologies, and the Catholic Church

The movement of European economies from an agrarian to an industrial base was coupled with political transformations, including a shift from monarchies to representative forms of government. In the midst of these tumultuous transformations, Karl Marx (1818–1883) offered a provocative analysis of social structures, economies, and governments that would change the world. Marx's thought revolved around a materialist analysis of history:

- Social development is based on the development of productive forces, which are material.
- The forces of production and the corresponding social relationships they produce progress independently of the human will.
- Society at every level is organized and stratified for production.
- The state is an instrument of repression used by the ruling class.
- When social relationships, determined by the forces of production, become a hindrance to further progress of production revolution occurs.

Marxist analysis of economic suffering and dehumanization at the hands of governments and economic interests has become an effective tool for many

Continued

Marxism, Liberation Theologies, and the Catholic Church *Continued*

theologians. In Latin America, liberation theology has frequently embraced a Marxist analysis of economic forces. The materialism of such an analysis has caused concern for many, especially among authorities in the Vatican. Liberation theologians have consistently responded that they do not subscribe to Marxism or Marxist philosophy per se, but they find Marxist analysis a useful but limited tool to do social analysis.

The rise of liberation theology in Latin America in the 1960s and 1970s, by contrast, resonated with many Christian leaders, especially the Roman Catholic bishops of Latin America. The conference of Roman Catholic bishops in Latin America (CELAM) began to express its concerns about poverty and the Catholic Church's silence on the suffering of the poor. In several conferences CELAM echoed the themes of liberation theology. The conferences at Medellin, Colombia (1968), and at Puebla, Mexico (1979), spoke of the Church "listening to the cry of the poor and becoming the interpreter of their anguish." These conferences were important moments for the articulation of the theme of liberation in Catholic theology.

During the pontificate of John Paul II the Congregation for the Doctrine of the Faith (CDF) issued a document on liberation theology expressing suspicions about the use of Marxist tools of analysis, however. "Instruction on Some Aspects of Liberation Theology" (dated August 6, 1984, and published September 3, 1984) praised the purpose of liberation theology but warned against an uncritical acceptance of atheistic Marxism as a dominant principle. This document expressed the fear that the gospel would be reduced to materialism and its call to transcendent value would be ignored. The harsh tone of this document generated a backlash. In response, the CDF issued a second document, "Instruction on Christian Freedom and Liberation" (1986), which was much more positive in tone and affirmed the Church's obligation to serve the marginalized.

Feminist Christology

Not only politics and economics have been scrutinized for their exploitative aspects. Many contemporary philosophers have analyzed the exploitative dimension of communication.[12] Within this philosophical focus on language and society, philosophers have noted that any effort to create an ideal speech situation must be preceded by an examination of the prevailing patterns of discourse within a given community. The community tends to marginalize or exclude certain voices in its discourse while canonizing certain terms and symbols that become normative. Although the field of feminist theology is quite

---

12. Elisabeth Schüssler Fiorenza, *Bread Not Stone: The Power of Feminist Biblical Interpretation* (Boston: Beacon, 1984); Rebecca S. Chopp, *The Power to Speak: Feminism, Language, God* (New York: Crossroad, 1992).

diverse, Catholic theologian Elizabeth Johnson has steered a course in her theology and especially in her Christology that makes her generally representative of the major concerns and trends of reformist Christian feminist theology.

Hermeneutics of Suspicion

Think about the pressure high school students feel to dress and act a certain way—and how those who do not conform are marginalized until they conform. The right clothes, music, movies, and friends are all part of the language of school, and that language sets up some brutal boundaries between who and what is accepted and who and what is not. Those who experience marginalization in high school understand well the power of language and symbols to exclude and brutalize.

As dominant forms of discourse are established in society, some forms of speech and symbols are privileged over others on the basis of a set of preconceived notions of what is normative. The result of this privileging is the linguistic oppression of minority voices and their identification as "dangerous" or "subversive." Linguistic oppression then becomes "natural." It achieves objective status, so that any challenge to the hegemony of a cultural symbol system is understood as a challenge to the larger social order.

Feminist hermeneutics attempt to unmask the ideology inherent in contemporary theological discourse. Feminist theologians note that theological language is necessarily imprecise and cannot "capture" the experience and reality of God directly, but it may do so analogically. Elizabeth Johnson, along with many other Catholic feminist theologians, makes use of the Thomistic tradition's approach to the limits of language.[13] Thomas Aquinas, in his work on the *analogia entis* (the analogy of being), observed that all statements about God must first be negated; this he termed the *via negativa*. To say that God is Father means first of all that God is not a father: God does not contribute genetic material to create a new life; God does not have a spouse. Rather, one's experience of fathers provides the basis for saying that God is like a father: God is faithful, strong, dependable, and loving. Such statements follow Aquinas's *via positiva*. However, every such positive statement must be rounded off by the conviction that whatever qualities fathers might possess, God's love, faithfulness, etc., are infinitely beyond that experience; this is Aquinas's *via eminentiae*.[14]

> Admittedly, in speaking about God like this, our language is using human modes of expression; nevertheless it really does attain to God

---

13. See Elizabeth A. Johnson, *She Who Is: The Mystery of God in Feminist Theological Discourse* (New York: Crossroad, 1992), 113–17.

14. Aquinas's teaching on this subject has been accepted as doctrine in the Roman Catholic Church. See also the decrees of the Fourth Lateran Council in H. Denzinger, *Enchiridion Symbolorum*, 806.

himself, though unable to express him in his infinite simplicity. Likewise, we must recall that "between Creator and creature no similitude can be expressed without implying an even greater dissimilitude" (Lateran Council IV: *DS* 806); and that "concerning God, we cannot grasp what he is, but only what he is not, and how other beings stand in relation to him" (St. Thomas Aquinas, *Summa Contra Gentiles* I, 30). (*CCC* 43)

The analogical nature of "God-talk" relativizes propositional claims about God as "Father" and "Son" and leaves room for creativity and the recovery of alternate language—including images of God as "mother" (e.g., Isaiah 42:14; 46:3–4; 66:13; Psalm 131:2; see also *CCC*, 239).

Central to feminist hermeneutics, both in the hermeneutics of suspicion and in the retrieval of the tradition, is the analysis of symbolic language. In this area, Paul Ricoeur, the French philosopher of language and symbol, has provided some key insights about the symbolic nature of language, insights commonly advanced within the context of feminist theology. Ricoeur emphasizes a "surplus of meaning" within symbolic discourse. The symbol goes beyond itself and pushes the mind of those who encounter the symbol. It provokes new ways of thinking. Feminist theology's emphasis upon the symbolic and analogical nature of theological discourse enriches the tradition by offering a wider range of language while also correcting the stagnant and distorting language of a male-dominated church.[15] Paul Tillich's account of the six characteristics of the symbol adds further dimensions to a feminist account of symbol in theology:

1. The symbol directs one to that reality which is beyond one's grasp.
2. The symbol participates in that reality.
3. The symbol opens up levels of reality that would otherwise be inaccessible.
4. The symbol emerges from a region beyond reason.
5. The symbol is dynamic, not static.
6. The symbol points to that which transcends the world.[16]

This account relativizes the symbolic discourse of the past and makes androcentric (i.e., "male centered") language open to change and improvement. The limits of such change, however, have become a source of controversy.

---

15. For a powerful discussion of this dynamic in feminist theology, see Chopp, *The Power to Speak*, especially chaps. 1 and 2.

16. Elizabeth A. Johnson, "The Symbolic Character of Theological Statements about Mary," *Journal of Ecumenical Studies* 22 (1985): 312–35, 321; see Shannon Schrein, *Quilting and Braiding: The Feminist Christologies of Sallie McFague and Elizabeth A. Johnson in Conversation* (Collegeville, MN: Liturgical, 1998), 28–29.

The Hermeneutics of Retrieval

Many feminist theologians engage the Christian tradition with a hermeneutics of suspicion and reach the conclusion that the entire tradition is so saturated with patriarchal bias that it cannot be redeemed. This radical wing insists on the creation of an entirely new religious system centered on the experience of women—only then can the misogyny of the Christian tradition be eradicated. These theologians (e.g., Mary Daly or Daphne Hampson) now describe themselves as post-Christian.

Most feminist theologians insist that the Christian tradition has not always been misogynistic. They assert that the tradition provides women with the resources to resymbolize Christianity in a way that is in keeping with the concerns of women but also preserves the integrity of the tradition.

Elizabeth Johnson does not soft-peddle the problems of the Christological tradition: "At root the difficulty lies in the fact that Christology in its story, symbol, and doctrine has been assimilated to the patriarchal world view, with the result that its liberating dynamic has been twisted into justification for domination."[17] The maleness of Jesus has been used to reinforce a patriarchal image of God, and the maleness of God marginalizes women. She quotes a passage from Augustine's *De Tinitate* to illustrate her point:

> Woman does not possess the image of God in herself, but only when taken together with the male who is her head, so that the whole substance is one image. But when she is assigned the role of helpmate, a function that pertains to her alone, then she is not the image of God.[18]

The maleness of Jesus and the patriarchal image of God, in turn, reinforce an androcentric anthropology in which the male sex is made normative. Within many Protestant churches, the differentiation between men and women and their corresponding roles in both church and society is warranted by certain passages in the New Testament (e.g., 1 Timothy 2:12; Ephesians 5:22–33; 1 Corinthians 11:7–12), but the ontology of those differences finds more robust and philosophical exposition within the Catholic tradition. For example, in Roman Catholic theology the priest acts "in the person of Christ," in the celebration of the sacraments. Consequently, the Catholic Church argues that women cannot be priests, because they cannot represent or symbolize Christ appropriately. Thus the ecclesiastical participation of women is limited in the Catholic Church, and the justification of that limitation is grounded in the essential differences between men and women. The following passage comes from a statement from the Vatican's Congregation for the Doctrine of the Faith on this issue.

---

17. Johnson, *She Who Is*, 151.

18. Augustine, *On the Trinity* 12. 10. Quoted without citation in Johnson, *Consider Jesus*, 101.

It is indeed evident that in human beings the difference of sex exercises an important influence, much deeper than, for example, ethnic differences: the latter do not affect the human person as intimately as the difference of sex, which is directly ordained both for the communion of persons and for the generation of human beings. In Biblical Revelation this difference is the effect of God's will from the beginning: "male and female he created them" (Genesis 1:27). (*Inter Insigniores*, n. 5)

For Johnson and others, a normative, male-centered anthropology puts the salvation of women in jeopardy—"What was not assumed was not redeemed" (recall Gregory Nazianzen's famous quote in the midst of the Apollinarian controversy). Christians must, therefore, reject a dualistic anthropology that envisions male and female as unique and essentializing aspects of human existence and adopt a "single-nature" anthropology. Such an anthropology does not identify an abstract "humanness" and relegate sexual difference to mere biological function (i.e., sexual difference exists only insofar as it allows humans to procreate). Rather, Johnson argues that human nature exists in "an interdependence of multiple differences," or a "multi-polar" anthropology.[19] There are many ways in which individual humans differ—height, class, religion, age—sex being merely one of them; why, then, should humans be defined by sex rather than some other factor? Differences define individual humans. If one changes any one of the differences that constitute an individual human, one in fact changes the person. One ought to celebrate diversity in order to celebrate humanity and live authentically.

In the hermeneutics of retrieval, feminist theologians seek to uncover forgotten voices within history and move them to the center. The Wisdom tradition of Israel provides an important resource for reconstructing or "resymbolizing" Christology.

The Wisdom of God in this literary tradition is figured as female in both Greek (*sophia*) and Hebrew (*hokmah*). As such, the wisdom tradition counters exclusively masculine references to God and is a powerful and often used resource for the reconstruction or resymbolization of the Christian tradition.[20] Johnson envisions several benefits to Wisdom Christology:

1. A relation to the whole cosmos is built into the Wisdom tradition so that Christology is not simply centered on humans, but also includes all of creation;

2. Wisdom Christology is able to respond favorably and inclusively to other religious traditions;

---

19. Johnson, *She Who Is*, 154–56.

20. See Elisabeth Schüssler Fiorenza, *Jesus, Miriam's Child, Sophia's Prophet: Critical Issues in Feminist Christology* (New York: Continuum, 1994), ch. 5.

3. Wisdom is connected to the poor and the oppressed;

4. Through Wisdom Christology the significance of women within the ministry of Jesus and the early church is emphasized. Johnson's retrieval and cultivation of Wisdom Christology and her movement away from Logos Christology reflects her concern to ground Christology, and indeed all theology, in the effective use of analogy and symbol.

Some Other Forms of Contemporary Feminist Theologies

The following chart shows some major forms of feminist theology that have not been discussed in this chapter. They are, in some ways, species of the more general concept "feminist theology."

Name	Basic Concerns
Eco-feminist	• Addresses the connection between patriarchy and the exploitation and violence done to the natural order • Views technological progress and globalization with great suspicion and concern, particularly for its impact on the environment
Mujerista	• Emphasizes the experience of Latinas, particularly Hispanic American women, whose stories are taken as the primary material for constructing a theology of empowerment
Womanist	• The experience of black women, viewed as being significantly different from that of the European women around whom modern "feminism" revolves, defines this liberationist theology.

Central to the Christology of many feminist theologians is the retrieval of Jesus' attitude toward women. Johnson and other reformist theologians contend that the egalitarian nature of the community of disciples was gradually lost and replaced with an imperial model of discipleship in the early centuries of the Christian era. Ideas of "lordship" and submissiveness became normative while the role of women became increasingly marginal. However, the crucified Christ enables the egalitarian and liberating character of Christian discipleship to be recovered: "The crucified Christ embodies the exact opposite of the patriarchal ideal of the powerful man, and shows the steep price paid in the struggle for liberation."[21]

In her assessment of Elizabeth Johnson's Christology, Shannon Schrein concludes that Johnson, unlike many of her fellow theologians, remains robustly within the Christian tradition and "Christ-centered" as she labors to "braid a footbridge" between Christian theology and the concerns of feminist theology. Her commitment to the principles of analogical language and the control of analogy in theology, as well as her recovery of Wisdom Christology and the egalitarian practices of Jesus and the earliest disciples, all ground her commitment to the Christian tradition. At the same time, the concerns within her Christology provide a footbridge to other religious traditions and create the possibility of transforming dialogue with religious "others."[22]

Postcolonial Christology

Colonialism had a devastating impact on the way Christianity was spread around the world in the modern era. The remnants of this impact can be observed at almost every level of the Christian church even as colonialism still pervades some forms of evangelization. In contemporary evangelical churches throughout Latin America, there has been an acute Americanization of Christianity. American missionaries not only import American technologies and organizational structures, but also their theology reflects American values and even American politics. This phenomenon is by no means new or restricted to Latin America or to evangelical Christianity. In Roman Catholic circles, the evangelization of the Americas was coextensive with the imposition of Spanish culture and Spanish Catholicism, and that influence persists.

The experience of cultural marginalization is acutely felt throughout the regions of the world in which a European or North American image of Jesus and the church have been identified with colonial powers and colonial violence. The political emancipation of many colonized nations over the past half century has been accompanied by a cultural and religious emancipation. The Eurocentric assumption of Christianity, i.e., the assumption that Christianity is *essentially* expressed within Western culture, have been called into question among indigenous peoples in South America, the Philippines, Africa, and especially, Asia. What has emerged is often called postcolonial Christology, because it addresses the violence and structural marginalization of indigenous or native peoples throughout history, especially in connection with the colonialism of European nations in the past several centuries. The following discussion will concentrate on developments in Asian postcolonial Christology.

---

21. Johnson, *She Who Is*, 161.

22. Schrein, *Quilting and Braiding*, 105–6.

⚹ Postcolonial Christology in Asia

Peter Phan has offered some important reflections on the legacy of colonialism in Asia and its impact on the church there.[23] He writes, "Imagine that the earliest disciples of Jesus had turned to the East rather than to the Greco-Roman world to carry out the Lord's 'great commission.'"[24] Previous chapters have discussed the decisive role played by Greco-Roman culture in the emergence of classical Christology.

Phan's overview of postcolonial Christology takes account of the unique factors that characterize so much of the Asian context: poverty, totalitarianism, and religious pluralism. Oppressive political systems often neglect indigenous sensibilities reflected in folklore and religion. Phan lists five neglected features of Asian religious life that might help address the violence and suffering that define the existence of most Asians: (1) introspection, (2) the religiousness of the poor and the poverty of the religious, (3) the practices of Asian religion, (4) monasticism, and (5) Asian culture in general.

⚹ C. S. Song and the Crucified People

One of the most influential postcolonial Asian Christologies is offered by the Taiwanese-born theologian Choan-Seng Song. His theology and particularly his Christology are essentially narrative. For Song, these stories serve as the vehicle for theological *satori*, a Japanese Zen term expressing sudden insight or enlightenment. Because the stories of the Asian people are stories of poverty, suffering, and powerlessness, an authentic Asian theology is necessarily a liberation theology. As such, it must not begin with abstract doctrines but with the particular sociopolitical and cultural situations of the people in which God's love and suffering are manifested in the work of liberation.

Song uses traditional Asian narratives to unpack his theology. In *The Tears of Lady Meng: a Parable of People's Political Theology*, Song retells a famous Chinese legend about a woman whose husband was conscripted to build the Great Wall.[25] After a year of waiting in vain for his return or news of his well-being, Meng decides to journey to the Great Wall. She eventually learns that he has died and is buried under a portion of the wall. At this news, she weeps so prodigiously that her tears bring down a section of the wall—the section where her husband had been buried. The workers are ordered to rebuild that section of the wall, but it always collapses. Eventually, the emperor becomes infatuated

---

23. Peter C. Phan, "The Asian Face of Jesus," *Theological Studies* 57 (1996): 399–430.

24. Ibid., 399.

25. C. S. Song, *The Tears of Lady Meng: A Parable of People's Political Theology* (New York: Orbis, 1981).

with Lady Meng and seeks to marry her. She agrees, on the condition that the emperor build a large funeral pyre for her husband. When the emperor arranges for the pyre, Lady Meng throws herself onto the fire; as her body is consumed by the flames, the ashes fall into the river and turn into silver fish.

For Song, the story illustrates both the power of the people's suffering, symbolized by Lady Meng's tears, and the political power of self-sacrifice, symbolized in Lady Meng's act of defiance against the emperor. Meng's self-sacrifice illustrates the political power of Christ's crucifixion—the power to resist and subvert the forces of oppression and tyranny and promote liberation.

Song bases his Christological trilogy (*Jesus, the Crucified People*; *Jesus and the Reign of God*; and *Jesus in the Power of the Spirit*) on the liberation theology concealed in the people's stories, folklore, mythologies, art, dance, and music.[26] Underlying his Christology is the attempt to discover how the event of the Word-becoming-flesh (John 1:14) is being continued today in the life of Asian peoples. To this end, Song suggests, the Christological hermeneutic has to be a "people hermeneutic"—one needs to discover who Jesus is by connecting to the lives of the poor, the outcasts, and the socially marginalized. For Song, God is the story of Jesus, and Jesus is the story of the people—the people who suffer.

For Song, the cross of Jesus brings together the suffering of the people with the love of God expressed in Christ, and also tells the story of human rejection and unmasks that suffering as the work of social and political powers defending their privilege and power. Song denies that the cross represents an event in the life of God (contra Moltmann); rather, the cross is the quintessential example of human violence against other humans.[27] The life and ministry of Jesus stands out in sharp contrast to such violence. In Song's meditation on Jesus' temptations, Jesus rejects the powerful and coercive tactics offered to him by satanic powers (Matthew 4:1–11). At the end of the day, Jesus stands with humanity, sharing a meal at a round (Asian) banquet table at which all have an equal place and an equal share. The question of Jesus' identity and religious significance can only be answered through negation—"Jesus is not. . . ." The question to be asked, however, is not Who is Jesus? but Where is Jesus? Song's response identifies Jesus with the marginalized and suffering, and no other continent or set of cultures has experienced the scale of suffering that has unfolded in Asia.

Chung Hyun Kyung and *Minjung* Christology

Through a variety of works, Chung Hyun Kyung has offered a comprehensive presentation of Asian women's theology as a plea to God in search of justice and

---

26. C. S. Song, *Jesus the Crucified People* (Minneapolis: Fortress, 1990); *Jesus and the Reign of God* (Minneapolis: Fortress, 1993); *Jesus in the Power of the Spirit* (Minneapolis: Fortress, 1994).

27. Ibid., 98–99.

healing.[28] Her theology begins with critical reflection on Asian women's experiences, not with the elements of the Christian tradition such as scripture, doctrines, and liturgy. Chung presents these experiences as stories of Asian women she identifies as *minjung*, a Korean word meaning "the popular mass." She identifies herself as a "second generation liberationist." The previous generation concentrated on dealing with colonialism and its impact on Asian peoples. Chung says her generation does theology autonomously, "from [their] own feelings and experiences." She argues that if Asian women theologians do not permit themselves "to fully experience who [they] are, [they] will not have the power to fight back and create [their] own space."[29]

Cosmic and Metacosmic Religiousness

The Sri Lankan Jesuit Aloysius Pieris distinguishes between "cosmic" religiousness and "metacosmic" religiousness.[30] For Pieris, cosmic religiousness is a religious disposition that is oriented toward the management of our natural environment: making the crops grow, protecting the clan or the family from enemies, ensuring procreation, etc. Cosmic religiousness is ultimately oriented toward metacosmic religiousness, in which the practical concerns of day-to-day living are subordinated to more transcendent concerns. Within metacosmic religiousness, a greater systematization of ideas and a concern for reality beyond the practical exists.

Metacosmic religiousness is able to accommodate the questions and concerns of cosmic religiousness so that many of the rituals and theologies endure within the framework supplied by the metacosmic religion. If one looks at Buddhism as it is practiced throughout Asia, then one can easily identify the interplay of shamanistic (cosmic) religions and the metacosmic concerns of Buddhist teaching: one can go to the shaman in the morning and then visit the Buddhist monastery in the afternoon for instruction from the monks without contradiction.

To what extent can Christianity accommodate cosmic religiousness with the Christian (metacosmic) system? Historically, the pre-Christian religions of northern Europe continued to influence people long after they began to embrace Christianity. Could the same hold true today?

---

28. See especially *The Struggle to Be the Sun Again: Introducing Asian Women's Theology* (Maryknoll, NY: Orbis, 1991).

29. Chung Hyun Kyung, "'*Han-pu-ri*': Do Theology from Korean Woman's Perspective," in *Frontiers in Asian Christian Theology*, ed. R. S. Sugirtharajah (Maryknoll, NY: Orbis, 1994), 52–62, 53.

30. See Aloysius Pieris, SJ, *An Asian Theology of Liberation* (Maryknoll, NY: Orbis, 1988).

Chung contends that as Asian women live through the hardship and suffering of obedience to family and society, they need a language that can give voice to that suffering as well as to their poverty and oppression by colonial forces. The most popular image of Jesus in this context is that of liberator and revolutionary, but these images are tempered with feminine images of Jesus as mother. As mother, Jesus is confrontational in the face of oppression while also compassionately suffering with those who suffer. Such images, Chung argues, help to give strength to Asian women in their struggle for justice and freedom.

In addition to passing on traditional symbols and images, Asian women theologians create their own images and symbols out of their experiences and use their own resources. One such image is of Jesus as shaman—a priestess of indigenous religious tradition who primarily offers healing and protection. Jesus is a Korean shaman who helps Asian women release the *han*, or unresolved resentment, indignation, and sense of helplessness and total abandonment in the face of the cumulative injustice and suffering of the *minjung*. In the context of Korean folk religion, *han*-ridden ghosts often wander the country looking for justice and revenge. Chung sees in such lore the politics of memory and the need to address the countless thousands who have died unjustly and who cry out for justice. As the shaman who rids people of *han*, Christ signals the importance of memory and exorcism through resistance, suffering, and witness.

Chung points to the problem of a "high-descending" approach to Christology for the *minjung*. In an Asian context, with the blend of folk religion and forms of Buddhism, such a Christology makes little sense. Chung cites Lee Oo Chung and her account of how traditional Korean gods achieved their status after death.[31] For these figures, divinity came about through a series of trials and suffering. With persistence and through suffering, these figures successfully negotiated a variety of challenges to achieve divine status. Chung Hyun Kyung identifies this as the approach of an Asian women's Christology: not by looking for "rescue" but through faithful witness, through suffering, and even through bloodshed, Asian women can find union with God.

Conclusion

Can contemporary Christians still affirm the traditional Christological doctrines? Can the truth affirmed in these doctrines be separated from the way they are formulated? Are modern Christians free to innovate in their theology? If so, are there any limits? This chapter has explored contemporary concerns regarding the credibility of the Christian faith and the desire to reappropriate the tradition

---

31. Lee Oo Chung, "Korean Cultural and Feminist Theology," *In God's Image* (1987): 34, cited in Chung Hyun Kyung, "Who Is Jesus for Asian Women?" in *Asian Faces of Jesus*, ed. R. S. Sugirtharajah (Maryknoll, NY: Orbis, 1993), 230–31.

in a manner and language suitable for the present age. It has also noted that such a reappropriation can also collide with core beliefs. The attempts to negotiate the limits of innovative interpretations of traditional Christianity can raise troubling theological and ecclesiological issues. The work of Asian postcolonial theologians further complicates matters as it reappropriates the tradition while at the same time engages non-Christian religious traditions as a primary source for doing theology. In the following chapter, the limits of a Christian commitment to Jesus are pointedly explored as we raise the question of Jesus' unique offer of salvation and the presence of other religions and their savior figures.

Questions for Understanding

1. What is bias? Distinguish between individual, group, and general bias.
2. Describe Girard's notion of mimetic desire and the scapegoat mechanism.
3. What are the three steps or moments in Lonergan's "law of the cross"?
4. Contrast the soteriology articulated by Lonergan and Loewe with the approach offered by Anselm and the Reformers discussed in chapter 6?
5. Why is an appreciation of the analogical nature of language and theology so central to feminist theology?
6. Describe Johnson's "multi-polar" anthropology. Why is this so important for her Christology?
7. What are the distinctive factors that make doing theology in an Asian context unique?

Questions for Reflection and Action

1. Do Christological doctrines help to transform lives, or are they an obstacle to such transformation? What Christological doctrines do you think most effectively promote transformation? Explain.
2. Moltmann has leveled a robust critique of modern accounts of history as "progress" and the way the Christian church has been co-opted in such accounts of history. Stanley Hauerwas, an admirer of Moltmann's theology, has argued that Christians must live "out of control" in order to challenge the prevailing notions of progress and success. Can you think of people famous or not so famous whose "out of control" lives helped to subvert prevailing assumptions about "progress"?
3. Chapter 5 mentioned the Apollinarian controversy and Gregory Nazianzen's famous maxim, "What was not assumed is not redeemed." At the end of that chapter, one of the review questions asked if the depiction of Christ as a woman was problematic. Given what Elizabeth Johnson has

written, has your opinion changed? Explain. Do such "resymbolizations" of Christianity pose any problems? Are there any limits to resymbolizing the Christian faith?

For Further Reading

Moltmann, Jürgen. *The Crucified God: The Cross of Christ as the Foundation and Criticism of Christian Theology.* Minneapolis: Fortress, 1994.

Phan, Peter C. *Christianity with an Asian Face.* Maryknoll, NY: Orbis, 2003.

Schüssler Fiorenza, Elisabeth. *Jesus, Miriam's Child Sophia's Prophet: Critical Issues in Feminist Christology.* New York: Continuum, 1994.

CHAPTER 8

Jesus and Other Religions

"I am the way and the truth and the life. No one comes to the Father except through me" (John 14:6). Passages such as this, found throughout the New Testament, testify to the faith of the earliest Christians in Jesus' decisive role as mediator of God's offer of salvation. The discussion of soteriology in chapter 7 emphasized that for Christians this offer of salvation is made real and effective in the lives of people through transformation, or conversion. The story of Jesus mediates this transformation, but can Christian theology envision one having this experience of conversion apart from an explicit faith in Jesus?[1]

Some Christians worry that an affirmative response to that question makes Jesus' role irrelevant or, at best, merely pragmatic—if his story helps one to be converted, great; if not, one can find something else. The Christian interpretation of biblical passages like the one just quoted has shifted in recent decades as Christians become increasingly aware that they are not alone. Christians no longer have to imagine non-Christians in a distant land and theorize about how they might or might not be saved. Non-Christians are no longer a hypothetical or imaginary construct; for most Christians living in North America, for example, non-Christians are now neighbors, classmates, best friends, spouses, parents, or children. Religious pluralism has become a much more concrete and intimate reality than in previous eras.

Two factors have contributed substantially to this development: (1) the collapse of an exclusively Christian culture has led to more privatized religious commitments and has brought to an end social pressures to self-identify as Christian; (2) technology has dramatically increased the mobility and interactions of the world's population. These changes have put Western Christians increasingly in direct contact with non-Christians. No longer must churches send missionaries to remote and exotic lands to "discover" non-Christians.

---

1. See William P. Loewe, "Lonergan and the Law of the Cross: A Universalist View of Salvation," *Anglican Theological Review* 59 (1977): 162–74.

The significance of religious pluralism for Christians can be grasped more appropriately when considered in light of the experience of suffering. Christians believe that much of human suffering is the result of sin (e.g., injustice, oppression, greed), and that salvation—the solution to the problem of sin—is accomplished in Christ. As previously discussed, Christian silence in the face of that suffering represents one of the greatest obstacles to the credibility of Christian faith and the intelligibility of Christianity's claim that salvation has come to the world in Jesus. Christians are called to address the problem of suffering; does this not require Christians to cooperate with non-Christians to eliminate suffering? What can Christians say about those who, out of their own (non-Christian) religious convictions, join with Christians to address the problem of suffering? This chapter will explore the question of religious pluralism by first discussing theologies of religious pluralism and the controversies surrounding them.

Traditional Christian Response to Religious Pluralism

The second-century bishop Cyprian of Carthage famously wrote, "Outside the church there is no salvation."[2] Originally Cyprian directed this statement at Christians who threatened to leave or left the church community to practice the faith on their own. Cyprian declared that such a move placed one outside the church or, employing Paul's metaphor, separated one from the "body" of Christ. Today, the maxim "outside the church there is no salvation" has come to signify a position called exclusivism. The exclusivist position states that without explicit faith in Christ and the correlative participation in the life of the church, one cannot find salvation. The rationale runs as follows: Christ is God's definitive offer of salvation. If there is salvation through some other means, then Christ would not be God's definitive offer of salvation but simply one option among many.

An exclusivist position may be articulated in terms of the institutional church, what is called an ecclesiocentric position: "You must be a member of the institutional church in order to be saved." However, that is not the only interpretation. Many conservative evangelical Christians articulate an exclusivist position without any reference to church membership. Instead, they focus upon an explicit faith in Jesus: one prays to God, confessing and repenting one's sins, accepting Christ as Lord, and receiving God's offer of salvation and "new birth" in Christ (John 3:5). Apart from an explicit faith claim, one cannot be saved, though in the case of one who has no possibility of articulating an informed faith—as, for example, in the death of an infant—pastoral practice has usually affirmed the child's salvation.

---

2. *Letter* 73 (To Iubaianus), 21. The phrasing usually cited in church history is, "*extra ecclesiam nulla salus est*," but the actual next of Cyprian reads, "*salus extra ecclesiam non est.*"

Some readers may be surprised to learn that the exclusivist position is still widely held today. Its logic is clear and simple, it reinforces the importance of faith in Christ, and it offers a rationale for missionary efforts (Matthew 28:16–20).

Christians have long reflected on religious pluralism and the theological principle of God's unbounded mercy and desire that all might be saved. At many points throughout the history of Christianity, Christians have articulated notions of faith and grace that included those outside the visible church. In the early church one finds the notion that God was present in other religions "preparing" people for the advent of the gospel.[3] Others, like Nicholas of Cusa (1401–1461), went even further. Nicholas offered a visionary treatise in which Christ (along with Sts. Peter and Paul) affirmed truth in the various religions and summoned them to unity and peace.[4] Official Roman Catholic teaching, though not always the champion of tolerance toward non-Christian religions, developed a theology of religions with two documents issued by the Second Vatican Council, or Vatican II (1962–1965).[5]

Religious Pluralism at Vatican II

Vatican II was a watershed in ecumenical relations and in the theology of religious pluralism, and its impact was felt well beyond the confines of Roman Catholicism. One of the most highly anticipated documents to come out of the Second Vatican Council was the Dogmatic Constitution on the Church, known by its Latin title *Lumen gentium*. Instead of defining "the church" through legal and structural models, as was the norm in previous centuries, *Lumen gentium* used a far more relational model. Rather than defining the boundaries of the church or the offices of ministry within the church, *Lumen gentium* emphasized the living presence of the Triune God in the life of the church. In so doing, *Lumen gentium* was able to offer a more expansive account of the church that included those who did not hold explicit faith in Jesus.

> Nor is God remote from those who in shadows and images seek the unknown God, because he gives to all [people] life and breath and all things (Acts 17:25–28), and because the Savior wills all [people] to be saved (1 Timothy 2:4). Those who, through no fault of their own, do not know the Gospel of Christ or his Church, but who nevertheless seek God with a sincere heart, and, moved by grace, try in their actions

3. E.g., Justin Martyr, Origen, Clement of Alexandria.

4. Nicholas of Cusa, *The Peace of Faith* (*De pace fidei*), various editions.

5. Translations are from A. Flannery, *Vatican II: Conciliar and Post-Conciliar Documents* (Boston: Daughters of St. Paul, 1988).

Religion, Tolerance, and Armed Conflict: Islam and Christianity

Islam terms Christians and Jews "People of the Book" and regards them as having heard the revelation of God, albeit imperfectly. While both the Moslem and the Christian faiths decree tolerance and love, the history of both religious traditions is marred by violence.

Since the time of the Roman emperor Theodosius I (around 381 CE) Christians inaugurated various forms of persecution against those who opposed them. For the most part, Christianity spread peacefully in its early centuries, largely through the missionary work of Celtic monks. However, after the leader of a tribe or nation had accepted the Christian faith, any member of that tribe or nation who resisted conversion was persecuted, often violently. In the second millennium, Christian armies embraced the notion of a crusade, a war undertaken as a religious duty. When Pope Urban II called for the First Crusade (1095), he employed the rhetoric of holy war: it was an obligation for Christian knights to secure the Holy Land from the Saracens, as Christians then termed followers of Islam. Throughout the Middle Ages and well into the modern period, European Christians regularly legitimated violence against non-Christians in crusades and in the colonization of Africa and the Americas. Even war against other Christians was embraced as a sacred duty, as in the Thirty Years War (i.e., the sixteenth century European wars fought in the wake of the Reformation).

An egregious example of Christian violence against Moslems and Jews occurred in Spain in the early sixteenth century. Following the conquest of the last Moslem outpost in Spain, the victorious Christians expelled those Jews and Moslems who would not convert to Christianity and persecuted with great vigor those who did convert because they feared that these conversions were not genuine.

The expulsion of Jews and Moslems from Spain stands in sharp contrast to the relative peace and religious tolerance that Spain had enjoyed in some areas under Moslem control. Places like Toledo, an ancient center of Christianity before the Moslem invasion in the eighth century, became diverse and thriving cities, with relative harmony between Moslem rulers and Jewish and Christian merchants and officials. In fact, many scholars today paint a portrait of religious toleration in the history of the Moslem world that stands in sharp contrast with the caricature of Moslem intolerance many Westerners construct based on generalizations and assumptions emerging from contemporary events. While the historical situation is complex, Christians, Moslems, and Jews have persecuted one another violently (one must include the Palestinian-Israeli conflict), but these persecutions should be kept in perspective and read in light of a nuanced reading of a complex and intertwined history. Tolerance and peaceful coexistence is not a utopian ideal, but a fact of history.

to do his will as best they know it through the dictates of their own conscience—those too may achieve eternal salvation (cf. DS 3869–72). Nor shall divine providence deny the assistance necessary for salvation to those who, without any fault of theirs, have not arrived at an explicit knowledge of God, and who, not without grace, strive to lead a good life. Whatever good or truth is found amongst them is considered by the church to be preparation for the Gospel and given by him who enlightens all [people] that they may at length have life. (*Lumen gentium*, n. 16)

In a related document, "The Declaration on the Relation of the Church to Non-Christian Religions," or *Nostra aetate*, a similar chord is struck.

The Catholic Church rejects nothing of what is true and holy in these [non-Christian] religions. She has a high regard for the manner of life and conduct, the precepts and doctrines, which although differing in many ways from her own teaching, nevertheless often reflect a ray of that truth which enlightens all men [and women]. Yet she proclaims and is duty bound to proclaim without fail, Christ who is the way, the truth and the life (John 1:6). In him, in whom God reconciled all things to himself (2 Corinthians 5:18–19), men [and women] find the fullness of their religious life.

The Church, therefore, urges her sons [and daughters] to enter with prudence and charity into discussion and collaboration with members of other religions. Let Christians, while witnessing to their own faith and way of life, acknowledge, preserve and encourage the spiritual and moral truths found among non-Christians, also their social life and culture. (*Nostra aetate*, n. 2)

The position articulated at Vatican II, and embraced by many Christian churches, has generally come to be termed an inclusivist position.[6] Like the exclusivist approach, the inclusivist position understands Christ to be the universal savior and the only means of salvation. However, unlike the exclusivist approach, the inclusivist model affirms that the saving mystery of Christ is not limited to those who explicitly express faith in Christ, neither is it limited to the visible boundaries of the church but reaches followers of other religious traditions as well. For the inclusivist, Christ is the unique mediator between God and humanity, but the saving action of God in Christ is realized through the Spirit, which brings the God-fearing people inside the church together with God-fearing people outside it. The church is not superfluous in this case; rather, the

---

6. Mainline Protestant theology is reflected in the statements from the World Council of Churches, particularly in the "Guidelines on Dialogue with People of Living Faiths and Ideologies" (1979), which is more practical than doctrinal in its inclusivism.

church is the visible sign of Christ's saving work in the world, but it is not the *exclusive* vehicle of that work. Those who are outside the visible confines of the church and have no knowledge of the gospel per se find the salvation that only comes through Christ, but they find it in the religious traditions to which they belong. These traditions inspire faith in God and offer the means to respond to God. The inclusivist model tries to demonstrate that Christ is present in these traditions, albeit anonymously.

Karl Rahner and the Anonymous Christian

Karl Rahner (1904–1984) strove to overcome the extrinsicism of popular Roman Catholic imagination and prominent Protestant theologians such as Karl Barth who emphasized God's "intervention" in the created order. An "extrinsic" view of revelation and grace understands God as "coming down from heaven" to achieve his saving work. Building upon the studies of scholars seeking to integrate the work of Kant and Aquinas (e.g., Joseph Maréchal), Rahner developed a theology in which the human was the focal point of God's revelation and the foundation of theology. This anthropological orientation focused on the act of knowing or understanding at the heart of human existence and emphasized the human capacity to know and love God.

Rahner believed that every act of knowing contains within it an orientation toward infinite Being as the a priori condition (the condition for the possibility) of knowing or understanding. Consider the following analogy: when reading this book, one focuses on the various clusters of letters that are read as words, and these words have meaning. However, there is also the paper "behind the letters," which allows the letters to have form and allows them to be read. The paper acts as a condition for the possibility of reading. Rahner uses the term *horizon* to describe the limit of one's field of knowledge, the background that makes knowing possible. Yet, there is always something more, something beyond, to be known. As finite things present themselves to one's senses one can inquire after them and know them, but one never get to the end of the horizon, for it is constantly moving back to disclose even more to be known. The infinitude of reality becomes increasingly apparent. In all acts of understanding or knowing, Rahner contends, there is already present a preapprehension of Being, or, what is ultimately real: God. Rahner is careful not simply to equate being human with knowing God; after all, there needs to be room for what Christians call "grace." Yet, for Rahner, there is a close connection between human nature's capacity to experience God's grace and the actual experience of that grace.

When discussing non-Christian religions, Rahner begins with humanity's capacity for and experience of God's self-communication. This anthropological starting point serves as the basis to account for the salvation of those who do not know Christ explicitly. Though he maintains his Christocentric theology—Christ is the lens through which everything is to be viewed—he does not negate other religions, for God willed these religions as a kind of preparation for the gospel. The salvific power of other religions, however, is to be understood and affirmed only through Christ. Therefore, other religions do not enjoy theological autonomy—their validity and salvific power are mediated by Christ. Practitioners of these other faiths are, in fact, "anonymous Christians." He grounds the logic of the "anonymous Christian" in the realization that the vast majority of humans in history have not known Christ. He asks,

> Can the Christian believe even for a moment that the overwhelming mass of his brothers not only those before the appearance of Christ right back to the most distance past (whose horizons are constantly extended by paleontology) but also those of the present and of the future before us, are unquestionably and in principle excluded from the fulfillment of their lives and condemned to eternal meaninglessness? He must reject any suggestion, and his faith is itself in agreement with his doing so. For the Scriptures tell him expressly that God wants everyone to be saved (1 Timothy 2:4).[7]

However, precisely how does this love embrace all? For Rahner, true Christian faith is often *lived* by many who do not possess the *name* "Christian."

> [The human], in experiencing [this] transcendence, [this] limitless openness—no matter how implicit and incomprehensible it always is—also already experiences the offer of grace—not necessarily *as* grace, as distinctively supernatural calling, but experiences the reality of its content.[8]

Perhaps the classic example of what Rahner means in this last passage would be Gandhi. As a devout Hindu, Gandhi was committed to nonviolence, identified with the cause of the oppressed, and heroically brought freedom and a measure of justice to a subcontinent reeling from more than a century of colonial exploitation and oppression. Gandhi is said to have remarked that it was a pity that Christians did not seem to listen to Jesus: "I like your Christ, but I do not like your Christians." For Rahner, and to some degree for all inclusivists, Gandhi was an example of a Christian in every sense of the word, only without the name "Christian." Inclusivists could, therefore, affirm the salvation of Gandhi—he was saved because Christ was present in his life through the power of the Spirit despite that he did not profess a Christian faith.

---

7. Karl Rahner, "Anonymous Christian," in *Theological Investigations* (New York: Seabury, 1974), 6:391.

8. Rahner, "Anonymous Christian," 391.

This is essentially the idea embodied in the documents from Vatican II quoted previously. It must be noted, however, that in the documents of Vatican II there is no affirmation of other religions as such—only of Christ being present in "elements" of the religious tradition.

Some Protestant theologians have espoused similar positions, albeit from very different theological starting points. Karl Barth, for instance, who utterly

Christian Perspectives on Religious Pluralism

Exclusivism	Inclusivism	Pluralism
This approach often focuses on the importance of the church, in which case it is termed *ecclesiocentric*, or church-centered. It states that without explicit faith in Jesus Christ and incorporation into the Christian church, one is lost. The famous phrase from Cyprian of Carthage summarizes this position: "Outside the church there is no salvation." This position was once the norm throughout the Christian church. It is still popular in many conservative Evangelical churches but is less popular in mainline denominations churches.	This approach emphasizes the unique priority of the Christian faith while at the same time acknowledging that elements of truth are found in other religions. The inclusivist position identifies those elements of truth as preparation for the gospel, and to the extent that adherents of these religions respond favorably to God's call, they can be saved. However, they are saved through the work of Christ. Karl Rahner coined the phrase "anonymous Christian" to describe those people who, without sharing in the public life of the Christian church or making an explicit confession of faith in Christ, nonetheless, share in the life of grace. Official Roman Catholic teaching is inclusivist.	This approach to other religions has emphasized the relativity of truth claims and claims of privileged revelation. The pluralist position suggests that the result of historical criticism of the doctrines and practices of any religious tradition reveals a culturally bound system rather than the deposit of a pure, unadulterated revelation. The pluralist position advocates a sense of silence and awe in the face of the divine mystery to which all human experience of religion is related. The pluralist position can be theocentric (centered on God), pneumatocentric (centered on the experience of the Holy Spirit), or regnocentric (centered on the experience of God's kingdom).

rejected the methodology of Rahner, nonetheless affirmed the basic tenets of anonymous Christianity and inclusivism.[9]

Christology and Pluralism at the Turn of the Century

The inclusivist position has many points of strength: it affirms the unique role of Christ as the mediator of God's saving work but also provides a way to understand the salvation of non-Christians. Yet many object to the idea of the anonymous Christian as patronizing and demeaning. They assert that this model says, in effect, "Although you think you are a devout Moslem, you are really a good Christian—you just don't realize it!" How would a devout Christian feel if a Hindu came up to her and said that she was a great devotee of Siva, it was just a pity that she did not realize it? Since Vatican II, many have moved beyond the inclusivist paradigm to embrace a real pluralistic theology.

The pluralist approach rejects the inclusivist model for its uncompromising affirmation of Christianity over and against other religious traditions. Pluralists also reject inclusivism's tendency to view other religious traditions in relationship to Christianity; other faiths are seen as incomplete realizations of Christianity and not as self-sufficient religious traditions in their own right. Inclusivism assumes that Christianity is the yardstick by which all other traditions must be evaluated. Consequently, inclusivism makes interreligious dialogue impossible because it refuses to accord equal respect to other faith traditions. A paradigm shift is, therefore, necessary.

Theocentric Pluralism

John Hick, a noted English philosopher of religion, has proposed just such a shift in Christian theology away from Jesus.[10] Hick urges that a "Jesus-centered" (Christocentric) approach to God and religious pluralism be replaced with a "God-centered" (theocentric) approach. He argues that every religious faith is a historical-cultural realization of the human experience of divine reality. He does not mean, however, that all religions are of equal value. Rather, Hick seeks to move the question of interreligious dialogue toward an assessment of religious

---

9. See Karl Barth, *Church Dogmatics*, 14 vols., ed. and trans. G. W. Bromiley and T. F. Torrance (Edinburgh: T & T Clark, 1956–75), vol. IV/1, 688. Although most read Barth's theology of revelation and the abolition of religion in volume 1 of his *Church Dogmatics* as expressing a thoroughgoing negative assessment of pluralism, Barth's ecclesiological humility and emphasis on the sovereignty of God nuances his position more than many would admit (see, *Church Dogmatics*, vol. I/2 section 17).

10. For most of what follows see John Hick, *God and the Universe* (New York: St. Martin's, 1973) and his essay "Jesus and the World Religions," in *The Myth of God Incarnate*, ed. John Hick (London: SCM, 1977), 167–85.

traditions on the basis of their relative ability or inability to approach two objectives: (1) effective mediation of the divine reality, (2) promotion of a soteriology that seeks a "limitless better quality of human existence which comes about in the transition from self-centeredness to Reality-centeredness."[11]

Jesus fits into all of this as a relative experience of God. For those who confess Jesus as Lord, Jesus may indeed save them insofar as their lives have been transformed according to the principles stated previously. The language of the Incarnation and the metaphysical concepts that governed the theoretical aspects of this doctrine must not be taken literally because they are, for Hick, merely historically conditioned (i.e., mythological) statements about God. This does not, however, mean that these statements and doctrines should not be taken seriously as "God-talk," but because one cannot have firm knowledge about God, all such talk must be circumscribed by humility and agnosticism.

Hick's proposal resonates with highly pluralistic religious culture like that found in India. Raimundo Panikkar, a Catholic priest born in Spain to Spanish and Indian parents, has lived in India for many years. He proposes an ecumenism, a unity among religions of the world, within a diversity based upon the acceptance of the "transcendental principle" that forms the basis for all religious experience.[12] Panikkar insists on the importance of religious diversity as a guard against any move to favor one particular tradition, or against simplistic understandings of the divine reality.

Within this diversity Panikkar develops the distinction between the "Universal Christ" and the "particular Jesus." For Panikkar, "Christ" is the universal symbol for salvation that cannot be objectified as a merely historical personage. However, what Panikkar calls "the cosmotheandric fact of Jesus" must be affirmed. That is, in Jesus, Christians recognize God's connection to the world and specifically to human nature but not to the exclusion of other concrete occurrences of this phenomenon (e.g., Shakyamuni,

Raimundo Panikkar

© Juliet Van Otteren

---

11. John Hick, "On Grading Religions," *Religious Studies* 17 (1981): 451–67; 463, 467.

12. For what follows see Raimundo Panikkar, *The Unknown Christ of Hinduism*, rev. ed. (Maryknoll, NY: Orbis, 1981).

The Incarnation of God in Hinduism: The Avatars of Vishnu

Vishnu, along with Shiva and Brahman, is one of the chief deities within Hinduism. He is often called "the Preserver" and is characterized as loving, benevolent, and playful. Vishnu, of all the Hindu gods, is concerned with humans and creation, so much so that he inserts himself into human events to bring about balance and harmony in the universe. Vishnu has several avatars, or historical manifestations, that have appeared nine different times, with one still to come. The major avatars include Rama, Krishna, and for many Hindus, the Buddha.

Krishna is one of the most popular avatars of Vishnu. In the Hindu epic the Puranas, Krishna is depicted as a playful, often mischievous, cow herder who attracts the beautiful Radha with his flute playing. Krishna leaves Radha to go on a heroic mission and never returns. In the Hindu festival of Holi, women from Radah's village ceremonially beat the boys from Krishna's village. Additionally, Krishna appears in the Bhagavad Gita as the charioteer of Arjuna on the eve of a great battle. Krishna instructs the young warrior on the importance of his duty as a warrior and warns him to shun all attachments.

Rama, the hero of the Ramayana, is another avatar of Vishnu. The Ramayana narrates the story. Rama has his wife, Sita, kidnapped by Ravana, the demon-king of Lanka. The Ramayana recounts how Rama, along with the help his brother-in-law (Lakshman) and the army of monkeys led by Hanuman, defeats the demon and rescues Sita when the powerful goddess Durga gives him the secret of how to kill Ravana.

Kalki is the tenth avatar of Vishnu. He is often pictured with a horse's head but also as a man riding a horse. He carries with him a sword with which he will judge the wicked and reward the virtuous at the end of the world.

Krishna, etc.). Panikkar adopts the Hindu concept of the avatar, or the incarnation of deity common among Vaishnavites in Hinduism. Vaishnavites are devotees of Vishnu who recognize that Vishnu has been incarnated at various points in history as the humans Rama and Krishna, among others. Panikkar applies this concept of episodic incarnation to Christ and suggests that there is a functional equivalence between Christ and other saviors.

The theocentric perspectives of Hick and Panikkar place God at the center of all the religious traditions of the world and stress that God has been manifested or revealed in various ways to different peoples in history. The diversity of religious traditions manifests the intersection between the divine mystery and the diversity of cultures and histories through which that mystery has been mediated. For example, all of the religious language used to describe Jesus in the New Testament has its origins in the Jewish and Greek world of the first century. Additionally, the classical Christological doctrines of the fourth and fifth centuries were all formulated within the particular contexts of philosophical and theological disputes characteristic of those places and times. In fact, the difficulty modern Christians experience in understanding and appropriating those doctrines bears witness to their cultural remoteness.

This phenomenon of historical contingency is true not just for the Christian tradition but also for Buddhism, Islam, Hinduism, and all other religious traditions. In other words, all religions are in the same historically contingent boat. So is everything relative? Proponents of the theocentric position assert that the variety of religious traditions serve to complement each other in their differences. Dialogue is not only possible in this context, but also essential. In that case, the dialogue envisioned by Vatican II is seen as real dialogue—Christians have nothing to gain or loose if they already possess the fullness of revelation.

Spirit Christology and Roger Haight

The contemporary problem of religious pluralism came to a head recently in the case of the prominent American Jesuit theologian Roger Haight. Haight issued his major work, *Jesus, Symbol of God*, in 1999 and has endured scrutiny and criticism ever since.[13] The book articulates a distinctive and challenging Christological vision that created a firestorm of controversy.

The book begins with a methodological proposal that theology must be done in dialogue with the postmodern world. It is through postmodern convictions about the intelligibility of ancient doctrines that Haight proceeds to narrate and assess classical Christology. He argues that the postmodern world is radically pluralistic in its outlook and challenges the Christian claim of religious superiority and Christ as the absolute savior inherent in ancient Logos Christology. Differentiating between faith (the trusting abandonment to the transcendent God) and belief (the historically conditioned formulas that give concrete expression to the experience of faith), Haight argues for a fundamental change in Christian beliefs. Creeds are themselves the product of dialogue with particular cultures—recall the Greek philosophical terms and ideas at the heart of the debates at Nicea and Chalcedon.[14]

The language of the great Christological councils was theoretical in some respects; recall how *homoousios* was used as a technical, nonsymbolic term, to overcome Arian interpretations of the creed. Nevertheless, symbolic language remained primary in Christian discourse. In fact, the classical statement of Christology affirms that Christ is both human and divine—not one or the other—so a tension remains at the heart of Christian faith. Haight's

---

13. Roger Haight, SJ, *Jesus, Symbol of God* (Maryknoll, NY: Orbis, 1999).
14. E.g., *ousia* and *hypostasis*.

characterization of Jesus as "symbol of God" is meant to capture this tension and make use of it constructively. For Haight, when Christians affirm that Jesus is the symbol or sacrament of God, they mean that in Christ they have had the experience of God.

Haight contends that such an affirmation neither puts Jesus in competition with other religious traditions nor precludes the possibility that God would be revealed in other concrete historical mediations. The Christian encounter with God in Christ, like all encounters with the divine, can only be critically grasped and expressed through symbol and metaphor. To deny this fact is to introduce a theology that does not respect the reality of human encounters with the Divine—encounters that are essentially analogical. Through such analogical perception, through the play of ideas and metaphors, through symbols, one is schooled in the things of God, in religious language, which is understood as the disclosure of God's real presence to us. For "without a sense of God's transcendent mystery, without a healthy agnostic sense of what one does not know of God, one will not expect to learn more of God from what has been communicated to us human beings through other revelations and religions."[15] Christian language concerning Christ must respect this sense.

Haight believes that a Spirit Christology is the appropriate direction for contemporary Christology. In Spirit Christology, it is the Spirit of God who dwells within the human Jesus from the first moments of his existence. Such an approach is in keeping, he argues, with the best insights of the Antiochene school of Christology.[16] He argues that a Spirit Christology is faithful to the biblical testimony, as well as the decrees from Nicaea and Chalcedon, while at the same time providing the capacity to affirm the salvific presence of God in other religious traditions. For Haight, Jesus mediates a revelatory encounter with God. Yet God is immediately and immanently present to all creatures, and this immanent encounter with God is always described as the presence of God's Spirit. The Spirit, universally present in the history of the world, is revealed in Christ, works for the salvation of all and is not confined to one historical moment.

Salvation is, therefore, not so much caused by Christ as it is revealed in Christ. Christ *causes salvation for Christians* insofar as he enacts God's saving presence among them, but this is not to the exclusion of other mediations—mediations that can act independently of Christ. Haight sees this move as preserving Christian convictions regarding the saving work of Christ while at the same time affording recognition of God's saving presence, equally active and effective, in other religious traditions.

---

15. Ibid., 417.

16. See, e.g., the orthodox theology of Theodore of Mopsuestia, discussed in chapter 5.

Jacques Dupuis and Participated Mediations

Jacques Dupuis (1923–2004), a Belgian Jesuit, articulates a highly nuanced position that moves beyond the affirmations of Vatican II but does not go as far as the pluralist position.[17] For Dupuis, a Christian theology of religious pluralism must always affirm that Jesus is at the center of God's plan of salvation for the world. However, such an affirmation must also be nuanced and move beyond the inclusivist talk of "anonymous Christians." Dupuis affirms that Christ is the way of salvation and the universal mediator of God's universal offer of salvation. Dupuis affirms, along with Vatican II's *Lumen gentium*, that Jesus Christ is the sacrament of God. Through Jesus, God acts in history to bring about salvation, and this action reaches people in a variety of ways. However, the precise articulation of this "variety of ways" remains elusive. In an effort to construct a more Christocentric and pluralist theology of religious pluralism, Dupuis surveys a variety of modifications to the theocentric approach previously discussed.

One such modification emphasizes the "reign of God" as the appropriate paradigm. Chapter 2, on the ministry of Jesus, described how the reign of God denotes a relationship with God that is present now but will find fulfillment in the eschaton. Through this approach, Christians can affirm the relationship with God found and promoted in other religious traditions and that the fullness of that relationship is still to come. This approach has the merit of showing that the followers of other religious traditions are already members of "the reign of God" in history and that together with Christians they are destined to meet in God as pilgrims at the end of time. However, such an approach, Dupuis concludes, neglects the fact that Christians affirm that the reign of God has broken into history in Jesus and that it is through Christ and the work of the Spirit that all humans come to participate God's reign. So, Dupuis concludes, the reign of God paradigm necessarily emphasizes the centrality of Christ.

Dupuis also considers the Spirit-centered, or pneumatocentric, proposal. This modification to the theocentric approach involves the recognition—taken from the language of Vatican II—that the Holy Spirit is universally present and active in the religious traditions of the world. God's Spirit has always been active and continues to be active in the religious life of humans outside the Christian community. The Spirit inspires people to obey God and accept God's grace. However, such an emphasis, though true in every sense, cannot be divorced from the Christian account of the universal role of the risen Christ. The work of the Holy Spirit is essentially bound to the universal action of the risen Christ. The Spirit's saving function consists in calling people to Christ: Christ, not the Spirit, is at the center. Thus Christocentric and pneumatocentric approaches cannot be alternatives; rather, they are essentially bound together.

---

17. Jacques Dupuis, SJ, *Towards a Christian Theology of Religious Pluralism* (Maryknoll, NY: Orbis, 1997).

For Dupuis, various attempts to move away from a Christocentric approach to the problem of religious pluralism are inadequate. When understood properly from a Christian perspective, all other paradigms lead back to a Christocentric position. A Christian theology of religious pluralism, as a *Christian* theology, must be Christocentric and bring out the full dimension of the mystery of God's self-disclosure in Christ. Such an approach must demonstrate that members of other religious traditions share in the reign that God established in history through Christ and that the Spirit of Christ is active among them working for their salvation.

Any account of the saving work of Christ, Dupuis argues, cannot posit a "personal" distinction between the divine Son and the historical human, Jesus of Nazareth. At the same time, however, one must always distinguish between the two natures of Christ. Without this distinction, the two operations of Christ become utterly confused: as a human, Christ cannot operate as infinite or divine. The Third Council of Constantinople (680) affirmed that Christ had two centers of operation and two wills. The "unconfused" natures, affirmed at Chalcedon, retain their proper operation and "energies."

This last point is important, for in the Incarnation, the divine nature of the Son is not lost or diminished, it does not lose its essential characteristics and

Pope John Paul II and the Relationship between Christians and Jews

Pope John Paul II (1920–2005) was born Karol Józef Wojtyła in the Polish town of Wadowice. In his youth, he was fortunate to be part of a community comprised of both Jews and Christians. In fact, one of his lifelong friends was a Jewish man named Jerzy Kluger. He witnessed first hand the impact of Christian anti-Semitism as many Poles turned on their neighbors and cooperated in Hitler's "Final Solution." When he became pope in 1978, he tirelessly devoted himself to the issue of interreligious dialogue. He encouraged dialogue with the representatives of non-Christian religions, particularly in several prayer meetings at Assisi. His care and concern for the Jewish people and for Jewish-Christian relations drew particular attention. He was the first pope since the first century to visit a synagogue; he prayed for the Jewish people at the Wailing Wall in Jerusalem; and he approved the letter that recognized and expressed contrition for the role Christians played in the Holocaust. Perhaps most importantly, he approved revolutionary guidelines for implementing in Christian catechesis *Nostra aetate*, Vatican II's declaration on non-Christian Religions, which also affirmed the continuing validity of Israel's call and covenant without neglecting the universal salvific mission of Christ.

functions. For Dupuis, the distinction between the two natures and their operations allows for a discussion of the Son's saving activity in human history both before and after the Incarnation. For the Son always remains present and active everywhere in the world, working for the salvation of all. This universal activity of the Son is not diminished by the Incarnation and the historical life of Jesus. Dupuis insists that the eternal Son remains universally active while also being personally identical with Jesus of Nazareth. The distinction rests in the operations and not at the level of person. It is the divine Son who enacts God's plan of salvation, and this plan is unique—humans are all called to participate in the life of God through the work of the Son and the Spirit.

Dupuis affirms the work of the Spirit in the life of the church and in the world bringing about salvation, but also asserts that although the outpouring of the Spirit is to be connected to the resurrection of Christ, it is not confined to it. Dupuis notes that before the Incarnation, the Spirit acted in a revelatory and salvific fashion. With the resurrection and Pentecost, the Spirit, though working in total communion with the glorified Christ, does not lose its universal activity. Rather, if the Incarnation of the divine Son did not mean that the divine powers of the Son were lost or diminished, the same must be true of the Spirit: though poured out through the Risen Son, the divine nature of the Spirit cannot be limited.

This activity of the Spirit reaches and enriches the members of various religions in and through their religious life and practice. How else could the Spirit reach them but through the elements of their traditions? Because these religions contain elements of truth and goodness, as Vatican II states, and the Spirit is mysteriously and powerfully present to them, it must be the case that members of these religious communities find salvation through their respective traditions. In other words, their religions are "ways of salvation" for them. Dupuis borrows an expression from John Paul II's encyclical letter *Redemptoris missio*: "Although participated forms of mediation of different kinds and degrees are not excluded, they acquire meaning and value only from Christ's own mediation, and they cannot be understood as parallel or complimentary to his" (n. 5).

The notion of "participated mediations of salvation" is central for Dupuis as he constructs an inclusive pluralist approach to the theology of religions. "Participated mediations" maintains the integrity of other religious traditions as vehicles for the salvation of their adherents, while also remaining Christocentric by emphasizing that Christ is the definitive source of salvation and is present within those traditions. Dupuis' inclusive pluralism relates the ways of salvation proposed by other religious traditions to the "event of Jesus Christ," the Incarnation, life, death, and resurrection. These participated mediations are intended by God and the various religious traditions play a positive role in the salvation of their adherents. Religious traditions, as traditions, are necessarily secondary. The same is true for Christianity; there is a difference between the faith that saves and the religious tradition that conveys that faith. No religious tradition saves. Only by the work of divine Word and the Spirit in history does God the Father seek out humanity and save them. In that one plan all things, all cultures, and all religions converge toward the eschatological "reign of God."

The Return of a High-Descending Christology

Christology from Rome: *Dominus Iesus*

The Congregation for the Doctrine of the Faith (CDF), the chief doctrinal office of the Vatican, issued a document in 2000 titled *Dominus Iesus* (*DI*) that addressed the question of religious pluralism and Christology. The document begins with the evangelical mandate to "teach all nations" (Matthew 28:18–20), and then presents the entire text of the creed of Constantinople (often referred to as the Nicene Creed) as the definitive statement of Christian faith. It goes on to warn of the danger the church is confronting from "relativistic theories which seek to justify religious pluralism, not only *de facto* but also *de iure*."[18] The problem arises from certain philosophical and theological presuppositions that challenge the acknowledgment of "revealed truth." Some of these problems include the conviction that divine truth always remains inexpressible, the allure of relativism (the belief that all knowledge and value are relative to place and time and can have no universal claim), and the problem with making transcendent claims about the nature of God based on the historically contingent experience of Jesus of Nazareth. The document's account of revelation and the response of faith deserves note.

> The theory of the limited, incomplete, or imperfect character of the revelation of Jesus Christ, which would be complementary to that found in other religions, is contrary to the Church's faith. Such a position would claim to be based on the notion that the truth about God cannot be grasped and manifested in its globality and completeness by any historical religion, neither by Christianity nor by Jesus Christ. Such a position is in radical contradiction with [the creed] according to which the full and complete revelation of the salvific mystery of God is given in Jesus Christ. Therefore, the words, deeds, and entire historical event of Jesus, though limited as human realities, have nevertheless the divine Person of the Incarnate Word, "true God and true man" (Council of Chalcedon, *Symbolum Chalcedonense*: DS 301;

---

18. *DI*, 4. The document differentiates between *de facto* religious pluralism (as a matter of fact) and *de iure* religious pluralism (in principle), which suggests that the nature of God demands a plurality of religions.

cf. St. Athanasius, *De Incarnatione*, 54, 3: SC 199, 458) as their subject. For this reason, they possess in themselves the definitiveness and completeness of the revelation of God's salvific ways, even if the depth of the divine mystery in itself remains transcendent and inexhaustible. The truth about God is not abolished or reduced because it is spoken in human language; rather, it is unique, full, and complete, because he who speaks and acts is the Incarnate Son of God. Thus, faith requires us to profess that the Word made flesh, in his entire mystery, who moves from incarnation to glorification, is the source, participated but real, as well as the fulfillment of every salvific revelation of God to humanity, (Second Vatican Council, Dogmatic Constitution *Dei verbum*, 4). (*Dominus Iesus*, n. 6)

The document goes on in section 7 to make another crucial distinction between the theological virtue of Christian faith and the belief that is experienced and expressed in other religious traditions. For the CDF, religious belief—a common feature of the human condition—can be affirmed as a relatively vague (though real) experience of God's presence and our response to that presence, but it is primarily a search, or a quest. Conversely, Christian faith is a supernatural gift whereby God offers nothing less than God's full self-communication. In Christian faith, humans are not simply searching, but rather God has definitively reached out to humanity and given the gift of God's very Self.

For this reason, the distinction between *theological faith* and *belief* in the other religions, must be *firmly held*. If faith is the acceptance in grace of revealed truth, which "makes it possible to penetrate the mystery in a way that allows us to understand it coherently" (John Paul II, Encyclical Letter *Fides et ratio*, 13), then belief, in the other religions, is that sum of experience and thought that constitutes the human treasury of wisdom and religious aspiration, which man in his search for truth has conceived and acted upon in his relationship to God and the Absolute (*Fides et ratio*, 31–32). (*Dominus Iesus*, n. 7)

Dominus Iesus privileges the revelation of God in Christ as the definitive act of God's self-expression. The document reaffirms that Jesus of Nazareth is the unique Son and perfect Word, and that the salvific mission of the Word is accomplished through Christ and no other. In other words, there can be no separation between an account of the Word and an account of the human Jesus of Nazareth.[19] Additionally, *DI* admits that the fullness of God's revelation will be manifest in the future, but this does not mean that the revelation of God in Christ is to be regarded as temporary, limited, or provisional.

---

19. *DI*, 10.

Moreover, *DI* asserts that the revelation of God in Christ is not subject to modification or completion from other religious traditions, although this does not exclude the possibility that other religious traditions might be worthy of emulation in particular practices—e.g., Buddhist nonviolence or Islamic submission to regular prayer. *DI* also states that the salvific action of the Holy Spirit does not extend beyond the one universal economy of salvation of the Incarnate Word. While one may affirm the presence of the Holy Spirit and the salvation of non-Christians through the "elements of truth and goodness" in diverse religious traditions, one cannot affirm the salvific character of those religious traditions as such.[20]

When *Dominus Iesus* was published, it was greeted with much rancor from a variety of quarters.[21] While many Protestant leaders rejoiced at the Christocentrism of the document, they were also offended by the way the document refers to Protestant churches as "ecclesial communities" rather than as "churches." The official Roman Catholic position is that these communities are not churches because they do preserve apostolic succession and do not validly celebrate the sacraments. Non-Christian leaders found the document offensive because of its reaffirmation of the superiority of Christianity over other religious traditions. They felt it rolled back the progress that had been made in recent decades in official and quasi-official interreligious dialogue. Most theologians feel that the most remarkable feature of the document was that it simply reaffirmed the teaching of Vatican II and the teaching of John Paul II.

The real question is whether changing cultural conditions demand a new theological approach to ecumenism and interreligious dialogue. For many Christian theologians, the issue of religious pluralism threatens to force Christians to marginalize their claims about Jesus.

The Drama of Salvation in Balthasar

The shift in recent years to a low-ascending approach to Christology (i.e., one that begins with the human Jesus of Nazareth), along with the corresponding focus of the human as the theological starting point of theology, led inexorably to the question of the uniqueness and universal mission of Christ. *Dominus Iesus* responded to this development by unambiguously reaffirming God's unique and universal self-communication in Christ. In this model, revelation becomes the key for Christology, and to many ears it seems to embrace extrincisim and exclusivism.

---

20. *DI*, 8; 11.

21. For a compendium of reactions and opinions on *DI*, see Stephen J. Pope and Charles Hefling, eds., *Dominus Iesus* (Maryknoll: Orbis, 2002).

Hans Urs von Balthasar was never interested in the Christological controversies of the twentieth century that emphasized the human experience of openness to divine revelation (e.g., Rahner and Schillebeeckx). Instead, he seized on the importance of divine revelation for understanding Christ, and used this focus to develop his understanding of the nature of beauty and its relationship to faith as an aesthetic act. For Balthasar, God permeates all existence so that the sensible universe is teaming with the presence of God; one can come to know God as creation announces the divine presence. Similarly, any understanding of Christ must place him at the heart of such aesthetic experience as the central actor in the drama, the unfolding narrative of salvation. For Balthasar, theology is less a philosophical science than a mystical art. Yet such an approach helps him articulate a Christology that resonates, in many ways, with some of the concerns expressed in *DI*. His theology may mark a way forward through the morass of problems inherent in the question for an authentically Christocentric approach to religious pluralism.

Balthasar's diverse and extensive writings are tied together by his commitment to the transcendental properties of Being—beauty, goodness, and truth—and their unity.[22] He sees human existence as beset by a fundamental duality: the finite and the infinite, the particular and the universal. Balthasar affirms that humans were created to seek the universal, or that which is ultimately transcendent, i.e., God. However, the human search for God can only find fulfillment if God has shared infinitude with humans. The question is whether humans will be able to receive God's infinite revelation. The God of creation made the senses of humans, the organs by which humans come to wonder about God and their own finitude. God has created humans with the capacity to know God, to find God through the experience of wonder, the experience of beauty, which is at the heart of their existence.

While the experience of beauty and wonder are significant in Balthasar's theological and philosophical refection, the doctrines of Incarnation and Trinity are his real starting points, in stark contrast to the low-ascending approach that has been so characteristic of contemporary Christology. In the doctrine of the Trinity, Christians affirm that God is love, and love supposes the one, the other, and their unity. Such otherness within God, i.e., the Son as "other," is echoed in the relationship between God and creation. Creation, like the Son, is an icon of God, though unlike the Son, creation is not God; it is "other" than God. The Son, as the eternal icon of the Father, can without contradiction unite himself with creation. In this union, Balthasar understands Jesus as the "concrete universal," the union of the finite and infinite. In the Incarnation creation is made pure and brought into communion with the triune God. Such an event does not

---

22. For an overview of von Balthasar's work, see Hans Urs von Balthasar, *My Work in Retrospect* (San Francisco: Ignatius, 1993).

result in the dissolution of creation into God; rather, creation retains its identity as "other" than God. This involves the descent, self-emptying, or *kenōsis* of the Son.[23] In this descent, the Son remains with the Father, and the Son continues to know "where" he is throughout his *kenōsis*, his Incarnation—he is with the Father. Additionally, Balthasar sees complete identity between Christ's mission and his person—he is the one sent from the Father. This distinguishes him from other subjects who have been personalized by being given a mission, for example, the prophets. Jesus acts accordingly; he does not communicate a divine plan, but throughout his life, he speaks as the personal Word of God. Christ is that plan.

The unity between Christ's mission and identity quite naturally links the Incarnation and the cross. For Balthasar, the Incarnation cannot be separated from the cross because God assumed our sinful flesh in Christ in order to heal it and unite it to God. Balthasar's account of the Incarnation, therefore, is cruciform. From the self-surrender on the cross he moves to the abyss of sin and the abandonment that is death. It is this experience that Jesus embraces on the cross and his descent into Hell. Through such death, Christ embraces obedience in death—what Balthasar calls "cadaver-obedience"—revealing and experiencing the full horror of sin. Jesus was truly dead, and only God could rescue him.

In death, Christ is in profound solidarity with each of us, and Balthasar rejects any notion that the human suffered apart from the divine Son, inasmuch as the Chalcedonian formula affirms a distinction between the natures in Christ but also affirms their union in the person of Jesus. For Balthasar, the self-emptying of the Son is not simply a way of describing the journey of the Logos from his celestial abode, but it is a description of what happens in the Trinity through the suffering and death of Jesus. The *kenōsis* of the Son is eternal.[24]

The Trinity, in Balthasar's theology, is a unity with real difference. That difference is not oppositional but relational. Balthasar describes it as weakness, humility, and *kenōsis*. These features of the Trinity account for the dynamism within God's very nature: God is active, not passive or remote. God is relational, and, above all, loving and gifting. Analogously, this is reflected within human nature, particularly in the social dimension of human existence and its openness to the "other." Such openness is the condition for suffering. The more loving, and so receptive, the relationship is, the more disposed one is to suffer. Yet this suffering is not a passivity or a defect regarding the "other"; rather, it is an activity at the heart of human perfection, namely love. The Trinity, then, is a communion in which there is room for active receptivity in which the suffering of Christ is contained. God is in solidarity with the universal experience of sin, which is suffering.

23. See the sidebar on *"Kenōsis* and Buddhism" in chapter 4.

24. John O'Donnell, *Hans Urs von Balthasar*, Outstanding Christian Thinkers (New York: Continuum, 1991), 46.

This solidarity produces a universalism in Balthasar's soteriology. Building upon Origen's notion of *apokatastasis*, or "the restoration of all things,"[25] Balthasar asserts that in Christ, God has destined all humans for salvation. The possibility of deadly sin, the total rejection of God's love and mercy, remains real, but one cannot know if anyone has actually so thoroughly rejected that love and mercy. Balthasar rejects the idea that one can ever know such things and rejects any such speculation that would divorce our love from our hope; the union of hope and love demands that Christians hope for the salvation of all.

Balthasar's theology may seem to represent a return to a precritical stage of Christological reflection, yet his proposal does not embrace the mythological language and worldviews that dominated precritical Christologies. Balthasar's Christology is mystical, yet rooted in the temporal and centered on the historic experience of God's self-disclosure in Christ. His emphasis on the aesthetic and dramatic nature of revelation and theology situate his thought within a post-modern context but located at some distance from the thought of someone like Roger Haight. The categories of beauty, drama, and logic provide fertile ground for reappropriation of the Christian tradition in a post-Christian, postmodern world, but also provide common ground on which to understand and dialog without co-opting or imposing itself on other religious traditions.

Conclusion

If the history of Christology is the history of forgetting, the emergence of Balthasar's Christology in recent years seems to recapitulate the history of Christology. The dangers inherent in a low-ascending approach to Christology are spelled out quite clearly in the thought of John Hick, wherein Jesus is a remarkable cipher, an arrow pointing to God, but traditional Christological doctrines are ultimately dispensable. Is there a viable alternative to this conclusion? Can one affirm the definitive revelation of God in Christ and at the same time revere religious difference as difference? How does one overcome the violence that some see as inherent in universal claims about Jesus? Such questions, as yet unanswered, will propel Christological reflection into the future. It is the responsibility of all who profess faith in Christ to wrestle with, argue over, and embrace new paradigms of Christological orthodoxy—not despite the theological achievements of the past but precisely out of reverence for those achievements and a willingness to be instructed by them. The formulations of past generations and the officially sanctioned teachings of Christian churches—the teachings of the Roman Catholic Magesterium, for example—set out guidelines

---

25. See the sidebar on "Origen" in chapter 4.

and limits for contemporary Christology. These are best viewed as conversation starters, as invitations to the next generation of Christians to reflect upon the power of Christ for the salvation of the world.

Questions for Understanding

1. Why is religious pluralism such a pronounced issue for Christians today?
2. Define the exclusivist position. Why do many Christians in our day reject this position? Why do other Christians retain it?
3. What is the concept of the "anonymous Christian," and why do many theologians find it problematic?
4. What are the main characteristics of *Dominus Iesus*? How do these characteristics make the document problematic in the eyes of some?
5. Identify two important differences in the Christological approaches of Haight and Dupuis.
6. Explain the place of beauty and wonder in the theology of Hans Urs von Balthasar.

Questions for Reflection and Action

1. Can Christians remain faithful to the gospel and adopt a pluralist position? Explain. How should Christians respond to Christ's command to "Go teach all nations" (Matthew 28:19)?
2. Construct a chart listing each of the proposed paradigms for dealing with the issue of religious pluralism discussed in this chapter. In a separate column, list the arguments in favor and against each of these positions. Which paradigm offers the best option for articulating a Christian theology of religious pluralism? Explain.
3. *Apokatastasis*, or "the universal restoration of all things," is a tempting idea. Discuss the advantages and problems it entails.

For Further Reading

Dupuis, Jacques, SJ. *Christianity and the Religions: From Confrontation to Dialogue.* Maryknoll, NY: Orbis, 2002.

Phan, Peter C. *Being Religious Interreligiously, Asian Perspectives on Interfaith Dialogue.* Maryknoll, NY: Orbis, 2004.

Tilley, Terrence W. *Postmodern Theologies: the Challenge of Religious Diversity* Eugene, OR: Wipf & Stock, 1995.

GLOSSARY

A

Adoptionists   This heterodox Christian group believed that Jesus was God's son through adoption, not essentially. In other words, at some point in the life of Jesus, God chose to grace Jesus with a unique relationship. The Jewish-Christian sect known as the Ebionites were Adoptionists as was Paul of Samosata. Another form of this heresy emerged in Spain shortly after the Islamic conquest in the eighth century.

Alexandrian [theology/roots/Christology, etc.]   The Egyptian city of Alexandria was a center for learning centuries before the Christian era began. In the third century, it became the most important center of Christian life and thought. Alexandrian theologians developed a highly allegorical method for the interpretation of scripture and emphasized a form of Platonism. The Alexandrian approach to Christology is often described as "logos-sarx" because it emphasized the importance of the divine Logos and tended to diminish the humanity of Christ, making it merely functional by reducing it to flesh (*sarx* is the Greek word for *flesh*). The chief representatives of this school were Origen, Arius, Athanasius, Apollinaris, Cyril, Eutyches, Dioscorus, and Leontius of Byzantium.

Allegory   This Greek word literally translates "to offer a different argument." It is a literary genre as well as a method of interpretation that sees a story within another given story. More precisely, an allegory is a narrative in which every element or character has a corresponding element outside that narrative and within another plot. Many early Christians, particularly those in Alexandria, emphasized an allegorical approach to the interpretation of the Bible, an approach that they inherited from Greek writers and from Hellenistic Judaism.

Analogia entis   This Latin expression is usually translated as "the analogy of being." For Thomas Aquinas, the created order reflects something of God's being. As such, humans can make analogical statements about God, but all statements about God must first be negated (*via negativa*). For example, to say that God is "Father" means that God is not a father: God does not contribute genetic material to create a new life and God does not, strictly speaking, have a spouse. Rather, the experience of fathers provides the basis for saying that God is *like* a father: God is faithful, strong, dependable, and loving (*via positiva*). But every positive statement of this sort must be rounded off by the conviction that whatever qualities fathers might possess, even the most idealized father, God's love, faithfulness, etc., are infinitely beyond our experience (*via eminentiae*). This represents official teaching within the Catholic Church on all speech about God, endorsed by the Fourth Lateran Council in 1215. It remains a point of emphasis, especially among contemporary feminist theologians.

Anonymous Christian This phrase was used by Karl Rahner to describe those non-Christians who have responded to God's grace and who live God's call faithfully. In Rahner's view, they are saved through Christ, even though they do not formally recognize that fact. Many have criticized this notion as patronizing and devaluing other religious traditions.

Antiochene school The Syrian city of Antioch was one of the oldest Christian communities (Acts 11:19–26) and quickly became an important center for Christian thought. The Antiochenes preferred a more historical approach to scripture rather than an allegorical one. They also preferred the philosophy of Aristotle to that of Plato. Their approach to Christology is often called "logos-anthropos" because it emphasizes the full humanity of Jesus (*anthropos* means "human being" in Greek). The Antiochenes approached the Christological question by beginning with the human being, Jesus, and then asking how the divine Logos is connected to or united with the man, Jesus. Some chief representatives of this school include Paul of Samosata, Diodore of Tarsus, Nestorius, John of Antioch, John Chrysostom, and Theodore of Mopsuestia.

Anti-Semitism This is the denigration or hatred of the Jewish people and their faith. The word *Semite* refers to the descendants of Noah's son Shem in Genesis 10:21–31. He became the father of the "race" of people in Mesopotamia, including both the Arabs and the Hebrews, or the Jews. Throughout the Christian era, many interpretations of Jesus' teachings have portrayed Judaism negatively and have thus provided a foundation for modern anti-Semitism. The experience of the Holocaust has given impetus to Christian self-criticism for theological positions and attitudes that have condoned anti-Semitism. Additionally, the work of scholars such as E. P. Sanders (*Jesus and Judaism*) has attempted to shine a bright light on Christian prejudices and set Jesus and his followers firmly within a Jewish context.

Apatheia This Greek word literally means "without suffering." It refers to the Greek doctrine that God is remote and unaffected by the plight of the world—unable to suffer. In his theology, Jürgen Moltmann challenges this doctrine and its appropriateness for understanding Jesus and the God of Israel.

Apocalyptic eschatology The theology that emerged within Judaism in the centuries around the time of Jesus. It is characterized by an anticipation of God's decisive act in human history to bring about the destruction of evil and the vindication of the righteous. This theology, emerging within a context of suffering and persecution, included the idea of a final cosmic battle with the forces of evil and the resurrection of the dead—the righteous to eternal reward and the wicked to eternal punishment.

Apokatastasis   This Greek word, meaning "restoration" (also spelled *apocatastasis*), was used by Origen to describe the hope that at the end of time all things would be restored to God, including Satan and the damned. Others also held positions that resembled Origen's, including Gregory of Nyssa, Clement of Alexandria, and the early nineteenth-century theologian, Friedrich Schleiermacher.

Apologist   The Greek word *apologia* means "defense." An apologist was someone who offered a defense of an idea or a movement. Because Christianity was largely unknown by many people who were naturally suspicious of the movement, many Christian apologists emerged in the early church (e.g., Justin Martyr).

Authenticity   Bernard Lonergan and many other contemporary theologians have used this term to express what humans are created to be; i.e., the full potential of human existence.

B

Babylonian Exile   Following the Babylonian capture and destruction of Jerusalem in 587 BCE, the Babylonian king, Nebuchadnezzar, led a significant portion of the city's inhabitants into forced exile, hundreds of miles away, in Babylon (modern Iraq). During that time, the people of Judah longed to return to Jerusalem and be restored as a kingdom. The exile ended around 539 BCE when Cyrus the Great conquered Babylon and allowed the Jews to return home.

C

Canon/canonization   The Greek word *kanōn* means "measuring rod" and has come to refer to the process of making something normative, or that which is normative. The word *canon* usually refers to the collection of texts a group regards as sacred; in the case of the Christian church, the canon is the Bible.

CCC (Catechism of the Catholic Church)   This is a compendium of the Roman Catholic Church's teachings presented thematically and used to help educators and those preparing educational material. It contains both highly authoritative material as well as basic material for teaching the truths of the Catholic faith. It is a helpful resource for exploring many teachings that are basic to Catholic Christianity as well as to other Christian traditions.

Chalcedon, Council of (451 CE)   Convened by the emperor Marcian in 451 near the imperial capital, the council affirmed the full humanity of Christ and the union of that humanity with the divinity of Christ. The substantial union of the two natures, divine and human, was affirmed over and against the Alexandrian position articulated by Eutyches and Dioscorus.

Christ   The Greek word *christos* translates the Hebrew word *messiah*, which means "anointed one." The title evoked Israel's hope that God would raise up a descendant of David, and perhaps even a new high priest, to restore the nation and usher in the final age. The title *Christ* was applied to Jesus early in the Christian tradition.

Christocentrism   In the discussion of religious pluralism, the Christocentric position emphasizes the place of Christ in the discussion and how other "saviors" might relate to Christ as the Incarnation of God.

Christological moment   This refers to any scene in the gospel stories that the evangelists used to express and crystallize their understanding of Jesus—an understanding that was the product of the resurrection. The scene, rather than a recollection of an event from Jesus' life, is a vehicle for the expression of a post-resurrectional Christology.

Concrete universal   This expression comes for Hans Urs von Balthasar and refers to the conjunction between the finite and the infinite at the heart of the human experience of God. For von Balthasar, Jesus is the concrete universal.

Constantinople   The imperial city that Constantine built to unite the eastern and western parts of the fractious Roman Empire. It became a place of great political and ecclesiastical intrigue when Antioch and Alexandria began to vie for influence in the imperial court.

Constantinople, Councils of   The *First Council of Constantinople* was held in 381 to deal with several issues including that of the Holy Spirit and various heresies, including Apollinaris's Christology. This council issued an expansion of the creed formulated at Nicaea, which is often mistakenly called "the Nicene Creed." The *Second Council of Constantinople* was held in 553 as an effort to reconcile the Cyrilian-monophysite churches, but it succeeded only in condemning the great Antiochene theologians (Theodore of Mopsuestia, Ibas of Edessa, and Theodoret of Cyrus). The *Third Council of Constantinople* was held in 680 when it was affirmed that because, in Christ, there is a union of both the divine and human natures, there must also be two wills and two "operations." Interestingly, Pope Honorius († 638) was posthumously anathematized, or condemned, for supporting the doctrine of "one will" in Christ.

Convenientia   This Latin word is often translated as *appropriateness*. It refers to a contingent matter of fact, not a matter of necessity, in God's plan of salvation.

Cosmotheandric fact   This expression was used by the Spanish-Indian Jesuit Raimundo Panikkar to describe the inherent connection between God (*theos*) and the world (*cosmos*) in humans (*andres*), particularly in the man, Jesus.

Counter-Reformation   Following Martin Luther's successful challenge of church authority and the success of the other reformers, the pope convened a council in 1548 at Trent to address the concerns and challenges of the Reformers. The Council of Trent met periodically over the course of two decades (1548–1563) and instituted many positive reforms in the life and theology of the church. The general tenor of the council as well as its implementation over the course of the subsequent century, however, was often defensive and aggressive. It was not until the Second Vatican Council (1962–1965) that a more positive posture towards the Reformation was adopted.

Creed   The Latin word *credo* means "I believe" and has come to designate any formal statement of faith.

Cultural imperialism   The practice of intentionally imposing cultural norms and practices on other cultures as a matter of policy. Alexander the Great's policies represent an important example of cultural imperialism.

D

Day of Atonement   This solemn Jewish feast that celebrates the removal of Israel's sins is called *Yom Kippur* in Hebrew. The biblical ceremony includes a sacrifice of purification and the transfer of sins to the "scapegoat," which is then expelled from the community.

Demythologizing   This is the term used by Bultmann and his disciples to describe the process of "peeling back" the elements of a first-century Jewish (apocalyptic) worldview that are no longer applicable or meaningful for contemporary humans. The process of demythologizing yields a contemporary existential interpretation of the gospel.

Deuteronomist/Deuteronomistic History   The Deuteronomist is one of the four or more individuals, or more likely schools, that edited the Pentateuch, or first five books of the Bible (Genesis–Deuteronomy). The Deuteronomic tradition emerged in the Northern Kingdom of Israel in the eighth century BCE and was carried to the southern Kingdom of Judah following the collapse of Samaria in 722 BCE. It became the basis for Josiah's reforms before the destruction of Jerusalem in 587 BCE. The account of Israel's history that runs through Joshua, Judges, 1 and 2 Samuel, and 1 and 2 Kings is termed the Deuteronomistic History because it reflects the concerns and emphases of the Deuteronomic tradition and is probably the work of the same school. The basic outlook of Deuteronomic theology was that God would grant long life and prosperity to those who were righteous and faithful, while the wicked would be destroyed. The weaknesses of Deuteronomic theology became apparent as Jews increasingly began to experience the suffering of the righteous. In some ways, apocalyptic eschatology compensates for the inadequacies of the Deuteronomic tradition by making the afterlife or the resurrection the primary place in which God's justice and mercy are vindicated.

E

Ecclesiocentric position   Literally, this means "church-centered." It refers to the approach of religious pluralism that is centered on membership and participation in a particular church for the attainment of salvation. Cyprian of

Carthage famously expressed the most extreme ecclesiocentrism: "Outside the Church there is no salvation."

Enoch, First Book of   This book is an example of apocalyptic eschatology. It is a nonbiblical book and was written in the second century BCE. It is attributed to the biblical figure, Enoch, who was said to have been assumed into heaven (see Genesis 5:21–24). The book was widely read in early Christian circles. It is particularly important for understanding the origins and meaning of "the Son of Man" figure.

Ephesus, Council of (431 CE)   When Nestorius, the bishop of Constantinople, argued against calling Mary "*Theotokos*," saying that she was only "the mother of Christ" (i.e., *Christotokos*), Cyril of Alexandria arranged for a council at Ephesus to condemn his teaching. The council met before the supporters of Nestorius arrived, and those present condemned Nestorius and reaffirmed the unity of Christ against the distortion of Nestorius, who argued against a union between the divine and human natures in Christ.

Essenes   This is one of the so-called sects within first-century Judaism. It is commonly thought that this group was responsible for the Dead Sea Scrolls found in a series of caves near Qumran. These scrolls contain a number of biblical books as well as commentaries on biblical books. However, perhaps the most important documents from the Dead Sea are the sectarian documents that reflect the distinctive worldview and theology of the Essenes. This group was composed mainly of those who believed that the Temple in Jerusalem, and the priests who operated it, were corrupt. God was about to visit his judgment upon the Temple, and the Essenes retreated to the desert to prepare themselves for this event.

Ethical monotheism   This scholarly term refers to the demands placed upon Israel through the prophets that their status as the people of God (Yahweh) was to be sustained through a very particular set of behaviors—those that mirrored Yahweh's behavior toward Israel. Some examples include protecting the widow and orphan, treating neighbors and foreigners with justice, worshipping Yahweh alone. The exclusive worship of Yahweh, however, is meaningless without the corresponding ethical behavior (Isaiah 1:11–17).

Exclusivism   This is the position on religious pluralism that contends that one cannot be saved from destruction without explicit faith in Christ.

F

Formula of Reunion (433 CE)   Cyril of Alexandria and John of Antioch created this document in order to end the schism between the Alexandrian and Antiochene churches that followed the Council of Ephesus in 431. The formula was a synthesis of Alexandrian and Antiochene Christology, brought balance to the question of the natures of Christ, and became a major source for the Formula of Chalcedon.

G

Gnostics/Gnosticism   A complex religious movement that emerged in the second century CE. Some forms of Gnosticism blended well with elements of orthodox Christianity. Among other things, Gnostics denied the goodness of the material world and emphasized that "knowledge" of one's true nature as a spiritual being can bring about liberation from the "prison" of the material world. Gnosticism was particularly insidious because it utilized aspects of Christian thought and appealed to Christian figures for the legitimacy of their own scriptures (i.e., *Gospel of Mary*, *Gospel of Thomas*, etc.).

H

Han   The unresolved resentment, indignation, the sense of helplessness and total abandonment in the face of injustice that have accumulated over years and even centuries of oppression suffered by the *minjung*.

Heresy   This word comes from Greek and means "sect." It has come to mean any false teaching or a teaching that contradicts a central doctrine.

Hermeneutics of retrieval   In liberation theologies (i.e., feminist, Latin American, black, womanist, and *mujerista*) this is the principle of interpretation whereby a central place is assigned to elements of the Christian tradition (i.e., texts, symbols, traditions, and practices) that promote the well-being and freedom of oppressed groups, even though such elements may have been forgotten or suppressed.

Hermeneutics of suspicion   In liberation theologies, it is the principle of interpretation whereby one looks for Christian stories, symbols, traditions, and practices that have been used to support or legitimate the oppression or marginalization of certain groups of people.

hilastērion   This Greek word translates the Hebrew word *kapporet*, which refers to the golden cover on the Ark in the "Holy of Holies" of the Jerusalem Temple. This cover became the object of Temple sacrifices as the place at which Yahweh sat and received the blood of the atoning sacrifices on Yom Kippur—the Day of Atonement.

Homoousios   This Greek term literally translates as "same being." This word was suggested to the bishops at Nicaea under imperial pressure as a way to describe the relationship between the Father and the Son. In this context, it says, in effect, that whatever makes the Father God, makes the Son God.

Horizon   The horizon is the place at which the earth appears to meet the sky. It is the limit of our field of vision—we cannot see beyond the horizon. For Bernard Lonergan, a horizon also defines our field of moral vision and our understanding of reality. When confronted by the world, our horizon of meaning and value determines our understanding of the world and presents us with possible courses of action. When our horizon is infected by bias, it becomes extremely limited. For Karl Rahner, a horizon represents the infinite presence of Being as the source and goal of all human knowing—at which the finite and the infinite meet.

Hypostasis   There is a rough equivalence between this word and the Latin word *substantia*, that is, "underlying reality or subsistence." This word was problematic in the Christological debates between the Alexandrians and Antiochenes because there was no general agreement about its meaning and precise relationship to words such as *physis* (nature) and *prosopon* (mask or person). Clarifications were made at Chalcedon between the concepts *physis*, *hypostasis*, and *prosopon*, so that one could begin to speak of a hypostatic union of the divine and human natures in Christ. Whereas *physis*, or *nature*, answered the question "*What* is it?" *hypostasis* and *prosopon* answered the questions "*Which one*, or *who* is it?"

Hypostatic union   This phrase is often used as shorthand for the doctrine of the union of the two natures (human and divine) in Christ. That this union was "hypostatic" is probably best attributed to Leontius of Byzantium's notion that the human nature of Christ had its hypostasis in the divine nature (the human nature of Christ was "enhypostatic").

I

Inclusivism   This is the position on religious pluralism that forms the heart of contemporary Catholic teaching. According to this perspective, non-Christians can be saved from destruction so long as they respond to God's offer of grace through Christ. This grace is offered, unknowingly, to women and men of good will who seek to do God's will but who, through no fault of their own, do not know Christ. Those who do so are what Rahner called "anonymous Christians."

Infancy narratives   This genre of literature is common in the ancient world. Important figures in history often had the story of their lives prefaced by a tale of remarkable birth. This literary tradition can be traced as far back as Sargon the Great of Assyria in the third millennium BCE. Two of the gospels (Matthew and Luke) contain infancy narratives and some material of historical significance and other material that is primarily a reflection of post-resurrectional Christology.

J

Jubilees   This is a nonbiblical book written in the second century BCE. It is a commentary and expansion of material found in Genesis and Exodus and offers us, at one point, an account of the afterlife as disembodied spirits.

K

Kapporet   This Hebrew word refers to the covering on the Ark of the Covenant on which God (Yahweh) was enthroned, otherwise known as the mercy seat, or *hilasterion*, in Greek. It was the focal point of God's presence with Israel and the place where blood was sprinkled on the Day of Atonement (Yom Kippur).

Kerygma   This Greek word literally means "proclamation." It refers to the faith proclamation of the earliest disciples of Jesus (stage two). This proclamation of faith also served to call or summon others to faith. In the theology of Bultmann, it takes on special significance as an existential summons to a decision in favor of faith or trust in God.

L

Liberal theology   This theological movement emerged in the nineteenth century and sought to accommodate the Christian tradition to the sensibilities of modern Western culture. The result of this blending was a form of Christianity that had only a diminished capacity to critique modern culture and a diminished sense of the supernatural and the holy, or transcendent.

Liturgy/liturgical   The Greek work *leitourgia* means "public work" and refers to the act of public worship as opposed to private prayer. Public worship tends to be formal, regular, and symbolic.

Logos   This Greek term means "word," "reason," or "speech." In late Second Temple Judaism (around 100 BCE), the Logos emerged as an important aspect of God and became personified as Wisdom. The Fourth Gospel begins with a hymn to the Logos and the incarnation of the Logos in Jesus.

Logos Christology   This approach to Christology emphasizes the idea that God's self-expression, God's Word, became incarnate in Christ. It has its origins in Greek (Stoic) philosophy and in the Hebrew Bible (Old Testament), and it is particularly associated with the creation story in Genesis.

Logos spermatikos   This Greek expression means "seminal word" and was an important concept in Stoic philosophy. It refers to the notion that the divine Logos permeated the created order—in particular, within human beings. It was the duty of every human being to cultivate *logos*, or reason, and thereby cultivate a connection with the Divine. Justin Martyr appropriated this expression in his apologetic works and linked Christ to the Logos and the cultivation of reason in Greco-Roman culture.

Lord   At the close of the Old Testament period the divine name, Yahweh, was never pronounced (except by the high priest on Yom Kippur—the Day of Atonement). Instead the word *adonai* (the Hebrew equivalent of *Lord*) was pronounced. For Paul, the title "lord" (*kyrios*) meant several things: (1) it was a way of referring to the glorified, risen Christ; (2) it expressed that this figure was due the same worship and honor as Yahweh; (3) it seems to refer to the Christ of the *parousia* (second coming) and only gradually came to be applied to earlier phases of Christ's existence; (4) it implies that Jesus is something more than human; (5) it expresses Jesus' dominion over people.

M

Maccabees/Maccabean   This is the name of a Jewish family who, in the second century BCE, lead a revolt against the Greek kingdom (the Seleucids) that controlled Jerusalem and had outlawed Jewish religious practice. During this period, many Jews suffered torture and death because they would not violate the commandments of Yahweh (2 Maccabees 6:18–7:42). Their deaths were seen as "ransom" for the sins of Israel from current and past generations (see 4 Maccabees 6:27–29). The Maccabees eventually defeated the Seleucids but eventually compromised their religious and nationalist idealism. Pious Jews in Jesus' time regarded the successors of the Maccabees, usually called the Hasmoneans, unfavorably because they had compromised their original zeal and corrupted the priesthood.

Messiah   The Hebrew word for "anointed one." It is translated in the New Testament with the word *christos* or Christ.

Messianic secret   This is a feature of Mark's Gospel first identified by William Wrede. In Mark, Jesus admonishes many people not to disclose his identity as Messiah to anyone. Wrede explained such secrecy as an early Christian response to the problem posed by that, in the course of his ministry, Jesus did not proclaim himself to be the Christ. Wrede argued that Mark solved this problem by claiming that Jesus did indeed understand himself as the Messiah but instructed his disciples to keep his identity a secret until after his resurrection.

Metanoia   This Greek word is often translated as *conversion*, and it designates the appropriate response to Jesus' proclamation of the nearness of the kingdom. William Loewe and Bernard Lonergan have argued that this religious conversion, a radical transformation of one's horizon of meaning and value, is made possible through the recognition of God's love flooding one's being, of "being in love in an unrestricted fashion." Thus, *metanoia* becomes the centerpiece of any account of salvation, any responsible contemporary soteriology.

Middle Judaism   This expression has come to designate a step in the process of transformation that Judaism went through following the destruction of the Temple in 70 CE. Middle Judaism thus signals when the diversity of the late Second Temple period began to give way to various battles to reorient Judaism without a Temple, which would eventually lead to the formation of normative Judaism—a form of Rabbinic Judaism.

Midrash   This is a distinctively Jewish style of writing popularized among the Pharisees. It is a homiletic or sermon-like exposition of a biblical text that usually attempts to address questions not directly answered in the biblical text. For example, *Jubilees* is a *midrash* on Genesis and Exodus.

Miracle   This word is derived from the Latin *miraculum*, which means "something to be wondered at." The New Testament uses Greek words such as *dynamis* (power) and *ergon* (work) or *sēmeion* (sign), rather than *miracle*. A miracle has often been understood as an observable event with religious meaning that can only be attributed to God because it is outside the natural order of things. In this book, miracles are discussed as symbolic acts whereby Jesus proclaimed the kingdom of God. They are dramatic parables in action in which Jesus confirmed the faith of the recipient and challenged onlookers to be converted and accept the advent of the kingdom.

Minjung   This is a Korean word that means "the popular mass" and has become a popular tem for describing the status and suffering of the vast majority of Asians.

Modalist   One who holds the heterodox position that denies any real distinction between Father, Son, and Spirit. All are seen as mere energies or modes of encountering God. Sabellius and Praxeus were two chief advocates of Modalism.

Monarchia   This Latin term means "power" or "authority." In the early church, many theologians attempted to explain the relationship between the Father and the Son with reference to how they shared the divine power or *monarchia*. Two different solutions emerged in the third century: the Dynamic Monarchians or Adoptionists believed that the Son's share of the divine power was granted to him because of his virtue. The other solution, Modalism, denied any real distinction between Father and Son.

Monophysitism   The word literally means "one naturism." It is the label given to the heresy of Eutyches, who insisted that any mention of two-natures in Christ necessarily meant that there were two persons, or *prosopoi*, in Christ. Eutyches' insistence that there was only one nature—the divine nature—in Christ was condemned at Chalcedon in 451.

Myth   The Greek word *mythos* has a wide range of meanings. In the context of this book, especially in regard to the work of Strauss and Bultmann, it becomes a technical term that refers to the symbolic narrative found in scripture. Myth, in this context, has to do with the attempt to communicate truth, not deception.

N

New quest   Ernst Käsemann launched a "new quest" for the historical Jesus in the 1950s. This quest, conducted mostly by formed students of Bultmann, focused on retrieving the historical Jesus for theological reasons. The theological motivations, as well as their devotion to Bultmann's thought, distinguished this quest from both the "old quest" and the "third quest."

Nicaea, Councils of   The *First Council of Nicaea* was held in 325 CE to address the Arian crisis. It resulted in the condemnation of Arius along with the articulation of the orthodox faith in the form of a creed. The *Second Council of Nicaea* was held in 787 CE to address the issue of breaking images or "iconoclasm."

O

Old quest   The original quest for the historical Jesus in the nineteenth century focused on attacking traditional Christianity and vindicating one or another contemporary philosophy. It was brought to an end with the work of Albert Schweitzer in the early twentieth century.

Orthodox   This Greek word literally means "correct opinion," and refers to correct religious belief. While the term is used positively in this book, it has also been used pejoratively to describe a firm, fixed, and unnuanced position that does violence to other ideas.

P

Parable   The Greek word *parabolē* means "comparison." A parable is a provocative story or image that teases or plays with the hearers' imaginations and expectations. In so doing, the parable begins to force the hearers to reconsider their position and their worldview. As such, Jesus' parables were an important tool in his proclamation of the kingdom.

Parousia   This Greek word means "presence" or "visitation." In the New Testament, it refers to the so-called second Coming of Christ, at which time the dead will be raised and judged and evil will be defeated. The parousia oriented one of the earliest patterns of New Testament Christology, in which Jesus would become Messiah, in the fullest sense, only upon his return.

Participated mediations   Jacques Dupuis uses this phrase from John Paul II's encyclical *Redemptoris Missio* (n. 5) to lay out his theology of religious pluralism in which other religious traditions are the means of salvation for their adherents, and as such, they participate in the saving work of Christ to bring about the salvation of all.

Penal substitution   The Reformers espoused this approach to soteriology. According to this approach, sin incurs punishment from God, and this punishment was inflicted upon Christ instead of upon humanity. Christ's suffering takes on cosmic dimensions—it is the punishment due for all the sins of the world throughout time.

Pharisees   This is another of the sects or groups within first-century Palestinian Judaism. The word *Pharisee* means "separate ones." This group emerged during the second century BCE as opponents of those who wanted to find some accommodation with Greek and Roman cultural forces that had emerged in Palestine in the Maccabean period. The Pharisees were the great "democratizers" of Judaism to the extent that they sought to make purity not just a goal for the priests who served in the Temple, but also a goal for all the people of Israel. The Pharisees were often very popular in the first century, though they often argued with one another over the appropriate interpretation of the Mosaic Law. Jesus seems to fit in with this group in some ways. Both Jesus and the Pharisees were laymen and they were addressed as "teacher" or "rabbi." Both Jesus and the Pharisees sought to instill in the people of Israel a sense of righteousness and complete dedication to God.

Physis   A Greek word often translated as "nature." In the context of this book, it is perhaps best understood as answering the question "What is it?" The response to that question will tend to involve identifying the nature of something. (See *Hypostasis*.)

Platonic   This word refers to concepts associated with the thought of the Greek philosopher Plato. A characteristic of his thought was his emphasis on the distinction between the "concrete" world and the ideal world of "forms" (e.g., Plato's *Republic*, book 7).

Pluralist approach   This approach to religious difference sees religious diversity as a natural outcome of human contact with the Divine. Pluralists resist any talk of the superiority of one religious tradition over another; they affirm the relative worth of religious traditions. Christian pluralists insist that Christ is the savior of Christians, but they also insist "other saviors" operate independently of Christ or the Christian church.

Pneumatocentric   This phrase literally means "spirit centered" and refers to the approach to religious pluralism that emphasizes the universal saving work of the Holy Spirit rather than emphasizing the role of Christ or the Church in mediating salvation.

Post-Christian   This expression has come to describe much of the Western world. It sees the history of the West as traditionally dominated by Christian faith and its institutions, but such dominance is a thing of the past. From a cultural perspective, the West can no longer be regarded as "Christian."

Postcolonial Christology   This theological movement addresses the violence and structural marginalization of indigenous or native peoples connected with the promotion of the gospel throughout history. Such an approach to Christology has rendered pictures of Christ that are a far cry from those indicators of Western privilege proffered in the pages of a children's Bible.

Praxis   The significance of this Greek word is derived from Aristotle. It refers to action upon which there has been critical reflection. Praxis also signals an ongoing engagement, rather than an isolated act, that is informed by ongoing critical reflection.

Prosōpon   This Greek term is often translated as *person*, though it did not always seem to have that meaning. It was used interchangeably with *hypostasis* and conveyed the idea of concrete existence. (See *Hypostasis*.)

R

Ransom   The Greek word *apolutrosis* is usually translated as *ransom* or *redemption*. It is a commercial term reflecting the buying of a slave's freedom. It is used frequently by Paul and throughout the New Testament to describe the saving work of Christ's death. It is also used in the Septuagint to characterize some sacrifices and in the intertestamental literature to describe the effect of the death of the Maccabean martyrs.

Rationalists   In the eighteenth century, many had come to accept the autonomy of reason over and against religious faith. Rationalism argued that the only things that are real, true, and good are what can be affirmed through scientific reason.

Religious pluralism   This expression simply describes the contemporary situation, which is defined by its pluralism of religious belief and practice. For example, the identification of North America or Europe as "Christian" belies the fact that these cultures have become more open to and permeated by people professing other religious faiths or none at all.

Reformation (Protestant)   Martin Luther inaugurated an attempt at church reform in 1517. The condemnation of Luther by the pope and other church officials precipitated a fracture within Western Christianity. Other reformers, such as Ulrich Zwingli and John Calvin, followed Luther and held very different ideas about how the church should be reformed. The Reformation is a complex religious, social, and political event (see Counter Reformation).

Resymbolization   In feminist theology, resymbolization refers to the construction of a theology, stories, liturgy, and symbols that can become the vehicle for transformation from an androcentric, or male-centered, church to an inclusive church.

Robber Council (c. 449 CE)   Also known by the Latin expression Pope Leo I used to describe it, *latrocinium*. It was the council engineered by Dioscorus, archbishop of Alexandria, and Emperor Theodosius II, to vindicate Eutyches and Alexandrian theology over and against its opponents (especially Antioch). The council condemned Flavian, the bishop of Constantinople, and even forced the pope's legates (i.e., his representatives) to flee for their lives. Leo and many others rejected the results of this council. When the emperor, Theodosius II, died unexpectedly, his successors convened the Council of Chalcedon in 451 and deposed Dioscorus and his supporters.

S

Sadducees   This is another sect or group within first-century Palestinian Judaism. The name "Sadducee" is derived from the name of King David's great high priest Zadok (2 Samuel 8:17). From the late second century BCE this group, largely comprised of priests, held control of the Temple, the Sanhedrin, and were the primary link with the Roman government in the region. The Sadducees were pragmatic and, while not as popular as the Pharisees, were highly influential.

Sanhedrin   In the Roman Period the Sanhedrin was that body of Jewish leaders, under the leadership of the high priest, who administered the Temple and oversaw the application of Jewish law and observance in and around Jerusalem.

Satori   The Japanese term C. S. Song borrows from Zen Buddhism to describe insight or enlightenment, it is the function of theologians to provide or provoke insight or enlightenment primarily through the art of narrative.

Scapegoat   In the Yom Kippur ritual (Leviticus 16), the high priest transfers the sins of the nation to a goat that is then driven into the desert to be destroyed by the demon Azazel.

Seleucid Kingdom   This was one of the kingdoms or empires that arose following the death of Alexander the Great. The center of this empire was in Persia and Syria, and its main cities were Antioch and Ecbatana. The Seleucids took control of Jerusalem in the second century BCE and a new king, Antiochus IV Epiphanes, outlawed the Jewish religion, which precipitated a major crisis.

Sheol   This is the Hebrew word for the abode of the dead. Sometimes it seems to be equivalent to "the pit" or "the grave." At other times, it appears to be a place, much like Hades in Greek mythology, not of torture or despair, but of silence, forgetting, and sleep.

Shema   This is the traditional Jewish prayer found in Deuteronomy 6:4–9. It has been recited daily by Jews for centuries, and it presented the earliest Christians with a challenge: how does one affirm God's presence in Christ and God's "oneness" at the same time?

Son of God   This is both a Christological role and a title. As a role, it refers to angels and any individual or group that has a special intimacy with God. As a title, it was an important way for early Christians to express their faith in Christ and their intimacy with God. The Fourth Gospel (i.e., John) and other early Christians go further by describing Jesus as "the only begotten son of the Father," thus stressing the uniqueness of Jesus' relationship to the Father.

Soteriology   The theological discipline that seeks to articulate an understanding of how Christ's life, death, and resurrection bring about salvation.

Spirit Christology   This modern approach to Christology has been espoused by many figures, including Roger Haight and Piet Schoonenberg. In this approach, rather than emphasizing the incarnation of the Logos, the emphasis is on the incarnation of the Spirit in Christ. To its proponents, Spirit Christology does not limit God's saving work to the historical life of Christ but transcends that particular history to include other "saviors."

Spiritualization   The term refers to the metaphorical interpretation of sacrificial ritual so that its meaning applies to the intimacy between God and the believer.

Suffering Servant   In Isaiah, there is an enigmatic figure that modern biblical scholarship has designated the Suffering Servant (Isaiah 42:1–7; 49:1–7; 50:4–9; 52:13–53:12). This figure is often thought to be a collective figure, i.e., a figure that represents a group of people, and is usually interpreted as Israel or the righteous in Israel. Through the suffering of the Servant, the covenant with God will be renewed. The Suffering Servant thus became an important image in Jesus' ministry and in the early Christian community for understanding the meaning of Jesus' suffering.

Subordinationism   The tendency within Christology, particularly with Tertullian and Origen, to understand the Son as something less than God, the Father.

Symbol   In Bernard Lonergan's thought it refers to an image that evokes feeling and aids in the apprehension of value. Symbols express that which is beyond logical thought by embracing tension and conflict. Symbols complement logic.

T

Theory   The Greek word *theōreō* means "to look at or contemplate." Theory, then, is abstract language that reflects formal clarity—it helps one to see things more accurately. Theory is contrasted with metaphor and symbol, both of which are essential, but both metaphor and symbol are examples of "thick" language—with a wide variety of meanings. Theory is just the opposite.

Theōsis   This Greek word is often translated as *divinization*. It reflects the soteriology operative in the work of theologians such as Athanasius who argued that in Christ, humans participated in the life of God: "God became human so that humans might become divine."

Theotokos   A Greek word that means "God bearer," this was a title given to the Virgin Mary and was popular among the Alexandrians. Nestorius caused a major controversy when he insisted that Mary could not be called Theotokos but only *Christotokos*, because she had given birth to Christ (the *prosopon* of the conjunction between the divine and human natures) and not God.

Third quest   This name, coined by N. T. Wright, designates a distinct movement in historical Jesus research. Among some of the elements that distinguish the third from the second or "new quest" for the historical Jesus are the consistent use of standard criteria, the emphasis on the Jewishness of Jesus, and the ecumenical and interreligious nature of the research.

W

Wisdom Christology   This approach to Christology borrowed heavily from the wisdom tradition of Israel and its emphasis on the personification of God's wisdom. The fact that the word for wisdom in both Hebrew and Greek is grammatically feminine, along with the feminine personification of wisdom in the Bible, has encouraged many contemporary feminist theologians to emphasize a "wisdom" approach to Christology.

Wisdom tradition   One of the movements within Judaism that contributed greatly to the development of Christology. The wisdom tradition is embodied in the Psalms, Proverbs, Ecclesiates, and Job. The wisdom tradition emphasized, among other things, the nearness of God in the practical, everyday world. In Second Temple Judaism, the wisdom tradition began to emphasize the personification of God's wisdom and the communication of that wisdom as God's Word—the Logos.

Y

YAHWEH (YHWH)   This is the name of God given to Moses in Exodus 3:14, and it is often translated as, "I AM." It is traditionally written without any vowels out of reverence (pious Jews in Jesus' day would not pronounce the divine name), and contemporary translations of the Bible often render it as LORD. In scholarly circles it is often used to differentiate the God of Israel from other conceptions of God.

INDEX

Illustrations, charts, sidebars, and footnotes are indicated with i, c, s, and n, respectively.